MUSIC IN THE
AMERICAN
DIASPORIC
WEDDING

MUSIC IN THE AMERICAN DIASPORIC WEDDING

EDITED BY
Inna Naroditskaya

INDIANA UNIVERSITY PRESS

This book is a publication of

Indiana University Press
Office of Scholarly Publishing
Herman B Wells Library 350
1320 East 10th Street
Bloomington, Indiana 47405 USA

iupress.indiana.edu

Library of Congress Cataloging-in-Publication Data

Names: Naroditskaya, Inna [date], editor.
Title: Music in the American diasporic wedding / edited by Inna Naroditskaya.
Description: Bloomington : Indiana University Press, 2019. | Includes
    bibliographical references and index.
Identifiers: LCCN 2018031205 (print) | LCCN 2018038314 (ebook) | ISBN
    9780253041791 (e-book) | ISBN 9780253041760 (hardback : alk. paper) | ISBN
    9780253041777 (pbk. : alk. paper)
Subjects: LCSH: Wedding music—United States—History and criticism. | Folk
    music—United States—History and criticism. | Intermarriage—United
    States.
Classification: LCC ML3551.9 (ebook) | LCC ML3551.9 .M87 2019 (print) | DDC
    781.5/870973—dc23
LC record available at https://lccn.loc.gov/2018031205

1 2 3 4 5   24 23 22 21 20 19

Cover page photo, courtesy of WSPhotography, Chicago.

To Zhenya and Pavlik

CONTENTS

FOREWORD

What a Wedding Song Tells Me

ALEJANDRO L. MADRID

I PRESS PLAY and the music blasts out of the speakers. It is a song that starts with the three most recognizable bars from Richard Wagner's "Treulich ge-führt" (the famous "Bridal Chorus" from *Lohengrin*) sung by a female choir to a piano accompaniment that quickly morphs into a full-blooded pop song. The march-like piano harmonies become a circular sequence in G major (I–vi–ii–V7)—the *círculo de sol* as Mexican popular musicians call it—the voice of the backing singers becomes child-like, and a bass and electric guitar join the ensemble to achieve the sound of early 1960s US rock-and-roll and British Invasion bands. The lyrics begin, "Quero me casar contigo / Não me abandones / Tenha compaixão / A coisa que eu tenho / Mais medo na vida / É saber que um dia / Posso perder teu curacao" (I want to marry you / Do not leave me / Have compassion / The thing I am / Most afraid in life / Is to know that one day / I can lose your heart); it is the warm voice of Roberto Carlos back when he was considered one of the rising stars of Brazil's Jovem Guarda. Listening to this song in Saint Petersburg, Russia, thousands of miles away from Guaymas, Mexico, where I lived when I heard it for the first time as a kid in the early 1970s, in a completely different social, cultural, and personal setting, makes me rethink the affect and meaning I used to associate with it.

The nineteenth century and its Romantic legacy have colored our modern understanding of marriage as an institution. Roberto Carlos's "Quero me casar contigo" seems to dwell on this cultural/historical heritage. The song's almost naive, upbeat feeling and apparently innocuous lyrics celebrate this wedding—pun intended—between romantic love and marriage; it shows the romanticization, sanitization, and even universalization of a specifically Western understanding of an intercultural practice with an otherwise very complex

history (the intention to appeal to a sense of universality seems clear in the use
of Wagner's music as a universal index of sorts of the wedding ritual). Paying
close attention to the song one realizes it could also obliquely comment on many
of the other social and cultural functions (both pragmatic and symbolic) that
weddings and the institution of marriage perform. "Não fale nem de brincadeira
/ Nem pense nunca nunca / Em me deixar assim" (Do not even joke / Or think
about ever ever / Leaving me like that) in the voice of the male singer is not
only an expression of the man's desperation about losing his beloved woman,
but it also implies that the woman should relinquish her agency and her right
to leave the man, whom she may or may not love, upon his request. Romantic
love in fact conceals a series of larger gender dynamics and power struggles that
marriage as an institution is intended to reproduce—and as such, the círculo
de sol mayor, the song's harmonic sequence, with its unavoidable circularity
and inevitable repetition, works as the perfect metaphor of the reproduction of
these dynamics. In that context, the male's proposal—to get married in order
to avoid losing her ("A coisa que eu tenho / Mais medo na vida / É saber que
um dia / Posso perder teu curacao")—actually reveals one of the oldest purposes of marriage: masculine dominance and the female body as possession.
Moreover, it unintentionally underlines that historically and transculturally,
marriage and weddings have been precisely about the transfer of property in
one way or another. However, listening to this music in detail in Saint Petersburg, a place I now get to call home for three months of the year precisely due
to my marriage to a Russian woman, makes me think of what weddings and
marriage do in the everyday life of diasporic individuals. In retrospect, listening to Roberto Carlos's song also made me reevaluate how my own wedding, as
my wife and I planned and prepared it, and as an actual space of transnational
encounters—with a bride and a groom coming from two countries different
from where the ceremony took place, with attendees from several nationalities
who fluidly moved back and forth between several languages, and with the
active participation of my Russian in-laws via Skype—was also a space for the
negotiation of how a wedding and a marriage could be emotionally and symbolically meaningful diasporically, beyond the reproduction of the values the
institution may sanction locally.

It was music, especially my emotional and historical connection to a song,
that made me wonder about these issues. Therefore, I find particularly appealing
that the subject of this book is precisely to investigate how diasporic individuals use music in weddings to negotiate a number of everyday dilemmas that life
in their new homes present them, from questions of individual and collective
identity to concerns about citizenship and national belonging at a historical moment in which globalization makes the boundaries between them increasingly

blurred. The themes explored in this volume range from multiculturalism to interethnic alliances, from inter-diasporic weddings (as Inna Naroditskaya calls them) in a foreign land to what I would call trans-diasporic weddings (among individuals from completely different diasporic experiences). It would be easy to take a congratulatory stance in the name of multiculturalism and write about these nuptial rituals in a celebratory tone, as if they were bringing peaceful resolution to interethnic conflict. However, besides the problematic that individual couples may bring into these unions, they could also be seen as dangerous by persons whose cultural horizon is narrower and less cosmopolitan due to more rooted experiences of place. In that sense, conservative folks may see these weddings and marriages as sources for the erosion of the essentialist values about nation, citizenship, and community they may hold dear. Evidently, weddings could be spaces of serious cultural contention. Music, with its perennial power to transcend borders and be reinvented, provides a perfect site and excuse for the exploration of the intersection of the emotional and the political in these rituals, because, to use Roberto Carlos's lyrics in a more critical manner, weddings are *não pra falar de brincadeira*.

ACKNOWLEDGMENTS

LOVE OF MY PARENTS, their boundless devotion to family, filled my life, the life of my sister, and our sons. Their romance, complex, uneasy, everlasting, through complex migration, aging, and losses, guided me in this project on wedding as a moment of celebration and joy. Only a moment but the one that marks a high point in the lives of people across times, places, traditions, diasporas.

The idea of diasporic weddings began shaping up in ethnomusicology classes I taught at Northwestern; graduates in my seminars on ethnic weddings conducted exciting fieldwork in Chicago, and undergraduates studied world musics through the prism of weddings. The idea of the book was honed in panels I organized with inspiring colleagues at Society for Ethnomusicology meetings, which also provided opportunities for informal meetings and discussions with collaborators. I am grateful to several editors who polished this volume. Beginning with the editorial assistance of Raina Polivka and completed under Janice Frisch, this book and my introduction in particular benefitted significantly from edits by Dee Mortenson and Janet Rabinowitch, Janet also providing overall conceptual advice on the book. I also appreciated the assistance of Kathleen Hood and am thankful to two production editors, Nancy Lightfoot and Pete Feely. It was thrilling to work with an excellent team of inspiring, enthusiastic, and reliable collaborators, and to every contributor I am profoundly grateful. Each author's writing bears a personal story (perhaps because of the topic), and I feel rewarded to become a part of these stories.

This book, like all my works, would not be possible if not for the absolute support of my husband. With him this volume began in lengthy conversations, discussions, arguments. Jamie, you are my most patient and encouraging listener, my most critical editor, and gracious generous reader. Please forgive that I did not include our wedding in this book; it remains between us, our sons, and a small group of participants.

MUSIC IN THE
AMERICAN
DIASPORIC
WEDDING

SAY YES TO US: MUSIC IN DIASPORIC WEDDINGS

INNA NARODITSKAYA

Have you ever been to American wedding?
Where is the vodka, where is the marinated herring?
Where is the musicians that got the taste?
Where is the supply that's gonna last three days?
Where is the band that like fanfare?
Gonna keep it goin' 24 hours.
Ta-tar-ranta-ta-ta . . .

—"American Wedding," Gogol Bordello / Eugene Hütz

HOPPING, DANCING, JUMPING, SINGER EUGENE Hütz belts out short melodic fragments of "American Wedding" with electrifying rhythm and speed. The dense crowd swaying below the stage vibrates as one. From the balcony, I see Hütz leaping into their midst, landing on their heads and outstretched hands, still singing as he clutches his guitar and a bottle of vodka.[1]

MULTIPLE CONFUSING DIASPORIC SELVES

An immigrant from the former Soviet Union (but not Russia), I have been frequently identified in the United States as a Russian. Though immersed in Russian cultural heritage, I only toured and vacationed in Russia. My parents' families migrated to Azerbaijan from Ukraine. I grew up and was educated in Azerbaijan, but I am barely connected with Azerbaijani Americans as I am neither an ethnic Azerbaijani nor a Muslim and speak only vernacular Azeri. I identify as Jewish, though my understanding of being a Jew is different from that of many Americans. "Jewish" as a national, not religious, identifier was written in my Soviet passport, which links me to Jewish immigrants from all parts of the Soviet Union. We share the richness of Russian culture and a strong Soviet education as well as memories of the USSR's endemic human rights abuses. Family roots in Ukraine make me an Ashkenazi Ukrainian. But with my intimate ties to a rich Azerbaijani soundscape and aesthetics, also associated with Azerbaijani mountain Jews, I am drawn to the music of Eastern Jewry. This self-reflexive puzzle makes me a Russian-Ukrainian-Azerbaijani-Eastern-Ashkenazi-Jewish-American—the order in this pile of identities flexible, any omission/addition circumstantial.

While undergoing different stages of immigration and diasporization, I began to think about weddings in immigrant communities as a metaphor for diaspora. Immigration—a bridge between past and future, between homeland and host country—is not unlike a marriage. Like marriage, immigration is messy, challenging, at times disturbing, and sometimes unsuccessful, but it also engenders loyalty, pride, and hope. The celebratory tone of a wedding may not carry over into the marriage, which often is a mixed bag of gender tensions, cultural disparities, and internal and external pressures. But however successful a marriage might or might not be, a diasporic wedding (like any wedding) is an ideal moment, a model for a perhaps unattainable perfect balance. Weddings link the bride and groom to larger cultural institutions, and by celebrating a couple's union, a diasporic community displays its perseverance and accomplishments.

In diaspora, separation from the homeland disrupts established social and cultural norms; living on the margin between cultures is filled with ambiguities. Assimilating to the new culture signifies reassembled stability, balancing old and new elements. Scholars of diaspora have used slightly different terms to describe these elements. Floya Anthias defines *diaspora* as a process of relocation, settlement, and adaptation.[2] She writes that "the original father(land) is a point of reference for the diaspora notion." William Safran identifies diasporic communities with several common characteristics that include (1) dispersal from a place of origin, (2) maintenance of a "memory, vision, or myth about their original homeland," and (3) a "continuous relationship with the homeland."[3] Analyzing rituals, Arnold Van Gennep identifies three similar phases: separation, margin, and aggregation.[4] Van Gennep's definition of three phases of ritual and Anthias's and Safran's characterizations of diaspora apply to many traditional marriages, which, at least for the bride, entail separation from a natal place, nostalgia, assimilation, accommodation, and possible tensions within a new family.

Weddings can be symbolically compared with diasporas that celebrate affinity with both home- and host lands. The neatly paired hyphenated American identities, however, are evasive, fleeting, and confusing. It seems to me that as the United States has moved away from the melting pot formula, perhaps multiculturalism is more open to diasporic diversity. In diasporas, nuptials bind immigrants to their host land, often celebrating their compound identities, whether African American, Chinese American, Ethiopian American, or Russian Jewish American.

THE DIASPORIC WEDDING AND MUSIC

Each diaspora, a nation within a nation, a community within a larger community, engages simultaneously in preservation and compromise. Each diasporic family endures multiple transitions—physical relocation, financial and social changes, new beginnings, alliances, and ongoing negotiations. What happens to weddings when a community, uprooted and dislocated, seeks a home in a new land?

The wedding is one of the three major life rituals celebrated in most cultures. Unlike birth and funeral rites, where the central figure is not privy to the proceedings, a wedding features two live, fully engaged protagonists and their families—a sizable cast in a spectacular production. Linking past and future, weddings secure the physical continuity of the community and, in Victor Turner's words, reinforce "cultural values embodied and expressed in symbols at ritual performances."[5]

Whether in a temple, backyard, or banquet hall or during the bridal procession, music defines the space of weddings. Music also determines the temporal structure of wedding events—for example, songs accompanying henna painting define a particular day in a traditional multiday wedding celebration and also set a pattern of events and their duration during the henna ritual. Ritualistic laments in the bride's home mark the completion of one segment of the traditional wedding and signal the progress to the next. Verses teasing a young groom, sword dances by brothers of the groom and/or the bride, religious recitations, and traditional dances guide the temporal sequence of weddings. And there are always verses one can add to extend the celebration or omit to speed it up.

How, in diaspora, do we choose and listen to wedding music: a tune from our youth in a faraway home that brings tears, a rhythm that pulls us from our chairs to dance with our children raised in the United States, a song that makes the heart stop and urges us to run and hug our elders, or a melody we learned in another diasporic community? Music is portable and thus easily brought by an immigrant from home to the host country. Instruments connect with distant homelands: the whistle, the drone, the high-pitched wailing of zurna, the fiery fiddle. Songs evoke precious childhood memories. Mark Slobin writes that music acts as "an extraordinary multilayered channel of communication, nesting language itself, that primary agent of identity, within a series of strata of cultural meaning: the erotic potential of the voice, the organizing capacity of rhythm and tempo, the time-stopping movement of melody, the space-subduing powers of instrumentation and sonic architecture, and the collectivist thrust of the dance."[6]

The diasporic wedding is both a celebration of immigrants' accomplishments and, as in any wedding, a hopeful foundation for the future. This chapter comprises three parts: (1) ethnographic observation of three weddings, (2) notes on weddings, diasporic weddings, and music in historical and cultural contexts, and (3) an introduction of the team of collaborators.

During the last decade, as I was thinking and working on this volume, I attended dozens of weddings, recording music, rituals, and receptions, and interviewing couples, their relatives and guests. Some of my ethnographic observations follow.

WEDDING ONE: THE BEATLES AS A VOICE
OF THE AZERBAIJANI HOMELAND

At Houston's Intercontinental Hotel, with "Sunrise Sunset" from *Fiddler on the Roof* played by a string quartet of the Houston Orchestra, my close friends from Baku walk their daughter toward a shimmering crystal *chuppah*.[7] A few minutes after her betrothal, my friends proceed again, now with their son, for his marriage vows, as the same quartet plays a medley of classical pieces. This double wedding includes over three hundred guests—fellow Baku immigrants now living in all parts of America, friends from Russia and Azerbaijan, and local Houstonians. Over half the guests are young; others belong to the generations of parents and grandparents. A number of guests speak only English or only Russian or other languages, so the toasts are delivered in both English and Russian.

After the ceremony, dressed in the psychedelic military uniforms from *Sgt. Pepper's Lonely Hearts Club Band*, the ensemble Fab5 plays a selection from the album, satisfying the Beatle-fanatic hosts and welcoming guests back to the grand hall, reconfigured from sanctuary to wedding reception room. Later, the Beatles tribute band performs songs from *Yellow Submarine*, changing costumes accordingly. The quality of the musical impersonation satisfies my friends, passionate fans of the Beatles.

Halfway through the evening, Mango Punch, a Latin band, takes the stage.[8] The group, including musicians from Guatemala, Puerto Rico, Mexico, and California, plays Latin dances mixed with Italian pop songs, paying respect to the groom's Italian mother. When Mango Punch begins "Hava Nagilah," both couples are lifted in their chairs, a traditional moment in Jewish weddings. Later, a recording of Azerbaijani music is played, and male friends of the two siblings' father get up, extending one arm, palm up with the other arm bent before the chest while engaging in rigorous footwork. Women join gradually, their arm movements smooth, wrists gracefully turning, small steps, heads tilted. I dance among them.

Afterward, I pondered over the musical selection in this wedding, the dia-sporic musical kaleidoscope. The music reflected composite identities of Jewish, Russian, Azeri, Soviet, American, and other elements molded by at least three generations: (1) the grandparents; (2) the parents, born and raised in Soviet Azerbaijan, who immigrated to the United States; and (3) the siblings, who, brought by their parents to the United States, grew up in Texas, have Texan ac-cents (different from my midwestern son's), wear cowboy boots and Stetsons, and compete in Latin dances.

My friends' son arrived in the United States as a teenager; he is fluent in both English and Russian and is adept in both cultures. He wedded a Muscovite ice skater and trainer who had recently come to the States. The son's wedding can be viewed as intradiasporic; both he and his bride were from the former Soviet Union. However, the families came from different republics, now states, with diverse cultural backgrounds and soundscapes. My friends' daughter, brought

Figure 0.1. Double Wedding in Houston Intercontinental Hotel, July 2006. *Courtesy of the Karash family.*

to the States at the age of four, married an American man of Polish and Italian descent; thus, hers was a mixed diasporic wedding.

The musical selection of the Beatles was influenced by the siblings' father, an accomplished engineer, the Soviet equivalent of a Renaissance man, and an amateur rock guitarist. During our student years, when Western popular music was both forbidden and desired, he managed to accumulate a large Beatles collection. For him, as for many of us, "home" may thus be associated not as much with any ethnic music as with the urban musical tastes of Baku's rebellious intelligentsia. The Beatles thus represent Soviet Azerbaijani cultural heritage along with Azerbaijani dances and Jewish songs—a fragmented sense of identity transmitted in music.

At this wedding, "Hava Nagilah" clearly represented Jewishness. In an Albanian wedding (Chicago, 1986) described by Sugarman, "most of the music was Albanian.... As a nod to the non-Albanian guests, one of the Prespa men sang 'Hava Nagilah' with the band."[9] There, the song represented Americanness. The ubiquitous melody seems to stand for Jewish and for American, for Jewish American, and for non–Jewish American.

WEDDING TWO: "MNOHAYA LITA" TO COUPLES CROWNED IN CHICAGO'S UKRAINIAN VILLAGE

Driving into Chicago, one cruises through nations not identified on city maps, invisible to passersby yet within well-defined borders: La Villita (Little Village, home to Mexican Americans), Little Italy, and Ukrainian Village. The citizens of these states follow distinct traditions, respect internal hierarchies, and create somewhat independent social structures. Though Ukrainian islands are found throughout metropolitan Chicago, Ukrainian Village is a center of Ukrainian culture, tradition, language, and religions, represented in the Ukrainian Institute of Modern Art, the Ukrainian National Museum, and three Ukrainian churches with choirs.[10] The children here study in Ukrainian schools, attend a Ukrainian scouting organization (Plast), and become members of the fifty-year-old Chicago Youth Association (CYM). Women shop in Ukrainian groceries, youth gather in Ukrainian bars, and a Ukrainian policeman from the Ukrainian American Police Association stands at the church door surveying the crowd at a Ukrainian wedding.

Traditional Ukrainian weddings in the Village, which are led by a designated pair of *starosta* and *starosinya* and include the crowning of the groom and bride, tying their hands with embroidered *rushniks* (handmade linen towels), affirm the unity of Ukrainian Village. At the same time, weddings reveal distinctions within the community—between Ukrainian Orthodox and Ukrainian

Catholics,[11] between different generations of immigrants, among customs brought from different parts of Ukraine, and among Ukrainians with varying degrees of assimilation. There are four waves of immigration; the oldest are third-generation American-born Ukrainians, and the youngest are "newcomers" who arrived in the United States in the quarter century since Ukrainian independence.[12] Each claims ownership of cultural authenticity, a concept that, challenged in scholarship, nevertheless captivates peoples' imagination.

Sonya, a Ukrainian American bride, is marrying Yuri, who came to the United States as a Northwestern University law student six years before their 2004 wedding. On the steps of the bride's house in Ukrainian Village, Sonya's grandmother and Yuri's mother lay down rushniks. As the young couple kneels on the rushniks, the two families' matriarchs present *caravai* (loaves of bread) and salt. Sonya's mother is an American-born Ukrainian, her father Slovenian. The service in Saints Volodymyr and Olha Church is conducted in Ukrainian, though some passages are read in Slovenian, honoring the bride's father's side. The groom's family speaks no English. The bride, who is taking Ukrainian classes once a week, understands but does not speak Ukrainian well.

The music selection for this wedding reception is curious. The groom fancies American rock, which he identifies with freedom. The bride's family wishes to hear music from their homeland. The musicians performing the Village's weddings have to confront the realities of mixed-diasporic and mixed-generation traditions. Weddings here also illuminate competition between two musical streams. Professionally trained musicians arriving in the last wave have begun to rival predominantly amateur church choirs and ensembles of American-born Ukrainians. "The two don't mix," asserts John Steciw, an American Ukrainian accordionist/keyboardist, composer, and bandleader. "We can meet and talk, but do not play together; the repertoire and listeners are different."[13] Yet Steciw's group during the last twelve years has included a Lithuanian saxophone player from the last wave of immigration. "He is a fantastic saxophonist. We invited him to play with the group; by now he speaks Ukrainian language and knows our tunes by heart," clarifies Steciw, who himself seems to be fluent in Polish repertoire.[14]

The young diasporic generation is introduced to homeland wedding traditions with debutante balls in the Ukrainian Village, which evoke the tsarist aristocratic style of the first ball in Leo Tolstoy's *War and Peace*. Ukrainian debutantes, seventeen-year-old girls dressed in long white gowns with matching gloves, shoes, and corsages, are escorted by tuxedoed fathers and chic mothers to the center of a large hall. After formally presenting their daughter and giving a blessing, parents pass her to a tuxedoed Ukrainian escort of approximately the same age. Songs and dances follow. The introductions are delivered in Ukrainian. Larrisa, a bride I interviewed after her wedding, says that these balls serve as a bridal market. Bringing local youngsters together, debutante balls recycle traditional songs and dances and set the stage for weddings within the community.

A focal element of the ball is the *kolomeika*, a dance performed collectively by men and women separately, then together. The men's movements emphasize strength and valor—skillfully jumping, kicking, leaping, and stamping in semi-seated positions, competing individually and in small groups. The women's movements are swift and graceful. At some point, men in circles of four to six spin with increasing speed, lifting their female partners from the ground. The kolomeika, a test of Ukrainianness, is performed at debutante balls and weddings; the younger generation learns and participates from childhood.

WEDDING THREE: ETHIOPIAN MUSLIM AMERICAN DEVON WEDDING

Store signs along Devon Avenue, Chicago, are written in at least a dozen languages. Diasporic neighborhoods intersect, and shared common spaces forge multiple networks among communities. Walking along this mile-long street, one may enter Jewish bakeries, Arabic halal stores, Indian groceries, Russian bookshops, Polish travel agencies, a Sikh temple, and endless Pakistani and Indian dress and jewelry shops. If Ukrainian Village seems to be a small nation-state within metropolitan Chicago, Devon is a point of intersection, evidenced by the variety of diasporic weddings held here by communities that inhabit this global market as well as by those who come in from the outside of Divan.

Bombay Hall on Devon Avenue hosts an Ethiopian Muslim wedding. The older married sister of the bride (the major sponsor of the reception) hands me an invitation picturing a smiling American Barbie doll in a sexy wedding dress with open shoulders. The bride on the card matches neither the real bride nor the setting for this wedding.

The wedding follows the Islamic tradition of gender segregation. The Bombay Hall banquet space is divided into men's and women's spaces, separated by a long, heavy curtain. After entering the female side, a number of women remove dark veils and long robes to reveal shining dresses, jewelry, bright lipstick, and makeup. The bride is dressed in a sparkly white gown, shoulders and arms covered with a festive white vest. Her head is covered by a dense veil, which is soon replaced with a lighter one. Together with her bridesmaids, she is seated on an elevated platform at the side of the hall.

Food is served in the foyer. The men are invited to the buffet first; the women wait. But the food line quickly disintegrates, and some men and women mingle—the dining space is desegregated. Ethiopian music is played through-out the wedding by a DJ, a young man firmly situated in the women's half. As women begin to dance, the emotional energy elevates. The characteristic dance movements remind one of an electric shock going through the female dancers' bodies, graceful at every moment. Having attended several Ethiopian weddings, I am familiar with the moves, tried them from time to time at home—unsuccessfully—and join the dancing crowd to share the excitement. The bride, who earlier shed her vest, now removes her light gauze veil. She joins the women who are dancing. When male ushers roll the table in and assemble the wed-ding cake, a group of young men, cautiously following the groom, walk into the female area to take part in a central ritual of an American wedding: cutting a multilayered cake that is topped with a figurine. A few minutes later, the sister pulls first the groom and then his male entourage one by one to the dance floor while encouraging and pushing women forward. Together, the men and women dance. Music and dance embody and facilitate the possibilities, even when un-predictable. This Ethiopian Muslim American Chicago Devon Avenue Bombay Hall reception is a space of liminality.

HISTORICAL PERSPECTIVE: WEDDINGS AS ROYAL ALLIANCES

Weddings throughout history and across cultures have defined the texture of social, cultural, and economical life. They led to wars, accomplished peace trea-ties, and served as an instrument of political negotiations. Royal weddings often served as a major political institution for internal state control and external al-liance. In European courts, weddings defined power relationships and forged cross-continental networks.

In 1710, a blasting German orchestra of trombones and horns led fifty boats down the river Neva. Ahead of the naval wedding procession, looming over sailors in red velvet attire with golden trim and silver crests, stood Peter I, seven feet tall, in full military gear, wearing a crimson coat with sables. Upending cen-turies of Russian tsars marrying native brides selected at bride shows, Peter the Great, having acquired access to the Baltic Sea and Europe, staged the wedding of his niece Anna to a foreigner, the Duke of Courland. Anna was the first of the family youngsters that Peter wedded to non-Russians. Their splendorous nup-tials, combining old Russian customs with the fireworks, spectacles, balls, and illuminations fashionable in the West, affirmed Russia's powerful military and political presence in Europe. Peter's heirs on the Russian throne continued to devise princely weddings as a political institution.[15] Anna's groom died within days. After years of miserable exile in Courland, Anna returned home to become

Her Majesty Empress and was crowned in the Orthodox ritual of *venchanie*—a wedding to the Russian patria.[16]

Weddings also connected the mortal with the divine in service of political and economic power, with music smoothing and solemnizing these societal mechanisms. While monks vowing celibacy rejected marital bonds, some nuns, as brides of Christ, underwent a wedding-like ritual of consecration. In seventeenth-century Bologna, a five- to six-hour group consecration of virgins in the church of Santa Cristina was accompanied by "fireworks, drums, and trumpets and . . . a choir of external musicians brought in specially for the occasion."[17] In the North German convent of Wienhausen, a nun's investiture "was followed by a great feast, with dance and song, hosted by relatives, which paralleled a bridal feast."[18] Theatrical productions staged as a part of the festivities were performed in richly decorated spaces before local notables and visiting dignitaries; the scene and attendees hardly differed from noble weddings.

Like courtly matrimonials, these monastic weddings involved gifts and transfers of property, dowries allocated to the church. The ritual itself served as an exhibition of the wealth and stature of the bride's family, as well as the power dynamic among local church, local community, and sacred authority.

FROM ROYAL TO CINEMATIC WEDDINGS

Queen Victoria's wedding (1840) provided a model for the "white wedding" that took root in the United States. Today, we are still allured by royal weddings, British ones in particular.[19] In May 2018, twenty-nine million people in the United States alone watched the intercultural, interracial, cross-continental wedding of Prince Harry and Hollywood actress Meghan Markle.

Hollywood and a royal wedding had merged before. Two events, a princely wedding and a cinematographic nuptial a few months apart, featured the same iconic bride, Grace Kelly. Amid Frank Sinatra singing "Because You Are Sensational," Bing Crosby singing "I Love You, Samantha," and Louis Armstrong jazzing up Mendelssohn's Wedding March, the heroine of *High Society* ended up wedding a groom different from the one she planned to marry. In the film, she wears the engagement ring given to her by the (real) prince of Monaco; at her actual wedding to him, she appeared in gowns made by the same costume designer who devised her dresses for *High Society*. Kelly's fairytale weddings, in the princely palace of Monte Carlo and in the film, cross-reference each other. The wedding performance was linked with the screen, royal nuptials tied to pop culture.

Diegetic music defines the twenty-seven-minute Italian American wedding scene that opens *The Godfather* (1972). With "The Godfather Tarantella" playing the family poses for photos, a crowd dances, and a grand wedding cake is carried in. The bride's parents dance to "The Godfather Mazurka" and the newlyweds to "The Godfather Foxtrot." Mamma sings "Luna mezz'o mare," and Johnny Fontana, an unmistakable Frank Sinatra avatar, croons to the bride, "I Have but One Heart," driving the crowd ecstatic. The music sequence includes Cherubino's aria from Mozart's Italian *Le nozze di Figaro*. The final Godfather Waltz accompanies the father-daughter dance. The scene is a full sonic portrayal of music-loving Italians in America. Love, sex, violence, money, procreation, generational unease—all is magnified and temporarily reconciled by the soundtrack. The film about an Italian American family was itself a family affair: Francis Ford Coppola directed *The Godfather*, his father Carmine Coppola composed the music and led the wedding band, Coppola's cousin sang, and several other relatives were filmed on the set.[20]

In *Funny Girl* (1968), Fanny, an East Side Jewish girl with skinny legs and a big nose—"Is a nose with deviation such a crime against the nation?"—rises to stardom in the Ziegfeld Follies. Following a parade of long-legged, high-heeled, narrow-waisted, skimpily dressed, perfectly groomed brides, all in white—winter brides, spring brides, summer brides, and brides of autumn decorated with feathers, pearls, flowers, veils—at the top of this bridal pyramid, the star shows up in a virginal wedding-white gown she had stuffed with a pillow. Profiling both her bulging belly and her nose, she sings about her "beautiful reflection"—indeed, funny Fanny.

In *My Big Fat Greek Wedding* (2002), the heroine, Tula, struggles to escape her controlling father's mantra—"nice Greek girls are supposed to do three things in life: marry Greek boys, make Greek babies, and feed everyone." The thirty-year-old takes computer classes, finds a job outside her family restaurant, and marries a non-Greek man. While she belongs to an immigrant family, it is her fiancé, Ian Miller, who becomes a male Cinderella, marrying into a Greek kingdom in the middle of Chicago. The dynamics of Americans and Others, majority-minority, here is reversed. The only Americans in the emotive Greek crowd are Ian Miller, his briefly appearing friend, and his nearly silent parents. The film is filled with music: traditional Greek songs, belly dancing, and the contagious Zorba dance at the wedding. The bouzouki (lute) plays as the father walks the veiled, all-in-white bride into the church. There, the bouzouki solo fades into Wagner's "Wedding March," and after the Greek Orthodox wedding ceremony, the couple recesses quickly to Mendelssohn's "March." This diasporic wedding movie was the highest-grossing indie ever.[21]

Varied in genre, with soundtracks including ethnic music or pieces authored by film composers, such movies may romanticize and exoticize diasporic weddings, but they also engage and dialogue with otherness. Weddings in film overlap not only with TV reality shows but also with family videos transmitted digitally and watched transnationally. Cinematographic weddings serve as models for real diasporic nuptials, turning spectators into "armchair matrimonial ethnographers."[22]

THE AMERICAN WHITE WEDDING

Diasporic nuptials are often wedded with the American "white wedding," which is not a racial term but one that denotes white dresses, flowers, veils, diamonds, cakes, and decorations. Beginning with Queen Victoria's wedding and gradually spreading through the United States in the mid-nineteenth century, white weddings in recent decades have evolved into a massive commercial trap, a web of multimedia productions, the pinnacle of American consumerism.[23] Like other traditional weddings, the white wedding endorses vital goals: procreation, continuity, alliances, property exchange, financial transactions, and communal order. And like other wedding traditions, it is fraught with family competition, personal ambitions, dissatisfactions, and anxieties. Magnifying every possible goal and exploiting every possible sentiment, the white wedding puts a price tag on them all. It may involve astronomical expenses and consume family savings and future earnings. Still, the white wedding maintains a strong hold over young and old, and it asserts a firm grip on diasporic nuptials in the United States.[24]

For a diasporic family, a white wedding may become a visible affirmation of the realized American dream. As two powerful signifiers, the white wedding and the American dream may thus align with the "American" part of composite diasporic identities. The white wedding may also symbolize internal tensions in diasporic nuptials. While complex wedding formulas repeated and polished from generation to generation in the homelands ease tensions, the new cultural context destabilizes formulaic rituals. Rebuilding their lives and homes in new places, young couples, their families, and their communities debate which elements of wedding rituals to embrace and which to let go. The wedding negotiation no longer involves just two individuals but draws on extensive camps of relatives, who bring along all their generational identity issues. Grandparents may be uncompromisingly attached to their old home; parents mediate their natal and American experiences daily; and the young brides and grooms may nurture affinity with their origin, which, however strong, is abstract. White weddings consumerize and commercialize this all; the "dream" is an extraordinarily profitable business.

ANCIENT TRADITIONS, NEW MARKETS

Carol Wallace states that "everyday romance is a luxury, possibly even an artifact of the industrial era, and it didn't cloud marriage decisions until well into the 1800s."[25] Although today weddings are paired with love, until the nineteenth century, nuptials often had little to do with romance. Property exchange has been central to weddings throughout the ages. Claude Lévi-Strauss wrote about marriages arranged by men "on the basis of an exchange of daughters" in western Papua.[26] His analysis of the passing of the bride from father and husband led to many focused studies on trading women for goods.[27] Bridewealth and dowry may involve money, livestock, or the "exchange of 'sisters' formerly practiced in parts of Africa and Australia."[28] My own dowry in Baku included an upright piano, which now stands in my Chicago home and symbolically links my first wedding and my diasporic journeys.

The typical American wedding celebrated today is preceded by dating, possibly intimate relations, and at times a couple living together. Love choices and wedding decisions belong to the two persons getting married. However, this pattern does not always apply to weddings in diasporic communities. Arranged marriages seem to be a tradition from other times and places. But the families' critical role in matchmaking and wedding choices remains essential within some diasporic groups. Among Assyrian Americans, as told by Peter BetBasoo (a Chicagoan), the first step toward a wedding is *mashmeta*, which means "sending a word."[29] A young man's cousin (not the parents, to avoid humiliation in case of refusal) conveys a proposal to the family of a potential bride. If the response is positive, a *taliboota* takes place, during which the groom's parents visit the bride's family. When after the course of a long ornate exchange the two sides seal the engagement, a phone call brings the groom to the bride's household.

Peter remembers how as a teenager he attended the taliboota of his cousin. The heads of two family delegations, the groom's grandfather and the bride's father, were from Ottoman Turkey and shared several languages. In the course of the conversation, they began singing Assyrian, Kurdish, and Turkish songs. The singing continued for a couple of hours while the anxious cousin waited by the phone until the two elders exhausted their shared repertoire.

Parental involvement in engagements takes other forms as well. The classified ads of local Chicago Indian papers feature matrimonial sections in which parents seek a partner for their "USA born daughter, slim, beautiful doctor," or "their daughter MD/anesthesiology," or "the green card holder daughter," or for a "Punjabi Brahmin boy in US with master's from University of Illinois." When a candidate is found and a tentative agreement received, the wedding sequence unfolds with many types of shops and services involved. Video clips on YouTube feature bridal fashion shows as well as tabla and sitar players, singers, videographers, stylists, and chefs. Each South Asian Bridal Expo (including Chicago, Phoenix, and DC) embraces electronic media, web pages, and Facebook but also addresses the music of Indian weddings, featuring traditional, semitraditional, and nontraditional bands, individual performers, and DJs.

Today, diasporic weddings are local (Devon Street in Chicago), cross-cultural (often performed in multicultural immigrant communities), transcontinental (played twice: in the United States and in the home countries), and digital (with families and guests far away attending the celebration via electronic connection). The internet, smartphones, and tablets capture and transmit live events on the spot via powerful new networks. Whether born abroad or not, the brides and grooms reach out to families in faraway homelands and embrace the ties with their places of origin, seeking an authentic diasporic American identity.

A LOOK AHEAD

The present volume about diasporic weddings in the United States focuses on the interconnection of three elements: weddings, diaspora, and music—each element illuminating and illuminated by the other two. Diasporic weddings proudly affirm the hardship of transition and a community's successful reconstitution in its new home. Signifying communal continuity, wedding rituals abandon some traditions and preserve others, testing ways to connect with their American surroundings. Music, fueling passion and touching nerves, mediates between generations and families, ritual and entertainment, immigrant lore and assimilation.

This book explores wedding sequences cross-culturally—from proposals and engagements to ceremonies and receptions. In the foreword, Alejandro L. Madrid weaves a musical canvas—Wagner's "Bridal Chorus" morphs into a Brazilian pop song with British Invasion–like accompaniment about getting married that he listens to in Russia—which makes him think about romantic love that conceals gender dynamics in marriage and diasporic wedding celebrations situated at the intersection of globalization and nationalism.

The following chapters fall into three groups corresponding to three interconnected elements identified previously: (1) *diaspora*: music and weddings in geoculturally specific diasporic communities; (2) *weddings*: ritualistic elements, roles, and music negotiation within individual weddings; and (3) *music*: wedding ethnography by musicians performing at weddings. However, all the chapters discuss diaspora, weddings, and music, as well as representation, construction, identity, ethnography, and mechanisms of assimilation/preservation.

The first four chapters by Jihad Racy, Carol Silverman, Lorena Alvarado and Frances Aparicio, and Ian MacMillen feature wedding celebrations in different diasporic communities. Racy explores theoretical issues emerging from his study and performance in Arabic weddings. Silverman writes how several thousand proud Macedonian Muslim Roma, a small fraction of the global Romani diaspora, celebrate their nuptials across their multiple homelands. Alvarado and Aparicio discuss the wedding celebrations and homologies of Latinidad, traditions identified with a population of 56.6 million.[30] Ian MacMillan focuses on the prominence of the Croatian flag in weddings in the North American diaspora and the Balkan homeland.

Each of the next three chapters explores a single wedding: two autoethnographic case studies by bride-ethnomusicologists Meredith Schweig and Tanya Merchant and an essay on a same-sex marriage, which Nina Öhman explores as diasporic. Schweig writes about her Jewish Taiwanese wedding. Merchant engages in a discourse on reflexivity, which frames her wedding narrative about the American Bosnian community in the San Francisco Bay Area. Öhman's chapter entwines two stories: a gala six-hundred-guest same-sex marriage celebration in New York and Aretha Franklin's performance at this wedding. Öhman links Franklin's powerful voice, inseparable from the long history of African American diaspora, with the long "internal exile" of the gay community.

The following chapters consist of the two written by musicians who play for diasporic weddings, Michael Allemana and Hankus Netsky; a collaborative chapter about musical labor by two ethnomusicologists, Kaley Mason and Ameera Nimjee, who is also a dancer; and, finally, an ethnomusicology essay by Timothy Cooley that defines and redefines engagement with a community and its weddings. Allemana, a jazz guitarist, converses with his fellow musicians about wedding music strategies that work or don't work and how to make the musical performances beneficial for both the wedding party and the musicians earning a living. Netsky, a jazz pianist and klezmer performer, entwines the hundred-year history of Ashkenazi American weddings with his own family saga of celebrated *klezmerim* musicians in a delightfully humorous tone. A stretch of Devon Avenue in Chicago is the focus of the chapter by Mason and Nimjee. Cooley writes about Polish weddings that re-create the Tatra highlands in proximity to Chicago's Magnificent Mile.

What complicates any structural grouping of the chapters is that, although all authors are dedicated insiders to the traditions they discuss, all have different positions vis-à-vis their data. In several cases, the authors play inside versus outside (analytical) roles, shifting, reversing, and at times experimenting simultaneously as both informer and ethnographer.

All chapters emerged from the authors' extensive studies of diasporic communities in their homelands and/or America. Conducting fieldwork, the scholars observed, participated in, performed at, and contextualized weddings. Some contributors are members of a diaspora; others participated in the diasporic wedding they narrate.

The scope of populations studied in this volume is wide. Several essays focus on large diasporic communities and pan-diasporic alliances, while others explore weddings in smaller diasporic groups or a single wedding. Racy engages with diverse Arabic weddings and music practices among Druze, Egyptian, Lebanese Americans—a community of "3.7 million Americans [that] trace their roots to an Arab country."[31]

Most of the field research was conducted in American cities. Racy converses about Arabic American weddings with his fellow musicians primarily in his American home, Los Angeles. Silverman focuses on New York's Belmont neighborhood, "a center of Macedonian Romani life in the United States." Most of the case studies dealing with diasporic intersections and wedding "industries" focus on cities, where banquet halls, wedding planners, ethnic ensembles, and musical venues cluster. On the other hand, some Chicago Górale from the Polish Highlands, Cooley notes, have moved a few miles away from the city, where "a handful of Górale are now grazing sheep and making the distinctive smoked cheese called *oscypek*, a delicacy that no wedding feast should be without."

Diasporic weddings are tightly woven into the diverse fabric of American society—featuring elements ranging from the mocking rap by Hütz, the Russo-Ukrainian Romani leader of the Gypsy punk band Gogol Bordello that introduced this chapter, to musicians flying across the ocean to authenticate ethnic American weddings, to televised *Bridezillas* episodes (with ethnic overtones), and to transnational electronic blogs streaming ads for floral decorations and overpriced wedding gowns. Weddings, and diasporic weddings especially, have permeated and shaped the political, social, economic, and artistic fabric of different societies.

At a time of global sectarian attacks and ethnic intolerance, the wedding, an institution common to all cultures and polished within each from one generation to the next, may show us how to resolve differences, at least temporarily, by connecting individuals, families, villages, communities, and states and celebrating unity. Carol Wallace writes that "the way we get married in America shows us what we think—and what we have thought—about women, about marriage, about family, and about love itself."[32] But we, in America, also think about marriages, families, and about love in many different ways. A kaleidoscope of verses, songs, dances—sounding, moving, and mediating cultures in diasporic weddings—articulates our many visions of America. In the context of twenty-first century modes of transportation and communication, diasporas challenge the concept of a nation as contained within state borders.

Ultimately, despite all the discrepancies, tensions, disputes, and ongoing negotiations, the wedding, once it takes place, provides a couple and community, however diverse, with an agreement (however long-lived), joy, stability, and peaceful compromise. This study of American diasporic weddings offers models of conflict resolution beyond weddings and music, which instills joy and unifies, capable of moving conflicting sides to a dance.

Diaspora is American history and is the American nation. In welcoming differences and appreciating musical heteroglossia, we find, deep down in our rich multiple composite identities, a sounding unified common core.

INNA NARODITSKAYA is Professor of Ethnomusicology at the Northwestern University Bienen School of Music. She is author of *Bewitching Russian Opera: The Tsarina from State to Stage, Song from the Land of Fire: Continuity and Change in Azerbaijani Mugham,* and coeditor of several volumes, including *Music of the Sirens.*

NOTES

1. Chicago, Riviera Theater, March 4, 2008.
2. Anthias, "Evaluating 'Diaspora': Beyond Ethnicity," 557 (24).
3. Safran, "Diaspora in Modern Societies," 83–84.
4. Turner, *Ritual Process,* 94.
5. Turner, *Ritual Process,* 8.
6. Slobin, "Music in Diaspora," 244.
7. The Intercontinental is now the Royal Sonesta Hotel. This double wedding took place in 2006.
8. For more information, see the band's Facebook page: https://www.facebook.com /mangopunch/.
9. Sugarman, *Engendering Song,* 298.
10. Sts. Volodymyr and Olha Ukrainian Catholic Church, St. Volodymyr Ukrainian Orthodox Church, and St. Nicholas Ukrainian Catholic Cathedral.
11. The Ukrainian Greek Catholic Church follows the Julian calendar. Ukrainian Orthodox churches are divided into those under the Moscow Patriarchate and those under the Kiev Patriarchate.
12. I learned about the four waves in conversation with members of the community. The first wave of immigration dates from before the twentieth century; the second wave took place during and after the Russian Revolution (1917); the third was an outcome of World War II; the fourth came after the fall of the Soviet Union.
13. Steciw, John. Interview with the author, Chicago, July 2004.
14. Telephone interview with Steciw, September 2016. An electronic link of one of his performances can be found at https://www.youtube.com/watch?v=8Tjs3GC-zVQ (accessed November 10, 2016).
15. Martin, *Bride for the Tsars.* In my previous research on Russian empire and opera, I found that princely marriages were political affairs of the state. Fairytale princely weddings also became a marker of Russian nationalist opera (Naroditskaya, *Bewitching Russian Opera*).

16. There was an apparent gender difference between Russia's female and male rulers. Russian tsars underwent venchanie to the state while married or being urged to marry. Female rulers remained single (widowed or unmarried), wedded to their fatherland.

17. Monson, *Disembodied Voices*, 185. The convent of Santa Cristina belonged to the Camaldolese order.

18. Bynum, "Crowned with Many Crowns," 18.

19. Such as the weddings of Charles and Diana in 1981; William and Kate (Catherine Middleton), 2011. See Richards, "The Hollywoodization of Diana."

20. "Even the man in charge of supplying police officers for the production, Sonny Grosso, reports that his whole family served as extras." Jones, *Annotated Godfather*.

21. "*My Big Fat Greek Wedding* cost about $5 million to make and took in $241 million in domestic box office," writes Robert Marich in *Marketing to Moviegoers*, 337. See also Georgakas, "My Big Fat Greek Gripes," 36–37.

22. Jensen and Ringrose, "Sluts That Choose vs. Doormat Gypsies."

23. See Dunak, *As Long as We Both Shall Love*; Howard, *American Weddings and the Business of Tradition*; Ingraham, *White Weddings*; and Glapka, *Reading Bridal Magazines from a Critical Discursive Perspective*.

24. The white wedding is impractical—the dress is not typically reusable, flowers wither, food is distributed or thrown away. The untainted white celebration may satisfy "a class-based desire to make the wedding . . . for public display." See Ingrassia, "Diana, Martha and Me,", 24–30.

25. Wallace, *All Dressed in White*, 75.

26. Levi-Strauss, *Elementary Structures of Kinshio*, 433.

27. Oyěwùmí, *Invention of Women*, 67.

28. Goody and Tambiah, *Bridewealth and Dowry*, 35.

29. BetBasoo, Peter. Interview with the author, Chicago, September 2016.

30. The US census data of July 1, 2016, identifies the Hispanic population of the United States as 57.5 million. See "Facts for Features: Hispanic Heritage Month 2017," US Census Bureau, August 31, 2017, https://www.census.gov/newsroom/facts-for-features/2017/hispanic-heritage.html.

31. This data is provided by the Arab American Institute, "Demographics," September 30, 2016, http://www.aaiusa.org/demographics. The US Census Bureau's American Community Survey gives very different numbers: 1.8 million Arab Americans living in the United States in 2011. Accessed September 30, 2016.

32. Wallace, *All Dressed in White*, 8.

BIBLIOGRAPHY

Anthias, Floya. "Evaluating 'Diaspora': Beyond Ethnicity." *Sociology* 32, no. 3 (August 1998): 557–80. http://maxweber.hunter.cuny.edu/pub/eres/SOC217_PIMENTEL/anthias.pdf.

Borgia, Lucretia. *Correspondence of Her Day.* Translated by John Leslie Garner. New York: D. Appleton and Company, 1903.

Bynum, Caroline W. "'Crowned with Many Crowns': Nuns and Their Statues in Late-Medieval Wienhausen." *Catholic Historical Review* 101, no. 1 (December 2015): 18–40.

Dunak, Karen. *As Long as We Both Shall Love: The White Wedding in Postwar America.* New York: New York University Press, 2013.

Georgakas, Dan. "My Big Fat Greek Gripes." *Cinéaste* 28, no. 4 (Fall 2003): 36–37.

Glapka, Eva. *Reading Bridal Magazines from a Critical Discursive Perspective.* Hampshire: Palgrave Macmillan, 2014.

Goody, Jack, and S. J. Tambiah. *Bridewealth and Dowry.* London: Cambridge University Press, 1973.

Gregorovius, Ferdinand. *Lucretia Borgia: According to Original Documents and Correspondence of Her Day.* Translated by John Leslie Garner. New York: D. Appleton and Company, 1903.

Howard, Vicki. *American Weddings and the Business of Tradition.* Philadelphia: University of Pennsylvania Press, 2006.

Ingraham, Chrys. *White Weddings: Romancing Heterosexuality in Popular Culture.* New York: Routledge, 1999.

Ingrassia, Catherine. "Diana, Martha and Me." In *Altared: Bridezillas, Bewilderment,* edited by Colleen Curran, 24–30. New York: Vintage Books, 2007.

Jensen, Tracey, and Jessica Ringrose. "Sluts That Choose vs. Doormat Gypsies: Exploring Affect in the Postfeminist, Visual Moral Economy of My Big Fat Gypsy Wedding." Accessed November 10, 2016. https://www.academia.edu/2441717.

Jones, Jenny M. *The Annotated Godfather.* Philadelphia: Running Press, 2007.

Levi-Strauss, Claude. *The Elementary Structures of Kinship.* Boston: Beacon Press, 1969.

Marich, Robert. *Marketing to Moviegoers: A Handbook of Strategies and Tactics.* Carbondale: Southern Illinois University Press, 2013.

Martin, Russell E. *Bride for the Tsars: Bride-Shows and Marriage Politics in Early Modern Russia.* DeKalb: Northern Illinois University Press, 2012.

Monger, George. *Marriage Customs of the World: An Encyclopedia of Dating Customs and Weddings.* Santa Barbara: ABC-CLIO, 2004.

Monson, Craig A. *Disembodied Voices: Music and Culture in an Early Modern Italian Convent.* Chicago: University of Chicago, 1995, 2012.

Okinyi, Nyaruri Paul, and Maangi Eric Nyankanga. "Traditional Marriage Customs among the Gusii of Kenya." *Historical Research Letter* 12 (2014). www.iiste.org /Journals/index.php/HRL/article/download/15035/15114.

Oyěwùmí, Oyèrónkẹ́. *The Invention of Women: Making an African Sense of Western Gender Discourses.* Minneapolis: University of Minnesota Press, 1997.

Richards, Jeffrey. "The Hollywoodization of Diana." In *Diana, the Making of a Media Saint,* edited by Jeffrey Richards, Scott Wilson, and Linda Woodhead, 59–73. London: I. B. Tauris, 1999.

Safran, William. "Diaspora in Modern Societies: Myth of Homeland and Return." *Diaspora* 1, no. 1 (Spring 1991): 83–99.

Slobin, Mark. "Music in Diaspora: The View from Euro-America." *Diaspora* 3, no. 3 (1994): 243–51.

Sugarman, Jane. *Engendering Song: Singing and Subjectivity at Prespa Albanian Weddings.*
    Chicago: University of Chicago Press, 1997.
Turner, Victor W. *The Ritual Process: Structure and Anti-Structure.* New York: Aldine de
    Gruyter, 1995.
Wallace, Carol. *All Dressed in White: The Irresistible Rise of the American Wedding.*
    New York: Penguin Books, 2004.

ONE

—∿—

THEORETICAL PERSPECTIVES ON WEDDINGS, LOCALLY AND BEYOND

A. J. RACY

THE TOPIC OF WEDDINGS evokes a certain air of familiarity. Speaking about weddings usually brings to mind a variety of related experiences and memories: of the venue, the limousine, the bride's dress, the jewelry, the food, and the music played, among others. Similarly, as a subject of research, the wedding theme may seem conceptually and methodologically discrete. As such, it may resemble a high aerial view of a city. However, the closer we descend toward the cityscape, the more expansive and intricately detailed the view appears. As we look more closely into the makeup and the significance of weddings, we may face a vast panoramic terrain of interrelated domains that are historical, social, and economic, as well as ceremonial, emotional, and aesthetic.

My interest in weddings at home and abroad reflects my own background as a Lebanese-born-and-raised performer and composer of Near Eastern music and as someone who has witnessed numerous homeland wedding events. Later on, in Southern California, I have occasionally played the role of a participant-observer while joining fellow musicians, or performing alone as guest artist, at wedding-related musical events. Meanwhile, as an ethnomusicologist, I have become increasingly cognizant of the social, conceptual, and symbolic layers that bear upon the wedding theme. In this chapter, I place the wedding within a broader theoretical and ethnographic framework that is multidisciplinary and thematically varied. In the process, I also draw on related examples from both the Arab world, especially the Levantine, or eastern Mediterranean areas, and the Arab American immigrant or diasporic experience.

SOCIAL STRUCTURE

As a starting point, I look into the wedding as a social institution. Weddings, like other comparable rituals or commemorative markers in people's lives, have been viewed as collective manifestations that are fundamentally linked to their respective all-embracing social systems. Accordingly, in weddings, as in religious practices, the underlying ideology supposedly gains compelling presence as it becomes a social entity, as Durkheim indicates: "Of course, since categories are themselves derived from concepts, we readily understand that they are the work of the collectivity. . . . Since the world expressed by the total system of concepts is the world that society represents, society alone can provide us with the most general notions according to which it must be represented."[1] Comparably, British social theorists, notably Alfred R. Radcliffe-Brown and Bronislaw Malinowski, and others in the field of ethnomusicology have upheld the theoretical premise that the various institutions reflect the community's shared societal values and, furthermore, perform complementary functions that together contribute to the organicity or interconnectedness within the larger social system.[2] Such a perspective, which has been frequently questioned or refined, calls attention to a certain mutual relevancy between the wedding as an institution and the all-encompassing social macrocosm. Accordingly, "The rite of marriage is also an end in itself that it creates a supernaturally sanctioned bond, superadded to the primarily biological fact: the union of man and woman for lifelong partnerships in affection, economic community, the procreation and rearing of children. . . . By giving monogamous marriage an imprint of value and sanctity, religion offers another gift to human culture."[3] However, the notion of an implicit normative symbiosis between the wedding and the presumably overarching systemic social order, although in a sense quintessential, I find to be rather restrictive, or at least theoretically limiting. For one thing, such a relationship seems to underestimate or overlook the tensions or variances between the two realms. In the Arab American context, the connection between the two may become particularly complex given the heterogeneities (in terms of ethnicities, countries of origin, and social and cultural orientations) within the Arab American communities at large. Similarly to be considered are Arab American weddings' departures from, as well as affinities with, the host country's social mainstream, which in turn is vast and internally diversified.

RITUAL PROCESS

Meanwhile, analytical research on rituals gives us a useful model for studying weddings. In Arnold van Gennep's classic *The Rite of Passage*, which addresses a variety of examples, including initiation rituals, weddings, funerals, pregnancy, and childbirth, the author examines how such events enable individuals or groups to pass from one status or social standing into another. In this case, three stages are involved: (1) "separation," in other words, detachment from a certain status or social realm; (2) "transition," or undergoing the transformational phase; and (3) "incorporation," namely, the passage or merger into the newly acquired status. These stages apply to the basic contour of many traditional weddings. Of particular interest to the present study is van Gennep's recognition of the intervening rites that permeate the broader ritual process. For example, "The passage from the transitional period, which is betrothal [that is, the mutual pledge to become married], to marriage itself, is made through a series of rites of separation from the former, followed by rites consisting of transition, and rites of incorporation into marriage."[4] Such a sequential progression reveals the numerous almost self-contained, albeit sequentially connected, episodes of liminality, temporality, and transition that usually occur within the wedding as a multiphased process. On a finer level, the wedding itself may be read or viewed in terms of separate phases, as well as linked processes.

Theoretically, the rite of passage model enables us to study the extended ritual in stages toward understanding the different weddings' internal idiosyncrasies, or departures from certain presupposed norms, in matters of structure and signification. Providing a focused perspective on the individual ingredients, the model is particularly useful for examining Arab American weddings in the West or in other contexts where the dynamics of acculturation and diversification pervade the different facets of the ritual process.

A further perspective to be considered is Victor Turner's work,[5] which, drawing on van Gennep's model, probes the transitory, or liminal period in the Ndembu culture of Zambia. Here, Turner speaks of an extraordinary context in which the neophytes are neither here nor there, or "betwixt and between."[6] Accordingly, they endure trying physical and mental experiences, while acquiring such "neutralizing" traits as being neither male nor female and neither living nor dead. "Their condition is one of ambiguity and paradox, a confusion of all the customary categories."[7] In the midst, allusions to particular community values are brought to the subjects' attention in preparation for their transitioning into the desired initiated status. Turner thus envisions the overall ritual process dialectically in terms of "structure and anti-structure."[8] Furthermore, he associates the transitioning or liminal phase with what he calls "communitas," a shared sense of collegiality among the subjects, or, as he writes, "What is interesting about liminal phenomena for our present purposes is the blend they offer of lowliness and sacredness, of homogeneity and comradeship. We are presented, in such rites, with a 'moment in and out of time,' and in and out of secular social structure, which reveals, however fleetingly, some recognition (in symbol if not always in language) of a generalized social bond that has ceased to be and has simultaneously yet to be fragmented into a multiplicity of structural ties."[9] The author also speaks of different types of communitas experiences as he finds them in a variety of world social and religious contexts.

Turner's ritual design adds a certain viewpoint to the study of the wedding as a dynamic process that is capable of acting on, or challenging, the social system. As a specialized cultural mechanism, or as "anti-structure," the wedding ritual produces new social realities through its compelling symbolic and experiential attributes. Furthermore, the state of communitas, as Turner presents it, may resemble the wedding's collective sense of camaraderie, which is enhanced by the emotional arousal or the effervescence that prevails among the participants. However, the celebratory ethos of the wedding ritual, at least in the Arab case, stands as a clear contrast to the mood of submission and deprivation that usually underlies the communitas state as it is represented. Commenting on "rites of affliction," Catherine Bell explains further: "Following Victor Turner, who frequently invoked this category of ritual, rites of affliction seek to mitigate the influence of spirits thought to be afflicting human beings with misfortune."[10] Arguably, the liminal ambiance of the wedding festivity grants the celebrated wedded couple extraordinary licenses and prerogatives. Similarly, I would add that the wedding-bound emotional experiences tend to be ineffably complex and varied. In Arab American, and other, weddings, I have seen deeply moved, teary-eyed individuals, as well as others who are ecstatically energized and manifestly jubilant.

SYMBOLIC SYSTEM

The profile of rituals, including weddings, as symbolically empowered expressions is linked to the interpretive or symbolic discourse.[11] Here we see a departure from the functionalist supremacy of "culture" in favor of a semiotically connected network within which such expressions as wedding events can be strategically loaded and meaningfully interpreted or decoded. In his work on "The Invention of Culture," Roy Wagner comparably speaks of dialectic processes that operate through "a critical readjustment of the tension between invention and convention."[12] Furthermore, the effect and affect of various cultural expressions have been widely noted by ethnomusicologists and others, in terms of poetry recitations challenging the male-oriented code of conduct, the momentarily achieved symbolic gender reversals through trance rituals, singing traversing physical or conceptual barriers between brothers and sisters, linking certain sounds of nature to crying, and using song to "engender" the social patterns and hierarchies at weddings.[13]

Along similar lines, throughout history marriage has provided means to establish new ethnic, familial, religious, and political alliances or, for that matter, to reconnect the immigrants with their homelands. Furthermore, viewed through an interpretive, or "thick descriptive," lens, the study of wedding events may reveal several layers of meaning. At an Arab American wedding party I attended in Northern California almost thirty years ago, the event, on the surface at least, seemed typical or ordinary, except for something that caught my attention. I noticed two groups in the audience competing in requesting dance songs from the musicians on the stage, with one of the groups seeming to be more assertive in making the requests. Upon discussing this pattern with fellow musicians who knew the people at the wedding, I began to make sense of the behaviors: the bride and the groom came originally from two different villages that shared old mutual rivalries, and more requests came from the family that had covered a larger share of the wedding expenses. Interpretively speaking, the festive event seemed to provide an arena for strategized or symbolic competition, entitlement, and power play expressed through the song and dance performance.

PRACTICE

Other related theories treat the ritual as a process of societal enactment. Significant input comes from poststructuralist thought, specifically Pierre Bourdieu's theory of practice and his notion of "habitus": a habit-like disposition that intuitively inspires people's actions (practice) and in turn is inspired by the people's action (agency).[14] In this regard, Jane Sugarman, in her well-researched and critically oriented ethnomusicological work on Albanian weddings adds a more dialectic perspective, that "we need a notion of culture as something that is multiple and disjunct in order to chart the ways that individuals and communities are incorporating, resisting, or reformulating these discourses and practices through musical means."[15] Meanwhile, the wedding practice allows for implementing gradual change through improvising or "editing" in the course of enacting the wedding event. Moreover, the related notion that the practice may exhibit significant changes when it is transplanted into a drastically different locality or social environment may be further studied or refined in the case of weddings among the various immigrant groups in North America.

CONTINUITY AND CHANGE

Wedding practice, although arguably tending to maintain a significant degree of integrity and longevity, does also change over time. In many world contexts, change develops through gradual intercultural assimilation and exchange. Sugarman's study is particularly interesting as it reveals the historical connections between Balkan communities and the Ottoman or Islamic East, as well as the adjacent cross-Mediterranean areas. Her research, for example, gives attention to the Arabic Ottoman–derived nomenclatures that refer to the emotional state experienced by the musicians and the participants, as well as sheds light on the links between the wedding practice and such basic notions as family, community, gender, patriarchy, generational differences, and social reciprocities. Moreover, change may occur, both locally and through geographic relocation. In this case, Sugarman examines the Albanian wedding scene in North America, for example in Chicago and Toronto. The themes covered include (1) traditional ritual retentions such as the shaving of the groom, performing line dances, and singing in praise of the bride; (2) ambivalence toward certain American-inspired practices, although in some cases accepting the use of both back-home and Western music and dance expressions; and (3) innovations, represented for instance in changing the sequential order within the wedding ritual, eliminating certain components, and a tendency for male and female wedding song to be rhythmically and melodically simplified.[16] Thus clearly revealed are the manifestations of both the traditional practice and the ensuing manifestations of urbanization, modernization, and Westernization in the new-world setting.

Comparable features of continuity and change in time and space appear also in Arab-world weddings. The relatively stable or commonly encountered wedding practices have been documented by a number of dance and music scholars, including ethnomusicologists. In her *Music in Druze Life: Ritual, Values, and Performance Practice*,[17] Kathleen Hood meticulously documents the wedding and funeral rituals among the Druze communities. The Druze religious sect, which emerged as an eleventh-century offshoot of Ismāʿīlī Shīʿism, now exists largely in Syria and Lebanon and, to a lesser extent, in Palestine/Israel and Jordan. In her extensive research in Syria, Jordan, and Lebanon, Hood covers the ritual practices that are typical of the Druze communities but also addresses the significant sharing of music, dance, and poetry repertoires with neighboring communities, notably the adjacent Bedouin tribal groups and the rural, especially Christian, areas in Lebanon.

Introducing the Druze social structure and theological tenets and hierarchies, Hood's coverage on Syria, and to a certain extent Jordan, highlights the importance of the wedding as a landmark for demonstrating the local values of chivalry, honor, heroic struggle, and hospitality. These values are expressed through the local variety of dances, songs, and solo performances by the male poet-singer who traditionally accompanies himself on the Bedouin *rabābah*, an upright single-string bowed instrument. Further discussions address such typical expressions as the *ḥidāʾ*, call-and-response, highly animated, war-related songs that the men may perform, for example at the groom's *zaffah*, or wedding procession. Similarly noted are the widely common *āwīhā* or *zaghārīd*, short declamatory songs that end with ululation (a high-pitched, trill-like vocal effect) traditionally performed by women in praise of the bride or groom. Also noted is the throwing of rice seeds at the bride and groom, especially during their zaffah processions.

Among the Druze, and also among a large number of local Arab communities, the most widely encountered are the *dabkah*, the collective line-dance varieties that are performed either by men alone or women alone or, in some urban and more recent contexts, jointly by both. In the traditional dabkah performance, for example in Lebanon, the dancers usually perform call-and-response songs that are associated with the dabkah dance genre and occur in between the short animated episodes that recur during the course of the dance performance. Similarly the supreme instrument that customarily accompanies the traditional dabkah is the *mijwiz*, the iconic embodiment of the Near Eastern folk musical ethos: a double-pipe single-reed instrument, sometimes technically referred to as a "double clarinet," which is played through the technique of circular breathing.[18] Another instrument that traditionally accompanies the dabkah dance is an edge-blown metal or reed folk flute called *minjayrah* (in Lebanon) or *shabbābah* (among Syrians, Palestinians, and Jordanians). During my teens in Lebanon, I witnessed and joined dabkah lines at weddings and other festive events and also learned to play the minjayrah and the mijwiz.

However, also introduced are relatively more recent wedding practices. One is the hiring of a *firqah*, or a musical band made up of a few instrumentalists who perform primarily during the zaffah procession. Usually appearing in traditional or "folkloric" attire, they play primarily outdoor instruments, such as the *ṭabl baladī* (large double-sided drum), the *darbukkah* (hand drum), the *mazhar* (a typically Egyptian large-frame drum with heavy brass cymbals), and the *mizmār* (oboe-type double-reed instrument). The firqah repertoire includes folk and urban popular tunes from the region, for example from Lebanon and Syria, and also Egypt. In terms of instrumentation and repertoire, the firqah ensemble is inspired by the familiar Egyptian wedding zaffah ensemble. As Hood observes, another relatively more recent phenomenon is the use of the Scottish bagpipe in Jordanian weddings, as well as in other festive events. Given the British influence on the country's military institution, the bagpipe has become part of the local folk musical domain.

In Egypt, comparable patterns have been studied. Traditionally, the wedding culture reflects the country's rich and diverse music and dance heritage.[19] The Egyptian wedding serves as a prime arena for various music and dance art forms. In her extensive documentary work, Aisha Ali, a well-known Los Angeles–based dancer, dance instructor, and dance researcher with whom

I have performed as a musician on occasions, has provided a vivid survey of Egyptian dances. As illustrated through a number of her released records and videos, including *Dances of Egypt* and *Wedding in Luxor*, the traditional wedding, for example in Upper, or southern, Egypt, a variety of folk music and dances may be featured. Traditionally included have been the dances of the *ghawāzī*, professional female dancers, usually two or three performing together, accompanied by a group of three or more mizmār players and a performer on the ṭabl baladī. Also entertaining may be singers and dancers who are accompanied by a group of *rabābah* players (Egyptian *rabābah* is a two-string spike fiddle) and percussion instrumentalists. Also documented is the bride and grooms's zaffah, which is a prime feature of the Egyptian wedding. This ritual procession, which may take place outdoors on the way to the festive wedding celebration indoors, or on a rooftop, or in a *khaymah*, a specially erected ornately embroidered cloth tent. In the procession, there is a group of musicians, or a firqah, of performers who sing and play folk instruments, usually including a number of large-frame drums most typically of the mazhar type. In one of Aisha Ali's videos,[20] a zaffah in Alexandria is celebrated with music by a few players on the Scottish bagpipes, a phenomenon that, as Ali has noted to me, is adopted from the Jordanian practice. Furthermore, in both of her documentaries, Ali covers a representative selection of indoor *farah* (wedding) festivities during which the bride and groom are shown seated in the background as they and the guests are entertained by urban singers and dancers. The typical accompanying ensemble includes instruments such as the microtonally adjusted keyboard "orgue" and the accordion, as well as traditional instruments, such as the *qānūn* (plucked zither).

The zaffah, meanwhile, has been closely examined by Carol Lee Kent (Sahara), a well-known Southern California–based dancer whom I have known for many years, especially when she studied at the University of California, Los Angeles (UCLA) Dance Department in 1983–1985. Having performed professionally for a number of years in Egypt, Kent, in a 1989 article,[21] describes three zaffah types. The first is associated with the *fallahīn*, or farmers from rural villages, in which the zaffah employs a folk-oriented military-derived brass band. The second is the Upper Egyptian, or Ṣaʿīdī, zaffah, which is common in the central areas of Egypt, and features mizmār ensembles with female dancers and at times with men's stick dancers. The third takes place in narrow city streets and is accompanied by professional musicians, who in turn will stay longer to perform for the following wedding festivity. We are told that "in these three outdoor *zaffah* forms, the female dancer is fully covered in a tight, straight dress with a hip sash."[22]

Kent looks into a fourth, recently quite prevalent model: the "hotel *zaffah*."[23] Here the context is a reception with entertainment held in an expensive hotel, a choice that reflects a certain wealth or social status. Inside, a shortened version of the zaffah takes place "as a short walk across the ballroom floor instead of a procession of the entire neighborhood taking the full afternoon."[24] Similarly taking place is a stage show by one or more belly dancers and popular singers with their tuxedoed firqah accompanists. Kent notes that "it is this fourth hotel style of *zaffah* that is most closely mimicked at the Arab-American wedding in the Los Angeles area."[25]

Broadly speaking, Arab weddings exist in a variety of forms that basically reflect the people's geographic, cultural, and economic backgrounds. Understandably, some weddings are held as "in house" events, in other words, initiated to a large extent by the family, the relatives, the acquaintances, and members of the local community, including the cooks and the entertainers. However, trends of professional servicing, commodification, and standardization are becoming more visible, especially in urban centers. Speaking of the artistic expression, besides the exposure to European and American films and videos, the Egyptian cinema since the early 1930s has gained wide popularity throughout the larger Near Eastern world. The film plots have, almost expectedly, included Egyptian wedding scenes. The featured stars have included the late memorable singer, composer, and actor Farīd al-Aṭrash and renowned belly dancers such as Tahia Carioca (Taḥiyyah Kāryūkā) and Samia Gamal (Sāmya Jamāl). The on-screen wedding depictions have inspired numerous Egyptian-style belly dancers in the United States and in various parts of the world.

IMMIGRATION—DIASPORA

Essentially, weddings in the diaspora reflect both the new-world experience and the connections to the place(s) of origin. However, immigrant or diasporic identities, the hyphenation notwithstanding, are more than cumulative combinations of traits from the Old World and the New World. Those who left their homelands to live in North America, among them Arab Americans, have been constantly negotiating and dialectically constructing their identities. As Stuart Hall explains, new-world ethnic identities are "far from being eternally fixed in some essentialized past, they are subject to continuous 'play' of history, culture, and power."[26] Given their particular constructs, such identities have been studied as "hybridities." The concept of hybridity has been widely discussed and, in some cases, critiqued.[27] Granted, the Hollywood film industry has produced a number of interesting and socially engaging feature films on weddings. In some cases, the typical behavioral traits and attitudes of certain ethnic groups have been highlighted or stereotyped, or even exaggerated and humorously caricatured. However, sometimes such apparent sweeping depictions include the untold story of the immigrants' weddings, as arenas for cultural negotiation and creative adaptation. After all, some of these films also parody the alleged American natives' naivete about the foreign world, as well as illustrate the immigrants' successful integration into the American mainstream.[28]

In the New World, music and the arts have been recognized as powerful tools of self-representation. Thus, "even though they are out of the ordinary experiences, music and dance (and talk about music and dance) do encourage people to feel that they are in touch with an essential part of themselves, their emotions and their 'communities.'"[29] Similarly suited for the projection of one's own image within the new cultural and political environment are the literature and the visual arts,[30] as well as the native visual symbols, including the attire and the cuisine.

Notably, such expressions have maintained a certain connection with the homeland.[31] Actually, definitions of the diasporic condition have recognized the place of homeland in the people's consciousness. Accordingly, one definition of the diasporic status has taken note of (1) people moving from a center to a peripheral locality; (2) keeping a collective memory of the place of origin; (3) feeling a certain alienation in the new environment; (4) having an idealized image of, and hope to return to, the homeland; (5) expressing strong interest in the livelihood and maintenance of the homeland; and (6) attempting to keep a consistent connection with the homeland and sharing a feeling of allegiance to the country of origin.[32] Although the theories on diasporas have since been qualified and refined, the topic of homeland has also been reassessed. Accordingly, the place of origin, which historically undergoes change, may be viewed with an aura of nostalgia. It may also be imagined, or mentally reconstructed, and even fetishized.[33]

Today, however, the images, memories, and perceptions of the homeland are more likely to be revised or updated. This is happening through direct contacts with the homeland, the relative accessibility of travel, and the electronic audiovisual mediation, or global "mediascapes."[34] The compelling presence of the land of origin within the diaspora is illustrated, for example, through the direct availability of Indian Bollywood films in Indian communities who now live in different parts of the world.[35]

THE NEW WORLD

Arab Americans have undergone notable changes since their arrival in the New World during the last decades of the nineteenth century, when the places they emigrated from were largely part of the Ottoman Empire. Many came from the province of Syria, which embraced today's Syria and the Mount Lebanon area, which is part of modern-day Lebanon. In the West, the designation "Syrians" lasted until 1917, when the Ottoman rule ended.[36] A vast number of immigrants were Christians of different denominations, many of whom left for North and South America to seek refuge and a new life, given the oppressive Ottoman rule and the economic hardships in the home region. During the early decades of immigration, many who came from the Near East settled in the American Northeast, in and around the major metropolitan centers.[37] In later decades of the twentieth century, additional immigrants came from other parts of the Eastern Arab world and North Africa and settled in different parts of the United States. By the late twentieth century, the community of Arab Americans, estimated to be about two and a half million, has been considered as one of the fastest-growing communities in the country.[38] Today, the Arab American presence is represented by a variety of people who have immigrated, or whose ancestors did, from countries around the Arab world.

In order to better understand the Arab American wedding as an event, we obviously need to look into the demographic configurations and the historical backgrounds of the Arab Americans. Although the earliest Arab American wedding ritual may not have been adequately documented, we can point out certain common traits. Since a large constituency of the early immigrants came from the Levant region, especially rural or village areas, it is likely that the newcomers followed their homeland wedding models, albeit with certain modifications or deletions. Similarly, the overall nature of the wedding rituals may have reflected the immigrants' respective religious denominations and allegiances. As historian Philip K. Hitti noted in the early twentieth century, "A Syrian is born to his religion, just as an American is born to his nationality. In fact, the church takes the place of the state for him. It is inconceivable to find a Syrian who does not profess to be a Christian or a Muhammadan—regardless of the nature of his private belief."[39]

A further consideration may be the desire of some early immigrant male bachelors to go back to the "old country" to find and marry women there, possibly from one's own family or home village. Similarly to keep in mind, many of the immigrants, whose names were sometimes changed or Anglicized upon entering the United States, have been eager to adopt the host culture. In fact, the link to the homeland, as well as the interest in becoming well established within the American social system, was reinforced by the immigrants' flourishing literary life, the numerous Arabic newspapers printed in America, and the influential writers, such as the Lebanese-born Gibran Kahlil Gibran (Jibrān Khalīl Jibrān) (1883–1931), whose works appeared in English and in Arabic.

Musically speaking, some of the early comers brought with them instruments that they played in America, including the mijwiz, as a prime musical emblem of the homeland. I have learned about specific individuals who played the instrument in some early immigrant weddings or other related events. During the 1930s and 1940s, the mystique of the mijwiz and its unmistakable association with homeland weddings was audibly evoked by Arab American musicians on commercial 78 rpm discs released by Arab American record companies. Emulated on the violin, with darbukkah accompaniment, the recorded performances carry titles that mention the dabkah and the raqṣ (singular, raqṣah, or "a dance"), which refer to the solo, typically female, dances performance at the Levantine wedding.[40] Also certain imported discs that were recorded in the homeland and included wedding-related popular songs became accessible to the immigrants.[41] As Anne Rasmussen writes, later media such as the LP discs, cassettes, and videotapes have played "a huge role in collapsing distance between peoples within the same cities, among communities across the country, and between nations separated by oceans, political boundaries, and government travel bans."[42]

By the mid-twentieth century, the typical Arab American wedding borrowed from the traditional homeland counterpart, but also embraced newly acquired features. Although certain portions of the wedding ritual may have occurred in a private home or in a place of worship, the main wedding festivity typically occurred in larger venues, for example in a reception hall connected to a church or in a more public space, such as a hotel ballroom or banquet facility. The event, which included the bride and groom, as well as their respective families and various invitees, unfolded roughly as follows: usually after dinner, which sometimes offered traditional dishes and possibly alcoholic beverages, the entertainment was provided by a typically small musical ensemble that consisted of players on traditional Arab instruments, such as the 'ūd (short-necked, plucked lute), the violin, the qānūn, and the darbukkah, and featured one or more singers. These basically hired professional performers may have included Arab Americans or others who have recently immigrated to the United States. In this context, the dabkah dance was a highly prominent part of the festivity.

However, in these events (as I have observed during the past several decades), the dance-music scene had already acquired a certain character of its own: the dance line was characteristically very long as it included several dozen or more men and women from the audience; the dancers danced to a diversity of urban songs or instrumental pieces that were not necessarily composed for the dabkah; and the dabkah steps seemed to follow a simplified and repetitive foot work that differed from the traditional and more nuanced dabkah steps that I have performed and observed in the homeland village context. Although occasionally some recent immigrants in the audience have performed in the homeland dabkah style, or styles, the immigrants' more accessible dance version seemed to suit all the audience members and possibly those who did not come from Arab origins.

During the late twentieth century, the Arab American wedding became both more attuned to the American wedding practice and simultaneously more conscious of the community's own roots. To illustrate, Rasmussen has intimately experienced and presented three Arab American wedding examples in Detroit during the 1990s. Detroit is known to host the largest Arab American immigrant community, numbering about 250,000 at the time of the writing.[43] In the first example, a Lebanese wedding party, Rasmussen notices several identifying features. Included are the bride and groom's musically accompanied zaffah procession as they enter the reception hall; the traditional performance of āwīhā, described earlier, being delivered by women, who in this case are garbed in Lebanese folk attire; and a poem being read in honor of the bride and groom. Furthermore, performances on the mizmār and ṭabl baladī by Detroit musicians lead the zaffah and also play on the inside dance floor. Local Arab musical bands with singers and instrumentalists using both traditional and electronic instruments provide the bulk of the entertainment. Also particularly central is the dabkah line dance.

By comparison, the second example, a Detroit Yemeni wedding party, highlights a comparable set of practices. Particularly notable are the following: a bride-and-groom zaffah procession in the public space where the party takes place; not Yemeni, but American cuisine revealing a certain acculturation in food preferences; predominantly Yemeni attendees or ones of Yemeni descent; and as typical of this and many other weddings, the bride and the groom being seated prominently apart from the regular guest seating. Rasmussen also observed a Lebanese musical ensemble and a Yemeni musical ensemble, both from Detroit, entertaining the guests. Belly dancers, joining the zaffah procession, also dance for the main wedding party. At this wedding, the celebration represents the highly conservative orientation of the Yemeni community. However, she notices the people's acquired interest in the music and culture of other Detroit immigrant communities, as best represented by the popularity of two locally well-known Lebanese musicians: a woman who sings and her husband who plays the ʿūd. "The Lebanese and Arab popular music that Rana and Naim [Naʿīm] perform might be referred to as the musical lingua franca of Arab American Detroit. Their songs and musical style are the most commonly heard music in the area."[44]

The third example brings to attention a different cross-cultural dynamic: a party celebrating a mixed marriage in Detroit. The attendees are Americans of Iraqi descent and others of Italian descent. In this case, the two persons getting married are compatible in terms of their religious orientations, since one is a

Christian Chaldean Iraqi and the other is an Italian of a Catholic background. Rasmussen particularly notes, however, the passionate interest in Iraqi, especially popular, music among the Detroit Iraqi public, as well as the diversity of musics heard throughout the different wedding phases, from the zaffah to the larger main festive event. The musical selections include Iraqi popular songs with accompaniment on electronic keyboard and other instruments, "a set of dance music featuring primarily Iraqi songs with a smattering of mainstream Arab music thrown in,"[45] and non-Arab musical items such as Italian tarantellas and American pop favorites. These three wedding orientations, besides representing the cultural, ethnic, and religious backgrounds of Arab Americans and other groups in the United States, set the scene for today's familiar wedding profile.

In the twenty-first century, the contours of the wedding tend to unfold as variations on a typical sequential structure that includes the following stages: (1) introductory or background mood-setting music, either live or recorded, when the guests are arriving prior to the formal wedding ritual; (2) the formal nuptial ceremony, either indoors or outdoors, during which the processional walk of the bride and her attendants takes place and when the bride and groom may take their vows; (3) possibly a zaffah, or a transitory procession, that may precede or follow the formal ceremony, in the latter case shifting the emphasis toward the large festivity, typically held in a rented public space, and (4) the elaborate festivity proper, during which food is served and the groups invited would participate in socializing and dancing to live or recorded music.

The variations tend to be flexible. For example, during the first phase, the introductory mood music can be provided either through a recording of suitable Arab or Western music, or performed live by a Western chamber ensemble, such as a string quartet. The second phase, which can be particularly solemn or symbolically meaningful, the music may be live or recorded. Then in the third phase, if a zaffah is planned, the options may vary. For the Egyptian wedding, the musicians may provide an Egyptian zaffah, with such instruments as the mizmar, mazhar, ṭabl baladī, and others. If the wedding is Palestinian or Jordanian, a zaffah with a bagpipe and percussion may be used. If available, a mijwiz player may perform for a wedding that is Syrian, Lebanese, or Palestinian.

However, the Egyptian zaffah style has emerged as a shared generic expression that occurs regardless of the wedding's national, ethnic, or religious orientation. Furthermore, the procession may have the bride or the groom riding on a horse or lifted on the palms of enthusiastic zaffah participants. I was also told by a fellow musician that at an Arab wedding in Texas, members of the hosting family arranged for having a camel, presumably to be paraded during an outdoor procession.

Figure 1.1. A zaffah musical group with typically Egyptian instruments. *Courtesy of Hasan Minawi.*

FROM DABKAH TO DJ

In the last phase, or the culminating festive gathering, the musical entertainment is provided by an American or Arab music band or by both. However, an additional particularly central component in the events is the DJ, who provides the soundtracks for the dance that is open for any of the guests and includes the bride and groom. In this context, the dabkah may be performed by the few who are eager to represent and to display an expression from the "old heritage." However, the predominant activity may be the familiar American free-style dancing, and at times other dance styles. A belly dancer (usually American) or a folkloric dance troupe may also perform. Evoking a night club atmosphere through the loud music, the dance, and the lighting effects, the DJ typically plays tracks selected from American rock material and Arab and other popular musics, in all cases recorded with a strong, rhythmic drive. In some ways, the music acts as a homogenizing dynamic that accommodates the cultural diversity within the large audience, including Americans or Arab Americans, adult women and men, or teenagers, all of whom may be seen dancing in the center dance space. Incidentally, some guests, usually adults, find the recorded or live music too loud

Figure 1.2. A zaffah musical group with bagpipe and percussion, Los Angeles. *Courtesy of Hasan Minawi.*

Figure 1.3. A view of a zaffah procession in Louisiana. *Courtesy of Hasan Minawi.*

to engage in normal conversation with others. The types of music, the food, and other details may be chosen to please the mixed attendees, especially when the bride and the groom come from different cultural, national, religious, and even musical backgrounds.

CREATIVE PRACTICES

Sometimes, however, the wedding embraces novel or creative components that depart from the convention or the routine. The bride or the groom (or both), may wish to bring to their wedding an air of individuality, or implicitly perhaps, to make a social or philosophical statement. Such intentions may apply to the physical location, the officiating (religious or secular) person, the text to be read, the decorative displays, the people invited, the food, the music, and so on. Musically speaking, in the Arab American context, especially among the intellectually oriented or culturally minded, I have been invited to play *taqāsīm* (classical modal improvisations) on the *buzuq* (a long-necked lute), or on the *nāy* (a traditional reed flute usually associated with mysticism and meditation).

Often thoughtfully considered, such gestures may also express deep-seated sentiments, memories, and nostalgias. In this regard, I have been particularly moved by a sequence of music-related events that have recalled the homeland, family, immigration, historical continuity, and the wedding ceremony. On March 30, 2007, when I went to give a musical concert in Knoxville, Tennessee, I met there Jim Harb, a young second-generation Arab American man, and we became friends. At that time, Jim told me that his family has kept the mijwiz of his late father and asked me if I would repair it and send it back to the family. I was delighted to do that.

After returning to California, I gathered information from Jim about his father, whose life sheds interesting light on the history of Arab immigration to the United States and the struggles and successes of the immigrants in the new world. His father, Wadie Yusef (Wadī' Yūsuf), or W. J. Harb, was born into a Christian family in Ramallah, Palestine, in 1902. He came to the United States in 1920 and passed away in 1983. Yusef played the 'ūd as well as the mijwiz. Although apparently recordings of Yusef's music were unavailable, Jim's reflections about the family history provided informative glimpses of the family's social and musical life:

> Dad was the first of his extended family to dwell in Knoxville. He was soon followed by his brother John (Hannah), and they were soon joined by their first cousin. Eventually, more and more cousins followed, and a small coterie of Ramallah-ites soon established themselves in Knoxville. These people, outliers in the larger, mostly WASP community of Knoxville needed each other for sustenance. So they would gather at each other's houses from time to time to speak their Arabic and to eat their Arabic foods. And when they did that, longing somewhat for their old homeland, they would sing the songs of the homeland that resonated with their souls. And dad would sometimes play the oud ['ūd] and either accompany that singing or play some of the instrumental songs that they all loved to hear.[46]

Upon repairing the mijwiz, I made a recording of myself playing the father's instrument and returned to Jim the instrument and a CD copy of my performance, with a note of dedication to the life and memory of the late father, Wadie Yusef.

In 2016, after almost ten years, I was deeply touched by a phone call from Jim who told me that he had just gotten married to an American woman. He added, "At our wedding ceremony, we played the recording of you playing my father's mijwiz."[47]

CONCLUSION

This study has addressed a widely familiar human expression that is saturated with meanings and associations. I have brought to attention the wide interest in studying the wedding as a concept, process, and institution. Over the decades, theorists have given us a range of perspectives on the wedding, as a sociobiological entity, a social structure, a rite of passage, a ritual, a symbolic system, an antistructure, and a poststructure/practice, among others. In this research, the critical analysis of such interpretations, combined with detailed ethnographic documentation, has led to valuable insights, as well as raised questions that tend to challenge, or problematize, the study.

Certain realizations stand out, especially the complexity of the subject matter. The different theoretical constructs have revealed the multifarious nature of the wedding in terms of its social, cultural, and psychological implications. Further considered are the changing complexions of the wedding. As clearly illustrated, neither the homeland nor the diasporic wedding profiles have been frozen in time. Thus the relationship between them, as "moving targets," needs to be carefully interpreted, especially since their mutual borrowings often acquire new meanings and nuances. For example, is the use of traditional practices in today's weddings consciously meant to pay tribute to the local heritage or is it done habitually, through some historical and customary inertia? Are such seemingly quaint practices as using a horse or a camel for the procession, or throwing rice at the bride and the bridegroom in a Houston, or Los Angeles, or Chicago Arab American wedding a way to affirm one's ethnic roots, or to express nostalgia for the past, or to momentarily parody bygone practices, or all of the these? Similarly, is having a DJ in Arab American weddings intended to project an Americanized image, or to have a suitable means for engaging the typically diversified multiethnic and multigenerational public, or to emulate what is currently a trend back home, or all of the above?

Finally, this investigation has shown a certain ambiguity in the relationship between the wedding and the broader cultural system. In certain ways, the wedding has been shown to have intimate ties to other life domains, for example in terms of enacting or engendering certain social patterns, family values, economic hierarchies, aesthetic criteria, and so on. However, I have also argued that the wedding as an institutionalized practice projects a certain aura of specialness. Particularly recognized are its existential undertones, being associated with living, procreating, aging, and ultimately dying. Its connotations are emotional, visceral, and pan-human. My coverage of Arab and Arab American weddings has, implicitly perhaps, demonstrated that the wedding, not unlike the funeral, occupies a venerated human space, or what I call a "power zone." Not to ignore the closely connected affective expressions, typically including dance, poetry, and music, the wedding, above all, is a *performance*. In this vein, I have recognized the role of human agency through the ritual experimentation, or creative play, initiated by the bride and groom or others who plan the event. Challenging or testing the norm, as well as observing a certain established decorum, contributes to the wedding's vitality and continuity as a human experience.

A. J. RACY is Distinguished Professor of Ethnomusicology at the University of California at Los Angeles and a multi-instrumentalist and composer. He is author of *Making Music in the Arab World: The Culture and Artistry of Tarab*.

NOTES

1. Durkheim, *Elementary Forms of Religious Life*, 335 and 337.
2. For other examples, see Merriam, *Anthropology of Music*, and "Ethnographic Experience."
3. Malinowski, *Magic, Science, and Religion*, 40–41.
4. Gennep, *Rite of Passage*, 11.
5. Turner, *Ritual Process*.
6. Ibid., 234.
7. Ibid., 236.
8. Ibid.
9. Ibid., 96.
10. Bell, *Ritual*, 115.
11. See Geertz, *Interpretation of Cultures*.
12. Wagner, *Invention of Culture*, 99.
13. Abu-Lughod, *Veiled Sentiments*; Roseman, *Healing Sounds from the Malaysian Rainforest*; Seeger, "What Can We Learn When They Sing?," 373–94; Feld, *Sound and Sentiment*; Sugarman, *Engendering Song*.
14. Bourdieu, *Outline of a Theory of Practice*.
15. Sugarman, *Engendering Song*, 32.
16. Sugarman, *Engendering Song*, 286–340.
17. Hood, *Music in Druze Life*.
18. Racy, "Dialectical Perspective on Musical Instruments," 37–57.

19. Saleh, "Documentation of the Ethnic Dance Traditions of the Arab Republic of Egypt."

20. Ali, *Dances of Egypt.*

21. Kent, "Arab-American 'Zaffah al-'Arusah' Procession," 24.

22. Ibid.

23. Ibid.

24. Ibid.

25. Ibid.

26. Hall, "Cultural Identity and Diaspora," 320.

27. Ashcroft, Griffiths, and Tiffin, *Post-Colonial Studies Reader*, 183–84; Bhabha, "Cultural Diversity and Cultural Differences," 209; Taylor, "Some Versions of Difference," 145–55.

28. Quite illustrative is the 2002 HBO hit *My Big Fat Greek Wedding*, with Nia Vardalos, John Corbett, Lainie Kazan, and Michael Constantine, with Andrea Martin and Joey Fatone. This film, which highlights a wedding of an American groom and Greek woman, deals with ethnicity issues in America, as discussed in this chapter. Of the many Hollywood films that deal with weddings, a few are particularly well known. A good example is the movie *Father of the Bride*, inspired by Edward Streeter's novel, which depicts the challenges and the rewards of holding weddings in modern America.

29. Stokes, "Introduction: Ethnicity, Identity, and Music," 13.

30. See Turino and Lea, *Identity and the Arts in Diaspora Communities.*

31. See Moser and Racy, "Homeland in the Literature and Music of Syrian-Lebanese Immigrants and Their Descendants in Brazil," 280–311.

32. See Safran, "Diasporas in Modern Societies," 83–84.

33. See Yazedjian, "Reconstructing the Armenian," 38–50, and Naficy, *Making of Exile Cultures*, 127–55.

34. Appadurai, "Disjuncture and Difference in the Global Cultural Economy," 336.

35. See Alessandrini, "My Heart's Indian for All That," 315–40.

36. See Naff, "Lebanese Immigration into the United States," 142.

37. See Hitti, *Syrians in America*, 66–68.

38. See Rasmussen, "Music of Arab Detroit," 74.

39. Hitti, *Syrians in America*, 34-5.

40. The imitation of the mijwiz on the violin was done by bringing two violin strings very close to each other to play in unison or in octaves so that a certain "beat" effect, or subtle pitch discrepancy, would create a nasal timbre similar to that of the mijwiz. This practice had earlier been heard on 78 rpm discs by the famous Syrian Egyptian violinist Sāmī al-Shawwā, who visited New York in the middle of the twentieth century.

41. Racy, "Sound Recording in the Life of Early Arab-American Immigrants," 41–52.

42. Rasmussen, "Music of Arab Detroit," 96.

43. Ibid., 81.

44. Ibid., 89.

45. Ibid., 90.

46. Jim Harb, written communication to author, September 27, 2016.

47. I am thankful to Jim Harb and Laurel Goodrich for their support and for giving me permission to include the material on the Harb family.

BIBLIOGRAPHY

Abu-Lughod, Lila. *Veiled Sentiments: Honor and Poetry in a Bedouin Society.* Berkeley: University of California Press, 1986.

Ali, Aisha. *Dances of Egypt* (DVD documentary and cover notes). Los Angeles: Araf DVDA-900, 2006.

———. *Wedding in Luxor* (DVD documentary and cover notes). Los Angeles, CA: Araf DVDA 905, 2014.

Alessandrini, A. C. "My Heart's Indian for All That: Bollywood Film between Home and Diaspora." *Diaspora* 10, no. 3 (2001): 315–40.

Appadurai, Arjun. "Disjuncture and Difference in the Global Cultural Economy." In *Social Theory Volume II: Power & Identity in the Global Era*, edited by Roberta Garner, 332–46. New York: Broadview Press, 2004.

Ashcroft, Bill, Gareth Griffiths, and Helen Tiffin. *The Post-Colonial Studies Reader.* London: Routledge, 1995.

Bhabha, Homi K. "Cultural Diversity and Cultural Differences." In *The Post-Colonial Studies Reader*, edited by B. Ashcroft, 206–9. New York: Routledge, 1995.

Bell, Catherine. *Ritual: Perspectives and Dimensions.* Rev. ed. Oxford and New York: Oxford University Press, 1997.

Bourdieu, Pierre. *Outline of a Theory of Practice.* Translated from the French by Richard Nice. Cambridge: Cambridge University Press, 1977.

Durkheim, Emile. *The Elementary Forms of Religious Life.* Translated from the French by Carol Cosman. Abridged with an introduction and notes by Mark S. Cladis. Oxford: Oxford University Press, 2001.

Feld, Steven. *Sound and Sentiment: Birds, Weeping, Poetics, and Song in Kaluli Expression.* Philadelphia: University of Pennsylvania Press, 1982.

Geertz, Clifford. *The Interpretation of Cultures.* New York: Basic Books, 1973.

Hall, Stuart. "Cultural Identity and Diaspora." In *Social Theory Volume II: Power & Identity in the Global Era*, edited by Roberta Garner, 318–30. New York: Broadview Press, 2004.

Hitti, Philip. *The Syrians in America.* New York: George Doran, 1924.

Hood, Kathleen. *Music in Druze Life: Ritual, Values and Performance Practice.* London: Druze Heritage Foundation, 2007.

Kent, Carol Lee. "Arab-American 'Zaffah al-'Arusah' Procession." *UCLA Journal of Dance Ethnology* 13 (1989): 23–28.

Malinowski, Bronislaw. *Magic, Science, and Religion: And Other Essays.* Garden City, New York: Doubleday Anchor Books, 1948.

Merriam, Alan P. *The Anthropology of Music.* Evanston, IL: Northwestern University Press, 1964.

———. "The Ethnographic Experience: Drum-Making among the Bala (Basongye)." *Ethnomusicology* 13, no. 1 (1969): 74–100.

Moser, Robert, and A. J. Racy. "The Homeland in the Literature and Music of Syrian-Lebanese Immigrants and Their Descendants in Brazil." *Diaspora* 19, nos. 2–3 (2017): 280–311.

Naff, Alixa. "Lebanese Immigration into the United States: 1880 to the Present." In *The Lebanese in the World: A Century of Emigration*, edited by Albert Hourani and

Nadim Shehadi, 141–65. London: Centre for Lebanese Studies, with I. B. Tauris, 1992.

Naficy, Hamid. *The Making of Exile Cultures: Iranian Television in Los Angeles.* Minneapolis: University of Minnesota Press, 1993.

Racy, A. J. "A Dialectical Perspective on Musical Instruments: The East-Meditteranean Mijwiz." *Ethnomusicology* 38, no. 1 (1994): 37–57.

———. "Sound Recording in the Life of Early Arab-American Immigrants." *La Revue des Traditions Musicales des Mondes Arabe et Mediterraneen* (RTMMAM), no. 5, part 2 (2011): 41–52.

Rasmussen, Anne K. "The Music of Arab Detroit: A Musical Mecca in the Midwest." In *Musics of Multicultural America: A Study of Twelve Musical Communities,* edited by Kip Lornell and Anne K. Rasmussen, 73–100. New York: Schirmer Books, 1997.

Roseman, Marina. *Healing Sounds from the Malaysian Rainforest: Temiar Music and Medicine.* Berkeley: University of California Press, 1991.

Safran, William. "Diasporas in Modern Societies: Myths of Homeland and Return." *Diaspora* 1, no. 1 (1991): 83–99.

Saleh, Magda. "A Documentation of the Ethnic Dance Traditions of the Arab Republic of Egypt." PhD diss., School of Education, Health, Nursing, and Arts Professions, New York University, 1979.

Seeger, Anthony. "What Can We Learn When They Sing? Vocal Genres of the Suyá Indians of Central Brazil." *Ethnomusicology* 23, no. 3 (1979): 373–94.

Stokes, Martin. "Introduction: Ethnicity, Identity, and Music." In *Ethnicity, Identity, and Music: The Musical Construction of Place,* edited by Martin Stokes. Oxford: Berg Publishers, 1994.

Sugarman, Jane. *Engendering Song: Singing and Subjectivity at Prespa Albanian Weddings.* Chicago: University of Chicago Press, 1997.

———. "The Nightingale and the Partridge: Singing and Gender among Prespa Albanians." *Ethnomusicology* 33, no. 2 (1989): 191–215.

Taylor, Timothy D. "Some Versions of Difference: Discourses of Hybridity in Transnational Musics." In *Beyond Exoticism: Western Music and the World,* by Timothy D. Taylor, 140–60. Durham: Duke University Press, 2007.

Turino, Thomas, and James Lea, editors. *Identity and the Arts in Diaspora Communities.* Warren, MI: Harmonie Park Press, 2004.

Turner, Victor. "Betwixt and Between: The Liminal Period in Rites of Passage." In *Reader in Comparative Religion: An Anthropological Approach,* 4th ed., edited by William A. Lessa and Evon Z. Vogt, 234–43., 1979: (reprinted and abridged from *Africa* Vol. 34, 1964, 85–104).

———. *The Ritual Process: Structure and Anti-Structure.* Chicago: Aldine Publishing Company, 1969.

van Gennep, Arnold. *The Rite of Passage.* Chicago: University of Chicago Press, 1960.

Wagner, Roy. *The Invention of Culture.* Englewood Cliffs, NJ: Prentice-Hall, 1975.

Yazedjian, Ani. "Reconstructing the Armenian: The Genocide as a Cultural Marker in the Reification of Armenian Identity." In *Identity and the Arts in Diaspora Communities,* edited by Thomas Turino and James Lea, 38–50. Warren, MI: Harmonie Park Press, 2004.

TWO

—⟶∿⟵—

NEGOTIATING GENDER, COMMUNITY, AND ETHNICITY

Balkan Romani Transnational Weddings

CAROL SILVERMAN

WHEN LEILA INVITED ME TO her daughter's bridal shower in a Bronx banquet hall, I was both honored and surprised.[1] As far as I knew, Muslim Macedonian Roma didn't celebrate bridal showers, and the American ones I had attended were small, in-home events for close family and friends. When I attended the shower for over three hundred guests, I was struck by how much it resembled a Romani wedding yet incorporated several American customs. In this chapter, I explore the process of performative creativity in this transnational community—that is, how Roma select and reconfigure ritual (embedded in music and dance) to produce meaningful expressions that address changing societal conditions while upholding traditional cultural values.[2]

Since the 1960s, a growing community of Muslim Macedonian Roma has migrated to the Bronx, New York, and has climbed up the economic scale. Weddings are the center of family and community life, bringing into focus kin relationships that are enacted across transnational borders. With live music, multiple days of dancing, and elaborate ritual symbolism, weddings pose the question of what it means to be a Romani man or woman in America. Changing gender roles in the United States, including gains in female education, have especially impacted how wedding customs are enacted and what they mean.

Weddings have a long symbolic life: community members plan them far in advance and discuss them long afterward. They figure clearly in how Roma performatively conceive of their identity and how they distinguish themselves from both non-Roma and from non-Balkan Roma. Moreover, weddings are motivations for and manifestations of diasporic migration: for example, Roma plan travel to coincide with weddings and thus participants typically hail from several diasporic locations. Weddings also performatively enact gender roles, ethnicity, community, social status, and class, displaying cultural values and serving as markers or organizing principles of the life cycle. They are complex events comprising multiple genres (e.g., music, dance, costume, food, and ritual). Many dramatic roles are conveyed enacted, reputations are established or questioned, conflicts and alliances emerge, and individual and family power is negotiated.[3]

ROMANI MIGRATION: INDIA TO MACEDONIA

Linguistic evidence reveals that Roma are originally from India and that they had migrated to and spread throughout Eastern Europe by 1400, some settling and others following a nomadic way of life.[4] They have been indispensable suppliers of diverse services to non-Roma, such as music, entertainment, fortune-telling, metalworking, horse dealing, woodworking, sieve making, basket weaving, comb making, and seasonal agricultural work. Many Macedonian Roma converted to Islam in the sixteenth to eighteenth centuries to pay lower taxes and ascend the Ottoman ranks. The Muslim religion and Turkish culture and language were the marks of civilization, and conversion often meant merely a change in name. Like other Muslims in the Balkans, Macedonian Roma were not very religious (until recently); in fact, Muslim Roma share many cultural patterns with their non-Muslim Balkan neighbors.

Initial curiosity about Roma by European peoples and rulers quickly gave way to hatred and discrimination, a legacy that has continued until today. Despite their small numbers, Roma inspired fear and mistrust and were expelled from virtually every Western European territory.[5] Petrova suggests that negative stereotypes of Roma blossomed in fifteenth-century Western Europe and spread eastward.[6] Roma were viewed as intruders probably because of their dark skin, their non-European physical features, their foreign customs, and their association with the invading Turks. The positive yet dangerous coding of Romani otherness hinges on their romanticization by non-Roma as free souls (outside the rules and boundaries of European society); their association with the arts, especially music and the occult; and their proximity to nature and sexuality. Using Edward Said's concept, we can claim that Roma are "orientalized" and exoticized.[7] Katie Trumpener emphasizes their association with an ahistoric, timeless nostalgia: "Nomadic and illiterate, they wander down an endless road, without a social contract or country to bind them, carrying their home with them, crossing borders at will."[8] Simultaneously Roma are reviled as unreformable, untrustworthy, dishonest, and rejected from civilization. "Feared as deviance, idealized as autonomy,"[9] Roma serve as the West's quintessential others.

With the Nazi rise to power, Roma faced an extermination campaign in which five hundred thousand to 1.5 million perished.[10] After World War II, Roma received neither compensation nor recognition as victims. The communist regimes in Eastern Europe defined Roma as a social problem—they were targeted for integration into the planned economy, forced to give up their traditional occupations, and assigned to the lowest-skilled and lowest-paid state jobs (e.g., street cleaners). Nomadic Roma were forcibly settled, settled Roma were forcibly moved, and in some regions aspects of their culture, such as music, were outlawed. The state provided cheap housing, but segregated ghettos were commonplace. On the positive side, under socialism Romani school attendance grew (despite inferior segregated schools), violence was rare, and Roma had steady employment and received the benefits of the paternalistic state.

In the postsocialist period, harassment and violence toward the Roma of Eastern Europe have increased, along with marginalization and poverty. They are the largest minority in Europe (with a population of ten to twelve million) and have extremely low standards of living in every country, with unemployment reaching 80 percent in some regions. East European Roma face inferior and segregated housing and discrimination in the education system, where their children often end up in special schools for the disabled. Poor health conditions—specifically higher infant mortality and morbidity, shorter life expectancy, and higher frequency of chronic diseases—plague Roma. Discrimination is widespread in employment and the legal system, and even educated people routinely express disdain for Gypsies. Hate speech and racial profiling are common in the media. Perhaps most troubling are the hundreds of incidents of physical violence against Roma perpetrated by ordinary citizens and also by the police. In response to this, a Romani human rights movement has mobilized in the last twenty years via a network of activists and NGOs (nongovernmental organizations).[11]

Macedonia, which was a republic of Yugoslavia until 1991, reported 52,000 Roma in its 2002 census, but the Council of Europe approximates the country's Roma population to be 134,000 to 260,000, comprising 9.6 percent of the population.[12] On the one hand, the constitution mentions full equality; the Romani language is spoken by 80 percent of Macedonian Roma; and there are several Romani-language radio programs and television stations. On the other hand, there is widespread police brutality and discrimination in hiring, education, service in public establishments, and the legal system; moreover, surveys show 59 to 80 percent of non-Roma have negative feelings toward Roma.[13] Recently, evictions and violent police attacks have been condemned.[14] Because of the discriminatory and dangerous situations they continue to face, Romani refugees from the crisis of postsocialism can now be found in every Western European nation and in the United States and Canada.

MACEDONIA TO NEW YORK: MULTIPLE IDENTITIES

The United States is home to Roma from every subgroup, but they do not coalesce as a pan-Romani community. Macedonian Roma rarely interact with other Romani groups, although occasionally they intermarry with other Muslim Balkan Roma. The center of Macedonian Romani life in the United States is located in Belmont, a historically Italian neighborhood of the Bronx. In the past fifty years, Hispanics, Albanians, Bosnian Muslims, Montenegrin Muslims, Serbian Muslims, and Balkan Roma have moved into the area while the Italian population has declined.[15] Currently, Balkan restaurants, groceries, photography studios, and pizza or *burek* (a doughy pie with feta cheese, spinach, or meat) parlors are interspersed with older Italian businesses. Roma began moving to New York City in the late 1960s, specifically from the city of Prilep but also from Bitola and Skopje. At the time, the Yugoslav government supported sending "guest workers" to Western Europe, the United States, and Australia to encourage hard currency remittances. Emigrants saw working abroad as a way to make good money, move up the social scale, and help relatives at home. After the guest worker policy ended, the sponsorship of relatives and the need for spouses continued. The wars in Yugoslavia (1991–95) brought economic crisis to the entire region, causing another wave of emigration. While push factors (out of Yugoslavia) in the 1960s were mostly economic, now they include lack of hope, lack of a political future, and fear of police brutality and other forms of discrimination. Pull factors (to the United States) include the need for spouses, better employment possibilities, and less outward racism.[16]

"Chain" immigration—that is, one family sponsoring another—was the common pattern until the mid-1990s, when American laws became more restrictive. Now, spouses are the only migrants. Although Macedonia is the nominal "home," New York Roma often travel to other diasporic locations such as Western Europe, Canada, and Australia to visit kin. The movement of people, things, and ideas occurs among several sites in the diaspora, occasionally even without reference to Macedonia. A woman in Toronto, for example, saved money to visit her sister in Melbourne, Australia, whom she had not seen for twenty-five years; this was more important than a cheaper trip to Macedonia, where she has many more relatives. Travel, of course, is contingent on having the proper documents and the money for tickets and gifts. Many Roma visit Macedonia regularly, but some younger Roma have no desire to visit. Romani families, then, are *transnational*, defined by Deborah Bryceson and Ulla Vuorela as those who "live some or most of the time separated from each other, yet hold together and create something that can be seen as a feeling of collective welfare and unity, namely 'familyhood,' even across national borders."[17]

In the 1960s, Belmont families were poor immigrants who relied on help from relatives who were themselves recent immigrants. The majority are still working class, but many families have reached the middle class and a few, the upper class (often through real estate investments). Well-to-do families have relocated from smaller apartments to private homes in nicer locations such as Pelham Parkway in northeast Bronx, New Jersey, Westchester, and Connecticut. While the emigrant generation typically had an eighth grade education, the second generation in the United States is becoming better educated, especially women. While mothers worked in factories or cleaned offices, many daughters are pursuing professional college degrees, in fields such as business, accounting, law, computing, and teaching.[18] Some men do manual labor, but there are also electricians, carpenters, welders, clerks, store owners, and businessmen.

The Belmont community is extremely close-knit; everyone knows each other face to face, sees each other often at celebrations, and socializes at home. Roma rarely have close friends outside the community. A middle-age woman, Leila, illustrated this insularity: "Family values . . . are very important. My family was everything to me. . . . This was always the main issue growing up." She saw family as defense against the hostile outside world:

> Not to feel alone in the world, like many Americans, that is the main reason I stayed within the family. I could not imagine going against the family and the tradition, and being out there on my own and being ostracized from everything I knew from the time I opened my eyes. Your family is who you are, and it is there forever. The family is a positive thing, and it is our only defense. We have no choice, especially in Europe. If you go and you try to become a part of somebody else's community as a Rom, they don't want you. So you have to make the best of it. The family is so strong because we are not accepted anywhere. It has become almost an obsession.[19]

Leila points out that kin orientation is an adaptive mechanism in a world filled with hostility against Roma. This is still somewhat true for young Roma. What defines the field of social relations is a "very high level of interpersonal and intercommunal investment and trust—economic, social, emotional and moral."[20] Community members "define their subjectivities as moral individuals through long-term relations of sociality such as marriage, family, and community."[21]

The Muslim religion is a strong cultural identification point, but the level of practice varies tremendously. In general, Macedonian Roma in the past were not very observant; even today, some eat pork, and many drink alcohol and do not pray. During the 1980s, I rarely heard of anyone going to a mosque except for a funeral. But in the 1990s, the Muza Mosque/Islamic Center in Belmont became a vital community focus, and many Roma have now become quite religious. Most weddings feature a ceremony in the mosque and a few non-alcoholic weddings have taken place. Some women are covered, many men pray or congregate at the mosque; a few have made the hajj to Mecca. Since 2014, the mosque has sponsored an outdoor fair at the end of the Ramadan fast.[22]

Romani identity is still very strong even as many young Roma are well integrated into American life. This is not a contradiction because Roma, like many other ethnic groups, make strategic choices about what to incorporate, what to reject, and what to refashion into their lives (as I will illustrate regarding weddings in what follows). Roma are well aware of the tension between American individualistic ethics and the collective family ethics of their community. Although some youth see freedom of movement, individual use of money and time, and sexual relations as attractive, most try to balance these American practices with respect for Romani values. Thus they are integrated but not assimilated.

Living, working, and going to school alongside non-Roma make Roma aware of what they claim distinguishes them from others: their culture, their language, family orientation, restrained sexuality, historical ties to Macedonia, music, dance, and rituals, especially weddings. Note that this list does not include all the usual features of ethnic identity, which are shared territory, history, and language; territory and history are missing. Most Belmont Roma know a little about their origins in India, but as mentioned earlier, they relate to Macedonia as a referential home. I contend that their home is wherever their community is; this diasporic attitude deterritorializes homeland. Because they are people-oriented more than place-oriented, they take their home with them wherever they are.

In the United States, Roma have more choices about identity compared to Roma in Europe because America provides a more mobile environment, and Americans pry less than Europeans: privacy is valued. In America, you can hide your family history, you don't live in an exclusively Romani neighborhood, few can pinpoint your foreign language, and there are other dark-skinned people around. As a result, in Belmont, Roma exhibit a diversity of self-presentational attitudes. Many community members do not readily reveal their ethnicity to non-Roma because of stereotypes of "Gypsy" criminality and nomadism. Some, on the other hand, are proud to identify as Roma. I hypothesize that success in America (e.g., fluency in English, home ownership, and a secure job) provides the security to openly display their ethnicity; they are less afraid of the Gypsy stigma.

In their own community, all are proud to be Roma, but exactly what that means is contested. For the older generation, it may be language and customs; for the middle generation, it may be finding appropriate spouses for their children; for youth, it tends to be family, music, and dance. But all Roma are forced to deal with their public identity because of the stigma associated with being Gypsy. In the Balkans, non-Roma readily identify (and discriminate against) Roma by where they live, what language they speak, how they dress, their music and dance, or the color of their skin. In the United States, stereotypes about Gypsies center on criminality, violence, exoticism, and romanticized "freedom."[23] Police departments in several cities have divisions specializing in "Gypsy crime," fashion houses feature "Gypsy styles," and tribal belly dance companies are commonly called "Gypsy Caravan." In the last decade, several reality TV shows such as *My Big Fat Gypsy Wedding*, *My Big Fat American Gypsy Wedding*, and *American Gypsy* have reinforced these stereotypes.[24] It is no accident that these shows focus on weddings. For the Western television public, the wedding is the window into the secret world of exotic custom, heightened sexuality, family strife, and lavish spending.

MOBILITY AND MARRIAGE

Marriage upholds the significance of the family and the perseverance of Romani identity and also enacts transnational ties via a Roma network to find spouses. Everyone is expected to marry, and those who don't are somewhat stigmatized.[25] One man told me he was derided by his family in the 1990s when he turned twenty-eight years old and still wasn't married: "I got married because of all the pressure my parents put on me." Now, however, Roma are marrying at older ages and more individual choices come into play, as discussed below. Young people congregate at ritual events, on dance lines, at the mosque, and at school. Officially, there is no "dating," but rather young people socialize in groups. In reality, couples do spend time together, sometimes with the blessing of their elders. At weddings, for example, teenagers meet outside banquet halls for one-to-one conversations. The ideal is a marriage within the diasporic community.

A few decades ago, parents looked for appropriate spouses and the children acquiesced. Now, young people are more proactive, and elders rarely force children into marriage, although they are definitely involved in every step. If two people want to marry, the elders visit each other to discuss the situation before the deal is sealed. Parents get involved because they claim they can see beyond romantic love—they check out the reputation of not only the prospective spouse but also his or her entire family. They obtain information such as the family's economic standing, level of respectability, and treatment of brides in the past. Women gather "people knowledge" by actively discussing community members and their relationships. Although men may be the public face of the family in marriage negotiations, they rely on women precisely for the information that makes marriage negotiations possible.[26]

If a young man or woman can't find a suitable spouse in New York, usually the family takes a trip to Macedonia or other locations in the diaspora to "look around." Of course, only people who have legal status can travel abroad. Word goes out, for example, "back home" in Prilep or in Vienna, and relatives network to arrange meetings with prospective spouses. These trips can be very stressful, considering their short duration. Leila, who met her husband in the 1980s on a three-month trip to Prilep, commented:

> I met my husband through relatives. It was a group choice. I hadn't met anybody that I felt would be somebody I could work with.... But eventually, as time neared for me to come back, I had to take a risk.... I was honest with him about who I am.... I told him: "I'm not going to be a typical Romani wife. I go to school, I have a mind of my own, and I'm not afraid to express it. I'll be working with men; I may have to go on trips. Sometimes you may have to clean the house. You may have to pitch in and be an equal partner, and if you can deal with that, fine. If not, it's not going to work." We kind of agreed. And here we are, still married.[27]

Leila is somewhat of an exception because she was older than the typical bride— twenty-five years old and in college. Her family insisted on both education and marriage. She had an aura of self-confidence and honesty that was rare for young women. Her philosophy continued for her children: "I won't force my daughter to go back home for a husband. It's so stressful especially if you don't have the support from home. Everybody is telling you what you should do. They don't approve of anybody, and you don't know anybody. How are you supposed to make a decision? One relative says—you can't pick this one—his family did something 250 years ago! I hope my daughter finds someone here in the community that she will be happy with. If not, if she chooses to go home, she'll have my support." When I organized a focus group in 2009 on the topic of marriage with Leila's eighteen-year-old daughter and her friends, they agreed that these trips are too stressful and should be avoided. Leila said:

> For my girls, I don't want them to do that because we're talking about two different lifestyles.... Marriage itself is difficult enough without having to go through cultural changes. Even though we're all Macedonian Roma.... they have different ideas.... And life is already difficult without marrying somebody you don't know.... I don't want my girls to go through that. I keep telling them, there are plenty of boys here—try to find somebody from here. If you can't, and you want

to go home, that's your choice, I leave it up to them. If they want to do that, good. I will not force them to do it.

Romani parents emphasize that Macedonia is so poor that everyone wants to leave—they all "line up" when a prospective match arrives from abroad. So it is difficult to trust what anyone says. Leila said that "I would not let a girl child go back there alone, especially when she's of marriage age because they will play with her. . . . I'll go with her. I won't let her go alone." Nurija, a nineteen-year-old, commented:

> It's the same for the boys. . . . They don't want to go back home and just marry anyone, because they're marrying you just. . . . for the money and to come to America. It's like we have a passport written on our backs. It's their way out. And I understand them—nobody wants to stay and live in poverty, everybody wants to save themselves! And for Roma it's so much harder to save themselves in Macedonia because nobody gives them the opportunity to do it, so their only way out is leaving. And the only way they can leave is through marriage.

In the last twenty years, with cell phones and with social media such as Facebook, young people are prolonging transnational marriage negotiations and becoming more cautious. Nurija explained: "You don't have to get married right away; you can keep in contact with the person and visit a couple of times. One of my friends visited . . . and found some guy, and after speaking with him for almost six, seven months, she found out he really was using her for her money. . . . So she broke up with him, she went back again, she found somebody else, she spoke with him for a while and she went back two or three times over two or three years, and she married him, and she's OK."

Another case illustrates how young people's individual judgments come into play. Rubija was a twenty-seven-year-old educated woman who was beginning to be considered by some Roma as too old to marry. She did not find a suitable spouse among the local prospects, and thus, urged by her parents, she took a trip to Macedonia with them. She met a man she liked, but after corresponding with him for more than a year, she broke off the relationship. Her parents were supportive but were worried about her future. They insisted on another trip, and via a relative in another city, Rubija found a very well-educated spouse from a family whom her parents hardly knew. Rubija corresponded with him, and after she felt certain, she and her parents went to Macedonia for the engagement and wedding. Rubija applied for a "fiancé visa," and her spouse finally arrived. However, some wedding rituals had to be delayed because of the six-month wait for the visa.

Intermarriage is discouraged but does occur in a minority of cases. Despite his parents' initial disapproval, musician Seido Salifoski married a Japanese woman (see the following). Young women in the 2009 focus group have now married Roma; they are very reflective about why they want to marry within Romani culture. Nurija said: "I never wanted to marry outside of my culture. Aside from the fact that my father would go crazy and not allow it, I wouldn't want to do it. I think that it is just a big, big change. . . . Because there are just certain things that I grew up [with], and I value. . . . and it would just be such a big clash with the family. So I think I never thought about marrying out of the culture." Leila's daughter agreed: "Our community is very small, so I wouldn't want to start mixing, because if I mix, and then someone else mixes, then we will no longer be Macedonian Gypsies in the Bronx. I wouldn't want my community to disappear." *Intermarriage* itself may be defined broadly; for example, some Prilep Roma consider marrying Roma from Skopje as intermarriage because the culture is different. Muslim Bosnian or Albanian Roma are also sometimes considered "not like us."

WEDDING RITUALS: TRADITION AND INNOVATION

By far, weddings are the most frequent and largest celebratory event and the focus of community attention. Bronx Roma also traditionally celebrate other life cycle events, such as circumcisions, and later I discuss new occasions for celebrating. As Sugarman points out for Prespa Albanians, weddings are seen as key to the growth of the family and the community.[28] Because the bride is ideally brought into the groom's family, weddings affirm patrilocal residency, patriarchal relations, and the reproductive capacity of women. The bride is thus the ritual focus and the most symbolically endowed personage. She is the person undergoing the most marked transition (she is "a stranger" to the groom's lineage), and because the alliance between two families depends on her, she is structurally precarious.

However, in New York, a groom is sometimes brought over from Macedonia to live with a bride's family, contradicting the ideal of patrilocal residence. Given the patriarchal nature of the family, it is awkward for a man to move in with the bride's family and depend on them for language, employment, and legal status. He is known as a *domazet*, meaning a live-in son-in-law, which has a pejorative connotation. Leila explained: "When he's a zet in the house, they are made aware of it from the moment the marriage is announced. They'll get the comments, *Sega ke bideš domazet. Žena ke ti se komandva* (Now you'll be a live-in husband. Your wife will command you). And, they'll get that cruel stare." The stigma, however, is balanced out by the man's opportunity to emigrate.

Although I do not have the space to describe the full range of Macedonian Romani wedding rituals,[29] I note that they follow the general structure of most Balkan weddings, regardless of religion and ethnicity. In America, many traditional rituals have been eliminated, while some new customs have been introduced. Rather than seeing diasporic weddings as lacking, I explore how weddings illustrate the principles of innovation and reinterpretation of meanings.

Being working Americans, Roma must confine their weddings to one to two weekend days; some rituals are omitted or combined, some find new locations and times, and new ritual occasions appear. For example, the bride's henna party that in Macedonia usually takes place in the bride's house a few days prior to the wedding is sometimes held at the groom's house.[30] At one 1990s wedding, approximately twenty-five women occupied the living room of the groom's family's tiny three-room apartment; the few men present were relegated to the kitchen. There was recorded music, and the women danced solo *čoček* with abandon. Solo *čoček* is a modest form of belly dancing with hip and shoulder movements. The bride's trousseau, consisting of clothing, jewelry, and household items such as appliances, was prominently displayed.

The night before Samir and Lebadet's 2004 wedding banquet, the groom's parents sponsored a large henna party in the courtyard of their apartment building. They beautifully displayed gifts for the bride in an adjacent room and hired a band of local and diaspora musicians. The clarinetist and singer, who were born in Macedonia and were relatives of the bride's father, were flown in from Germany. Lebadet led the first dance with a fancy handkerchief, and one by one, her female family members as well as the groom's female relatives led the line. Before each woman led, she tipped the musicians. Lebadet wore a gown, then *šalvari* (wide-legged billowing pants), then another gown. Ten years ago *šalvari* were infrequently worn in the United States, but in in recent years more brides are wearing them, especially for henna parties; new designs, particularly Indian-inspired styles, have become popular.

Because henna parties are female-centered events, men are usually absent or stay on the sidelines. The dancing sometimes becomes bawdy as the women loosen up, and the mothers of the bride and groom sometimes climb on chairs and mime humorous sexually suggestive movements. These New York events resembled the henna parties I attended in Macedonia despite the lack of full application of henna to the bride's head of hair. Instead, just a dab of henna is applied because New York brides prefer to go to the hairdresser. Sometimes a dab of henna is also applied to the hands and/or feet, while in Macedonia there is a second, separate henna ceremony for the hands and feet. As in Macedonia, the henna is displayed on a tray that is elaborately decorated with red cloth and money. Another innovation is holding the henna party in a banquet hall.

A sieve, which is purchased or decorated by the family (sometimes by each side), is a prominent female wedding symbol. The sieve (for sifting flour) stands

Figure 2.1. Sieve decorated with red scarf, nuts, and greenery. Macedonia, 2004. *Photo by Carol Silverman.*

for fertility, which ties the reproductive capacity of the bride to nature and the land. It is used to lead dance lines; close female relatives are given this honor, and the order of leading may be contested. Thirty years ago both in New York and Macedonia women would laboriously decorate the sieve with red cloth, greenery, flowers, and money. Today decorated sieves can be purchased in stores in New York and Macedonia.

The "taking of the bride" (from her house to the groom's, usually on Saturday morning) is perhaps the most dramatic ritual because it symbolizes the bride's departure from her parents; it continues to be done in New York. The groom's close relatives drive to the bride's house (with musicians performing on acoustic instruments); men engage in dramatic humorous bargaining for the bride, often with alcohol (decades ago a bride-price was exchanged). In New York, the parents of the bride or groom may be absent, due to lack of documents; in this case, substitute relatives enact the roles of the parents in a substitute home. In the United States, brides still perform rituals of respect for elders, such as bowing down and kissing their hands. Some brides have learned to "zema temana" (take *temana*, a Turkish word for a slow, arching hand movement), which signals respect.

Rituals incorporating the bride into the groom's house are quite important in Macedonia but are rarely performed in New York. However, one New York groom's mother insisted that the bride enter her apartment with a loaf of bread over her head (for fertility); the groom's mother also rubbed the threshold with sugar water (for sweetness). The groom led the bride in with a belt around her neck and gently knocked her head on the walls (to make sure she would obey him and to introduce her to the house); then he teased her with a knife, and kisses were exchanged. All this was done with the groom's mother's formulaic blessings for luck, happiness, and "a male child next year." Some young women balk at these "submissive" rituals.[31] Seido Salifoski's Japanese wife, for example, who planned their Romani/Japanese fusion wedding, rejected all "sexist" rituals. She asked me to describe traditional Romani rituals, and she chose the ones she liked. She rejected the test of virginity, the temana, and bowing for the elderly. Yet she chose to wear Romani šalvari because they were beautiful. Seido wore an Asian inspired suit, and they hired Romani musicians because they both love the music.

A mosque ceremony is now common in New York and Macedonia even among some nonreligious Roma. As Lebadet and Samir emerged from the neighborhood mosque, for example, they danced to a band of clarinet, accordion, and *tarabuka* (hand drum) in the middle of a Bronx street. Many relatives congregated, and although the dancing blocked city traffic for over an hour, everyone was very polite. The couple then got into a rented limousine and went

Figure 2.2. Dancing in front of the groom's house before departing for the bride's house. Musicians Yuri Yunakov, Sevim Umer, and Erhan Umer, wedding, Bronx, New York, June 2011. *Photo by Carol Silverman.*

to a park to take photographs. Hiring a videographer is now ubiquitous and video clips made by both guests and professional videographers are shared via Facebook and YouTube.

BANQUETS

The highlight of New York weddings is the evening banquet, sponsored by the groom's parents. Its structure mirrors American weddings in that it takes place in a rented hall with a dais, catered food, and a wedding cake. Typically banquets are an eight-to-nine-hour affair, starting at 6:00 p.m. with an opulent buffet plus cocktails followed by a sit-down dinner with Mediterranean foods. Other American customs include throwing the bouquet, throwing the bride's garter, drinking champagne, cutting the first piece of cake, and having bridesmaids and ushers. They may enter the hall in pairs, hold an arch decorated in greenery, and lead the bridal couple under it.

Sugarman points out that for Prespa Albanians in Toronto the focus on pairs, including the bride/groom, signals individualism and is a marked departure from the Balkan focus on the large extended family.[32] The same holds true for

Romani banquets, where the couple enters the hall to approving shouts and typically dances a slow American couple dance that morphs into a free form čoček and becomes more intense as relatives throw money over the couple. Note that money has replaced some fertility symbols like candy, wheat, and rice. Also note that the bride's family is invited to the banquet (although they bring a small number of relatives) while in Macedonia they may sponsor their own banquet, *igranka* (dance), a day earlier. Thus the newer focus is on the couple, while the older focus was the on groom's extended family and, by implication, the patrilocal principle.

In New York, brides' families sometimes desire to sponsor a large event of their own; thus, bridal showers, henna parties, and *blaga rakija* parties (sweet brandy) are becoming very lavish. My opening vignette illustrates how Leila shaped her daughter's bridal shower to reinforce ties with and respect for her extended family. She explained to me that at the wedding banquet, sponsored by the groom's family, she would be allotted only a small number of guests: "It won't be our event. I have such a large family and my daughter is the first in her generation to get married. It is so important that we gather and celebrate."

Leila's daughter's bridal shower had elements drawn from both Romani weddings and American showers. Leila ordered printed invitations, but she decorated them with candy and gauze and hand delivered them to scores of relatives in the neighborhood. As in American showers, the guests were mostly women; however, close male relatives were also invited, including the groom. The first ritual was a couple dance with the bride and her father, followed by the bride and groom, and guests showered them with money. The gift giving was a cross between American showers and Romani weddings: the bride sat on a large decorated chair in the center of the hall; guests were called up one by one, in order of closeness, by the mistress of ceremonies (her aunt), and their gifts were announced (in Macedonian). Most of the gifts were household items, but close family members gave gold jewelry displayed on velvet (as in Macedonia). As in American showers, ribbons and bows from the wrapping paper were as-sembled into a hat, which the bride wore as she did traditional Balkan line and solo dances. As in wedding banquets, there was live music, and families were called up to dance in the order of closeness. This event illustrates how meanings are refashioned into new constellations that reference the past.

Wedding banquets follow formulaic ritual sequences that are enacted via music and dance. Thus music and dance not only are valued in their own right as art forms but also as the means by which family and community relationships are performed. The first dance line of the evening is led by the most respected female elder, often the mother or grandmother of the groom. The leader of the line occupies the most visible place of honor. As in Macedonia, respected close

Figure 2.3. Bride with decorated hat leads dance line, bridal shower, Bronx, New York, April 2015. *Photo by Carol Silverman.*

Figure 2.4. Dance line led by a respected elder, with clarinetist Ismail Lumanovski, wedding, Bronx, New York, June 2011. *Photo by Carol Silverman.*

relatives dance solo čoček inside the curve of the line. The emcee calls up the relatives to lead dance lines in order of closeness and respect. This is a visual interpretation of the social structure of the extended family. However, conflicts also erupt over the order of leading; several weddings were engulfed in scandals involving guests' outrage at being called up to lead late in the event or not at all. Some guests have stormed out of weddings in protest.

Migration is also highlighted performatively—guests from diasporic locations are honored by being called up to lead dances. Typically dance line leaders are women—they request tunes—and men leave the line to tip the musicians and singers (who perform near the front of the line with wireless microphones). The momentum and visceral excitement build up at the front of the line; there is thick affective intensity, and often people cry from joy and deep emotion.

In my conversations, I found that young people consistently cited Romani rituals, dance, and music as defining features of their ethnicity. Elders more often spoke of language, religion, in-group marriage, and values (such as respecting the elderly) as core ethnicity features. While the Romani language is disappearing (and even the Macedonian language is declining), the interest in and commitment to music and dance is extremely strong in the younger generations. Young people are so involved in music and dance that they have sometimes organized stand-alone banquets that are unconnected to rituals; these parties (*zabavi*) often specifically feature famous musicians visiting from diasporic locations.

In the last thirty years Roma have added anniversaries and graduations and New Year's Eve to their roster of large banquets. In the last decade, they have added bridal showers, baby showers, March 8 (International Women's Day) parties, and sweet sixteen and first-year birthday parties. Women are often the focus of these newer celebrations; thus traditional ritual forms are molded to new settings in the service of newer values, such as honoring girls' birthdays or finishing college. In fact, rituals, though appearing traditional, uphold new values, such as female education and accomplishment.

Although I do not have the space to analyze musical repertoire and style, I note that the newest song and instrumental hits from Macedonia are immediately performed in New York. This flow of music in the diaspora is facilitated by both social media and the mobility of musicians. The best bands perform for banquets in Macedonia, Western Europe, and New York. Some musicians are family members and play only for airfare and tips; others require fees. A typical wedding lineup in New York might include a guest clarinet or saxophone player and singer from Europe paired with local back up musicians. Because no one rehearses, everyone needs to be totally up to date in repertoire, plus know hundreds of older songs and melodies. Wedding participants often request specific tunes when they lead dance lines, and band members keep abreast of new songs so they may serve their patrons well and receive tips. Tips are often several thousand dollars.

As in the Balkans, in New York women are the primary dancers; they dance for hours while men dance sporadically. Solo čoček is considered a female specialty, and talented women are encouraged and lauded by their relatives. However, a female čoček dancer's level of modesty and respectability is closely monitored by her family. Although the dance form čoček is inherently sexual, no skin is revealed and no obscene movements are displayed—this distinguishes it from belly dancing. More important, the dancer is surrounded by family members, not strange men.[33] At a 2004 wedding, the sponsoring family hired a non-Romani American belly dancer, costumed with much flesh showing. Wedding guests had mixed reactions to her; elders for the most part disliked it (because it was not part of their tradition), and younger guests either liked the novelty or criticized it for taking the focus off the couple.

Another important part of weddings is the procession of the couple around the hall to every table, accompanied by slow songs, a practice that sometimes takes several hours. The couple greets each elder family member with the customary kiss on the hand, and they receive money. The largest cash gifts, however, are given in envelopes at the end of the banquet to the sponsoring family, as each guest family lines up to bid farewell. In New York, the financial outlay of gifts is substantially larger than in Macedonia. A guest (even distant kin) has to provide gifts for the engagement, the henna party, the wedding banquet (in fact, several gifts during the wedding plus tipping the musicians), and the blaga rakija. The main gift is approximately $100 per adult. This represents a financial strain for most Belmont families, and they struggle to give honorably in spite of limited resources. They do, of course, expect to reciprocally receive gifts when they sponsor events. Putting on a wedding in New York is a huge financial commitment: if several hundred guests are invited, the cost of the rental hall, the caterer, and the musicians runs over $20,000, not including the gowns, gifts, limousine, and tips. According to CNN, the average cost of an American wedding in 2014 was $30,000. This is precisely why families save money.

THE BRIDE'S REPUTATION

Among Roma, the test of the bride's virginity remains a significant custom both in the Balkans and the United States. It presents the visible manifestation of a girl's reputation and the honor of her family. Moreover, it is a sign of Romani identity in terms of keeping the proper order of things in a changing world. Until the 1960s in the Balkans, this custom was practiced among virtually all ethnic groups regardless of religion, but today it has declined. One elder Romani woman in Macedonia commented: "The bride must be honest and honorable. . . . We want to see the stained sheet. . . . If the bride had brought us all of Europe's wealth, it would not have been worth as much as what she gave us, her honor. That was the most beautiful gift to us." Theoretically, in Macedonia, the consummation of the marriage takes place after the banquet. The mother-in-law looks for blood stains on the wedding sheet, and if she finds them, she publicly announces "the good news." According to this elder, "we send word to her mother and father's house that she is honest. . . . If the mother-in-law doesn't see blood, she will send the bride home riding on a donkey with pots and pans tied on, clattering. All gifts are returned." When I asked her if she ever witnessed this, she says she heard it did happen. Obviously, the threat is enough for most young girls to make them conform. Leila confirmed that the sheet is shown in Macedonia, and I myself witnessed it many times: "If they haven't eloped, then they show the sheet during the wedding. . . . They bring the sheet, that night, over to the mother's house, and then everybody celebrates. Technically, that's how it's supposed to be done." Of course, not every bride is a virgin, not every virgin bride bleeds, and not every mother-in-law cares about finding blood; plus there are many tricks to produce blood; thus the custom has many variations. However, it still has a symbolic function in upholding honor.

In Macedonia, after the test, the sheet is placed on a metal tray, covered with gauze, and the groom and his close relatives process to the bride's house to bring the good news to the mother of the bride. This is a very important moment because it vindicates not only the bride's but also her family's honorable reputation; it is the job of the mother to raise her daughter in preparation for this test. The entire ritual dramatizes the proper control of sexuality transmitted from mother to daughter. Termed *blaga rakija*, the ritual features a procession with music, led by the groom's women carrying a brandy bottle decorated with flowers, greenery, and red ribbons (fertility symbols). The mother tips the groom and feeds him feminine foods (sometimes literally placing a spoon in his mouth), most notably eggs. The groom eats fertility foods to display the transference of the bride's reproductive potential from her family to his. In addition he receives a *bovčalok*, gifts such as shirts and handkerchiefs sewn on a sheet that is draped over him.

Several years ago there was a campaign in Macedonia to eradicate this virginity custom, based on the human rights dictum that every person has inalienable personal rights, regardless of culture.[34] Activists claim that "the test" is a form of subjugation of women (since only women need to be virgins), is humiliating for both men and women, and often leads to psychological trauma. The campaign was spurred by Romani activist Enisa Eminova, who in 2001 conducted a survey of 660 Roma (parents and children fourteen to twenty-five years old from ten Macedonian Romani communities).[35] In New York, the custom of checking the sheet is simply called *adet* ("custom" in Macedonian and Turkish) and is widely practiced. However, it is rarely done during the wedding because the timing of rituals has been altered. The first intercourse and test may occur somewhere in the diaspora after the engagement or whenever the families arrange it. If the couple elopes, it may be done immediately. The blaga rakiya celebration is also often removed from the test and is celebrated whether the test is done or not. It has morphed into a separate banquet put on by the bride's side after the wedding. The bride's mother still decorates the brandy bottle and the groom still eats fertility foods and receives a bovčalok; the setting may be the bride's home or a rented hall, but virginity may not even be the issue. One New York bride's blaga rakija celebration happened many months after her wedding and adet in Macedonia. She waited for the groom to receive his visa, and then her family celebrated her honor.

I was surprised to learn that some educated women in New York approve of the custom. Leila said: "It is oppressive. I have mixed feelings about that issue.

I had to do it. And if I could do it, everybody should be able to do it. But, it's not necessarily a good thing. I was able to sacrifice, and remain a virgin and go through it, and it was a demand I had to meet. And if we're going to expect these girls to stay in the culture and in the community, then yes. It is still very important in this community. Very important." Leila explored the changes in her attitude as she aged:

> When I was growing up, I was against it. I felt, "Why do I have to prove it to everybody? Why does it have to be done so publicly? Why can't just I bring the sheet out after I do whatever I do with my husband?" I've learned to accept that it is part of the culture, that it is part of the tradition, part of proving you are what you are. And if you can't fight 'em, you join 'em. So, I've kind of learned to join them. I mean, a lot of the younger ones are against it, that is, until they become women and have children, and they have sons. And their sons are expected to bring home a virgin and then all of sudden it becomes a major issue.

Some young Roma who have read the Quran are not practicing the custom; they know it is not required in Islam.

CONCLUSION

Macedonian Muslim Roma in New York display their changing cosmopolitan identities in weddings and other large celebrations that are the focus of community attention. Via ritual, enhanced by music and dance, Roma perform multiple ethnicities/roles as Americans, Macedonians, Muslims, men and women, but above all as Roma. They may identify with all of these labels, but each is complicated by the stigma associated with "Gypsy." The community ritual sphere serves as a secure, familiar, and traditional context where stigma is transformed into pride. Weddings create a Romani public space and time that frames the performative aspect of ideal identity roles. However, negotiations of status, class, and gender are embedded in weddings; these are sometimes conflictive and may even contradict ideals. Participants dissect and evaluate reputations; and they are especially observant of male/female displays of the proper embodiment of sexuality in music and dance.

With increasing female education and independence, loss of heritage languages, and dispersal of homes away from the core Belmont neighborhood, weddings remain perhaps the most traditional aspect of public Romani life. They serve as multilevel symbols of the ideal cohesion of the community, and they inscribe the reproductive importance of women and the primacy of the patrilineal patrilocal family. However, the flexibility of negotiations leading to marriages (including the decline of "arranged" marriages), and the older age of marriages, all evince recent changes in female roles. Thus weddings have changed considerably: they are simultaneously traditional and innovative.

Large banquets featuring live music and participatory dancing are the ubiquitous form of entertainment for Roma. They are formulaic but also flexible enough to allow for the incorporation of American customs. Moreover, new motivations for banquets are cropping up every year, such as bridal showers, first birthday parties, and sweet sixteen parties. These new events allow female milestones to be celebrated and noticed, which supports female agency. Weddings and other celebrations physically enact transnational networks as relatives travel from diasporic locations to celebrate with kin. Furthermore, musicians trace diasporic paths even more frequently than guests because their profession requires travel to serve patrons; finally, new songs and dance tunes migrate almost instantly over social media, allowing diasporic Balkan Roma to share a common musical repertoire and style. These multiple mobilities create an intertwined constellation of expressive behavior with dense layers of meanings that form the dynamic core of the community.

CAROL SILVERMAN is Professor of Cultural Anthropology and Folklore at the University of Oregon. She is author of *Romani Routes: Cultural Politics and Balkan Music in Diaspora*.

NOTES

1. This chapter is based on fieldwork in New York from 1988 to 2017 (with comparative fieldwork in Macedonia, Germany, and Australia) partially supported by grants from the Open Society Institute and the University of Oregon Research Office and the Center for the Study of Women in Society. Some information is taken from Silverman, "Education, Agency, and Power," and Silverman, "Diasporic Ethnicity, Gender and Dance," with permission of the publishers. The author quotes fragments of interviews and focus groups with members of the community. She conduced these interviews during 2009 to 2016 in New York City in peoples' homes. Names used are pseudonyms (except for famous musicians), employed to protect the privacy of community members. The author, of Russian Jewish background, has been welcomed into family settings and sincerely thanks her hosts for their generosity.

2. By the 1990s, the assimilationist model, which assumed that immigrants eventually gradually blend into the majority culture, had been replaced by a more processual dynamic model. Scholars also interrogated a single-homeland diaspora profile. See Schiller, Basch, and Blanc-Szanton, *Towards a Transnational Perspective on Migration*. Both trends produced the more recent emphasis on transnationalism that focuses on communities living across borders and having ties to multiple sites.

3. Following Brettell, I take an anthropological approach to migration that emphasizes "both structure and agency; it should look at macro-social contextual issues,

micro-level strategies and decision-making, and the mesolevel relational structure within which individuals operate. It needs to articulate both people and process." See Brettell, *Anthropology and Migration*, 7.

4. See Matras, *Romani Gypsies*, and Hancock, *We Are the Romani People*. Macedonian Roma discussed in this chapter are all sedentary.

5. See Hancock, *We Are the Romani People*; Petrova, "Roma"; and Stewart, *Gypsy "Menace."*

6. Petrova, "Roma," 128.

7. See Said, *Orientalism*. Lee extends Said's argument: "Whilst Orientalism is the discursive construction of the exotic Other *outside* Europe, Gypsylorism is the construction of the exotic Other *within* Europe—Romanies are the Orientals within." Lee, "Orientalism and Gypsylorism," 132.

8. Trumpener "Time of the Gypsies," 853.

9. Ibid., 854.

10. See Hancock, *We Are the Romani People*.

11. Many cases of discrimination and violence targeting Roma have occurred in the past two decades; in 2008 Italy, France, and Denmark began deporting Romanian and Bulgarian Roma. See World Bank, Roma Labor Market, and World Bank, "Roma"; Kooijman, "Roma"; Stewart, *Gypsy "Menace"*; and "Briefing: Europe's Roma."

12. See European Roma and Travellers Forum.

13. Plaut and Memedova, "Blank Face, Private Strength," 16.

14. See European Roma Rights Centre.

15. I approximate that there are several hundred Macedonian Romani families in the New York area, with half of them living in Belmont.

16. Silverman, *Romani Routes*.

17. Bryceson and Vuorela, *Transnational Family*, 3.

18. See Silverman, "Education, Agency, and Power."

19. Silverman, *Romani Routes*, 65.

20. Werbner, *Imagined Diasporas*, 272.

21. Ibid., 272–73.

22. The revitalization of Islam is happening in Macedonia and in other places in the Balkans and Western Europe.

23. See Voice of America, "For Roma, Life in US Has Challenges," a three-part video focusing mostly on American Kalderash.

24. See Marafioti, "Why TLC's *My Big Fat American Gypsy Wedding* Doesn't Represent the Romani"; White, "Big Fat Gypsy Confusion"; Williams, "Help Support Protest of My Big Fat Gypsy Wedding."

25. There are several community members who have never married. Although homosexuality may be a factor, it is not discussed openly, as most Macedonian Roma are homophobic; on the other hand, families do not ostracize members who are perceived as outside the community norms.

26. Much of what I am describing about family life is not unique to Roma and is comparable to other Balkan ethnic groups. There is a huge cross-cultural literature on the topic of the negotiation of female power. See Silverman, "Music and Power," and Silverman, "Macedonian and Bulgarian Muslim Romani Women."

27. Silverman, *Romani Routes*, 72, based on interview, August 2009.

28. Sugarman, *Engendering Song*.

29. See Seeman, "Music in the Service of Prestation," and Silverman, "Education, Agency, and Power"; "Gender of the Profession": and "Transnational Chochek."

30. Henna is vegetable dye that is used on the hair, hands, and feet in several parts of the world for beauty.

31. Silverman, "Music and Power."

32. Sugarman, *Engendering Song*, 397.

33. Silverman, "Gender of the Profession"; "Transnational Chochek."

34. The uneasy relationship of human rights to culture has been discussed widely in the anthropological literature, see Abu-Lughod, *Do Muslim Women Need Saving?*

35. Nearly half of the surveyed parents said they would accept brides if they were not virgins, but 70 percent replied that they were not sure whether their sons would. Many respondents saw no need to maintain the custom. In short, the survey revealed much uncertainty on the issue and opened up an avenue of debate. See Eminova, "Raising New Questions about an Old Tradition," 13. Virginity is one of many issues regarding female subordination that activists are addressing, see Plaut and Memedova, "Blank Face, Private Strength," and Silverman, "Music and Power."

BIBLIOGRAPHY

Abu-Lughod. Lila. *Do Muslim Women Need Saving?* Cambridge, MA: Harvard University Press, 2013.

"Average Wedding Bill Hits $30,000." CNN, March 28, 2014. http://money.cnn.com/2014 /03/28/pf/average-wedding-cost.

Brettell, Carolyn B. *Anthropology and Migration: Essays on Transnationalism, Ethnicity, and Identity*. Walnut Creek, KS: Altamira Press, 2003.

"Briefing: Europe's Roma: Bottom of the Heap." *Economist*, June 21, 2008, 35–38.

Bryceson, Deborah, and Ulla Vuorela. *The Transnational Family: New European Frontiers and Global Networks*. Oxford: Berg, 2002.

Campbell, Alicia. "Police Focus on South Florida 'Gypsy' Crimes Sparks Criticism from Roma Advocates." *Sun Sentinel*, July 3, 2011. http://articles.sun-sentinel.com/2011-07 -03/news/fl-gypsy-crime-groups-20110703_1_gypsy-criminals-bunco-investigators -police-focus.

Eminova, Enisa. "Raising New Questions about an Old Tradition." *Open Society News* (Summer/Fall 2005): 13.

European Roma and Travellers Forum. 2015. Fact Sheet on the Situation of Roma in Macedonia. https://www.ertf.org/images/Reports/The_situation_of_Roma_in _Macedonia_01092015.pdf.

European Roma Rights Centre. "Victory for Roma: Macedonia Agrees to Pay Compensation for Roma Prison Death." June 15, 2017. www.errc.org/article/victory -for-roma-macedonia-agrees-to-pay-compensation-for-roma-prison-death/4584.

Glick Schiller, Nina, Linda Basch, and Cristina Blanc-Szanton. *Towards a Transnational Perspective on Migration: Race, Class, Ethnicity and Nationalism Reconsidered*. New York: New York Academy of Sciences, 1992.

Hancock, Ian. *We Are the Romani People: Ame Sam e Rromane Džene.* Hatfield, UK: University of Hertfordshire Press, 2002.

Kooijman, Hellen. "Roma: Bleak Horizon." *VoxEurop,* April 6, 2012. http://www .presseurop.eu/en/content/article/1757331-bleak-horizon.

Lee, Ken. "Orientalism and Gypsylorism." *Social Analysis* 44, no. 2 (November 2000): 129–56.

Marafioti, Oksana. "Why TLC's *My Big Fat American Gypsy Wedding* Doesn't Represent the Romani." *Slate Blog,* May 15, 2012. http://www.slate.com/blogs/xx_factor/2012 /05/15/is_my_big_fat_gypsy_wedding_unfair_to_the_roma_community_.html.

Matras, Yaron. *The Romani Gypsies.* Cambridge, MA: Harvard University Press, 2015.

Petrova, Dimitrina. "The Roma: Between a Myth and a Future." *Social Research* 70, no. 1 (2003): 111–61.

Plaut, Shayna, and Azbija Memedova. "Blank Face, Private Strength: Romani Identity as Represented in the Public and Private Sphere." In *Roma's Identities in Southeast Europe: Macedonia,* edited by Azbija Memedova et al. Ethnobarometer Working Paper, 2005. http://www.piemonteimmigrazione.it/PDF/ethnobarometer9.pdf.

Said, Edward. *Orientalism.* New York: Vintage, 1978.

Seeman, Sonia Tamar. "Music in the Service of Prestation: The Case of the Rom of Skopje." Master's thesis, University of Washington, 1990.

Silverman, Carol. "Diasporic Ethnicity, Gender and Dance: Muslim Macedonian Roma in New York." In *Oxford Handbook of Dance and Ethnicity,* edited by Anthony Shay and Barbara Sellers-Young, 161–80. New York: Oxford University Press, 2016.

———. "Education, Agency, and Power among Macedonian Muslim Romani Women in New York City." *Signs: Journal of Women in Culture and Society* (Symposium on Romani Feminisms) 38, no. 1 (2012): 30–36.

———. "The Gender of the Profession: Music, Dance and Reputation among Balkan Muslim Romani (Gypsy) Women." In *Gender and Music in the Mediterranean,* edited by Tullia Magrini, 119–45. Chicago: University of Chicago Press, 2003.

———. "Macedonian and Bulgarian Muslim Romani Women: Power, Politics, and Creativity in Ritual." *Roma Rights* 1 (April 2000): 38–41.

———. "Music and Power: Gender and Performance among Roma (Gypsies) of Skopje, Macedonia." *The World of Music* 38, no. 1 (1996): 63–76.

———. *Romani Routes: Cultural Politics and Balkan Music in Diaspora.* New York: Oxford University Press, 2012.

———. "Transnational Chochek: The Politics and Poetics of Balkan Romani Dance." In *Balkan Dance: Essays on Characteristics, Performing, and Teaching,* edited by Anthony Shay, 37–68. Jefferson, NC: McFarland Press, 2008.

Stewart, Michael. *Gypsy "Menace": Populism and the New Anti-Gypsy Politics.* London: Oxford University Press, 2014.

Sugarman, Jane. *Engendering Song: Singing and Subjectivity at Prespa Albanian Weddings.* Chicago: University of Chicago Press, 1997.

Trumpener, Katie. "The Time of the Gypsies: A 'People without History' in the Narratives of the West." *Critical Inquiry* 18 (1992): 843–84.

Voice of America. "For Roma, Life in US Has Challenges." April 6, 2011. http://www .voanews.com/content/for-roma-life-in-us-has-challenges-119394819/163156.html.

3

Werbner, Pnina. *Imagined Diasporas among Manchester Muslims.* Oxford: School of American Research, 2002.

White, Patrick. "Big Fat Gypsy Confusion." Media Diversity Institute, March 9, 2012. http://www.media-diversity.org/en/index.php?option=com_content&view=article&id=2178:big-fat-gypsy-confusion&catid=35:media-news-a-content&Itemid=34.

Williams, Mario. "Help Support Protest of My Big Fat Gypsy Wedding." *Gypsy Connection.* Accessed February 14, 2019. http://thegypsyconnection.blogspot.com/2011/06/help-support-protest-of-my-big-fat.html.

World Bank. "Roma." February 21, 2015. http://www.worldbank.org/en/region/eca/brief/roma.

———. "The Roma Labor Market—Why Europe Should Care." December 8, 2014 http://www.worldbank.org/en/news/feature/2014/12/08/the-roma-labor-market---why-europe-should-care.

THREE

—∿—

DISSONANT LOVE

Music in Latina/o Diasporic Weddings

LORENA ALVARADO AND FRANCES R. APARICIO

WITH BOMBA DRUMS AND MARACAS "thundering," bride Ana García and groom Gabriel Dionisio danced down the church aisle before "rapping the marriage vows" to each other. On June 17, 2000, the two New York Puerto Ricans got married at St. Cecilia's church on 106th Street, "right in the heart of El Barrio (East Harlem)."[1] Publicly known as B-girl Rockafella and Kwikstep, respectively, Ana and Gabriel are breakers, leaders of the Full Circle dance crew, and cultural activists. Raquel Z. Rivera, a witness to the ceremony, described it as an "impressive manifestation of a Nuyorican identity whose referents have as much to do with the Caribbean culture which our parents and grandparents transplanted to this New York soil, as with the urban youth culture out of which comes hip hop."[2] While the integration of bomba and hip-hop inside the hallowed space of a church may sound unusual and extraordinary, it allows us to frame our analysis of the hybrid mixtures of multiple sonic traditions in Latina/o diasporic weddings.

On the other coast, bride Mercedes, a modern professional woman, makes a traditional musical choice for her father/daughter wedding dance, which she says is the "second most important song in the wedding reception" (wedding in San Leandro, CA, 2010).[3] She grew up "loving the idea of dancing with [her] father," a ranchera music fanatic, collector, and connoisseur. Honoring him and his musical preferences, she chooses "La recién casada" sung by the legendary Antonio Aguilar, a popular banda and ranchera singer of her father's generation.

What are the musical expectations, standards, and motivations that inform musical repertoires in Latina/o diasporic weddings? What are the factors that influence the sonic innovations and disruptions that Latina/o couples make for their wedding celebration? How are the celebration and music connected and informed by literary and cinematic works?

One of the most memorable scenes in the Latino film *My Family* (Mi familia) is the wedding of Gerardo and Irene, the oldest daughter of the Sánchez family. The wedding reception and the family celebration help us introduce our analysis of the role of music in Latino diasporic weddings. Filmed in 1995 but set in the late 1950s—thus presenting traditions of an earlier generation—the wedding prominently features mariachi music, performed by the Mariachi Los Camperos, as the principal musical ensemble during the celebration. The repertoire includes the son jaliscience "La negra" and the Mexican polka "Jesusita en Chihuahua," two popular songs that trigger dancing among the guests. Tony, one of the daughters, performs a zapateado to the polka rhythms of "Jesusita," a moment that captures the traditional sounds and dancing movements associated with Mexican working-class weddings in the Southwest. Another Mexican classic, "Flor de canela," a Purépecha song, serves as the sonic background to a confrontation between Chucho, one of Irene's brothers, and a rival gang that takes place during the wedding party.

The scenes exemplify traditional expectations in the popular imagination of the sounds of a Mexican wedding, in particular, the homologies between mariachi music, Mexican sones, and ultimately, Mexicanidad. Given the film's historical setting in the late 1950s and its geocultural context of East Los Angeles, mariachis represented a more acceptable and proper expression of Mexican identity and family than the sounds of the mambo, the jitterbug, swing, and other forms of dance music of the times that were incredibly popular among Mexican American urban youth. Anthony Macías notes the popularity of swing bands among Mexican Americans in Los Angeles of approximately the same period that is pictured in the film: "Despite repeated exposure to mariachi, guitar trio, bolero, ranchera, and conjunto styles, Mexican Americans throughout Los Angeles were 'hooked on' and 'crazy about' swing bands." He also comments on the ways in which "listening and dancing to swing" allowed Mexican Americans to forge "their own freestyle expression" that was neither "performing blackness" nor "assimilating whiteness."[4]

Deploying Deborah Vargas's critical concept of "dissonance," "an interruption, or disruption of the heteronormative and cultural nationalist limits of la onda by Chicana/Tejana singers,"[5] this chapter will examine the heterogeneous musical repertoires featured in US Latina/o weddings that trouble or "disrupt" the dominant sonic imaginaries—like Mexican mariachi—that conflate national identity with musical traditions.

Tracing the musical repertoires in US Latino weddings, this essay juxtaposes a survey we conducted with eleven couples and four Latino grooms with our own readings of weddings in films, novels, and poetry. Defining Latinidad as a conceptual framework that allows us "to document, analyze and theorize the processes by which diverse Latinas/os interact with each other, subordinate and transculturate each other," analyzing what each couple's musical selections tell us about the discontinuities and ruptures of Latinidad.[6] For many couples, curating the music for their wedding day is no easy, simple task, nor is it devoid of politics. They weigh and negotiate, they compromise and insist, they honor and dismiss. In their selections, they theorize Latinidades that challenge our understanding of the heterogeneity and power continually shifting not only in their families but also within the larger communities to which they belong.

Given the lack of scholarly attention to weddings as social rituals within US Latina/o communities, and in order to offer a broader picture of music in Latino weddings, we weave textual and ethnographic approaches as an intervention that can only begin to suggest new ways of thinking about the social meanings of musical repertoires in these weddings. While the literary and film texts served as a (limited) archive, they helped us frame our analysis of the survey narratives as examples of the ways in which weddings are produced by social imaginaries that construct US Latinidades. Set against the backdrop of reified imaginaries of Latino weddings as expressions of a segmented ethnicity or national sonic tradition, as the scenes of *My Family* suggested, our narratives and interviews propose that the younger generations of Latinas/os who marry across Latin American nationalities as well as across other racial and cultural borders, selected musical repertoires for their weddings that unsettle national sonic imaginaries and express the increasing heterogeneity in our ever-shifting and dynamic communities. The tensions between tradition and modernity, between national and global sounds, generation-informed musical taste and predilections, and gendered norms, surfaced in the film and literary texts studied as well as in the surveys completed by young Latina/o couples.

GENERATIONAL TENSIONS / TRADITION AND MODERNITY

"La recién casada," the music Mercedes chose for her father-bride dance, is lovely and upbeat. The lyrics are a different matter. The song tells the story of a recently married woman who complains to her father about her spouse. The most important thing in the song is not the young wife's unhappiness, but her father's message, given "in a loving yet stern way," urging his daughter to stop complaining and instead to accept and submit. The general idleness of the new husband, his coldness and unwillingness to collaborate are suggested in the spoken sequence Aguilar inserts in his singing. In the lyrics, the woman appealing to her parents and saints is described as crying "as if she were a child."

The song integrates the father's message that his married daughter should accept the burden of unhappy marriage with the comic sonority that makes the patriarchal authority palatable and much easier to accept as the norm. The combination of a young woman's tearful appeal with a light melody and bouncy rhythm also creates a discursive space trivializing the woman's feelings. At the same time, while masking the text, the song releases the tensions through laughter that makes this song safe for celebratory rituals and for having fun.

Mercedes is well aware of the text. Born in her parent's home state of Michoacán and raised in California's Bay Area, she recalls that since her early teens she discussed the topic of the song with her parents. A young woman, she can relate to the way the young wife "in the song felt—learning to live with another person is challenging and it pushes your limits beyond anything imaginable." Yet Mercedes grew up believing that "a person has the right to choose to decide what their limit is and when they feel they are ready to walk away and not feel like a failure, not just from a marriage, but from a career, a friendship, or a project." By choosing this song for her wedding Mercedes continued negotiating a traditional view of gender with her parents, specifically with her father. While her father's face "lit up" when he heard the beginning of the song, and Mercedes described this moment as "priceless," she remembers this song as a text that "stirred some controversies" with her parents. She explains: "This is where my parents and I would argue about its meaning, and they disagreed with my view. That sometimes you don't have to stay in a marriage if one is not happy. Whereas they felt that marriage is for life and one should do whatever it takes to keep it intact."

By playing "La recién casada," the newlywed daughter is acknowledging her father's values, which are deeply grounded in Mexican patriarchy. Yet simultaneously, by surprising her father with her own musical choice, Mercedes ironically had the last word. She honors her father while she is also reminding him that the decision to marry and to stay in the marriage is ultimately hers.

Many Latino brides and grooms give serious consideration to, demonstrate respect, and honor their parents' and grandparents' musical preferences. For Vicky (wedding in Racine, Wisconsin, 2011), the inclusion of music to please her relatives was the result of family expectations. She shared with us the sense of pressure she felt to play their music: "I needed to have Spanish music or else my family would be upset. For my family, it was important to me (not my husband) that we incorporate Latino music. I wanted my guests to have fun, and this was part of it." Vicky had to negotiate between mariachi, Mexican banda, and a DJ, as in her sister's wedding, and a more hybrid selection, which reflected not only her own love for salsa, bachata, and hip-hop since she grew up in a more urban, black culture but also her Caucasian husband's preference for country music.

Bride Bárbara and her husband (wedding in Cancún, Mexico) were both born in the United States and raised in Chicago. Growing up in Pilsen and Little Village, they both share a love for the varied sounds of Mexicanidad: *rancheras* (dramatic ballads of love and/or regional pride, associated with mariachi), *cumbias* (a dance-oriented genre originally from Colombia, popular throughout the Americas), *norteñas* (a northern Mexican genre characterized by its accordion sound), and banda (a genre and ensemble consisting of wind, mostly brass, instruments). Thus it was a clear decision for them to include music to embrace their "Mexican culture that went beyond our Mexican neighborhoods in Chicago"; that is, they visited and engaged with family on both sides of the border frequently throughout their lives. The richness of the neighborhood sounds also speaks to the deep social segregation that characterizes Chicago. Keenly aware of regional differences, Bárbara and her husband wanted to honor both the southern and northern regions of Mexico from which their families originated. They played "El corrido de Monterrey," as well as norteño musicians like Ramon Ayala and Los Tigres del Norte for her family and "Caminos de Michoacán" for his. They never had any doubts about including a mariachi, since this ensemble had always been a part of their family celebrations, from baptisms and quinceañeras to weddings. Not having a mariachi would be like "something was missing in our wedding." This evocation of absence emphasizes the ubiquity of mariachis in their family celebrations. Indeed, the presence of, or desire for, mariachis in a wedding ceremony echoed other participants' responses, particularly, though not entirely, those with familial connections to Mexico. It also reaffirms the dominant sonic imaginary cemented in the film *My Family*.

In addition to the foundational Mexican repertoire, Bárbara and her spouse included other musical traditions as important as the one "inspired by their parents and families." The couple chose and enjoyed house, New Wave, rock en español, hip-hop, and reggaeton—all musics that they also claim as their own and that convey a "sentiment" that resonated with their upbringing as second-generation Mexicans living in urban Chicago. As US-born Mexican Americans, they did not choose to reject traditional Mexican sounds, nor did they cater only to their parents' generation; indeed, the hybrid sounds of their wedding articulated their historical and social experiences. Bárbara acknowledged it was "no easy task," but the "end result made it all worth it, as it brought all [our] wedding guests from different generations and ethnicities on to the dance floor." Even when a couple belongs to the same national/ethnic group, generational dissonances can be further complicated by families' geographic disparities. For example, Guillermo, who was born in Jalisco, Mexico, married a third-generation Mexican American woman from Southern California (wedding in Long Beach, California, 2001). While they had mariachi music during the dinner, they also played oldies, hits popular among youth during the 1950s and 1960s, "to honor [my] father-in-law and his generation."

Alejandro and his spouse live in Texas and embraced their Mexican roots by getting married in their hometown of Tequila in Mexico (wedding in Jalisco, Mexico, 2004). Not much concerned about satisfying the musical tastes of their guests and older relatives, they "never thought about a specific tradition." They said that their goal "was not to make guests happy with chosen music [but to] enjoy ourselves our selections and to share our happiness with our guests."

Alejandro questioned the existence of a Mexican musical tradition. His own predilections revolved around American popular music, which offered him "refuge, peace, and pleasure" during his teenage years. His wife's musical taste was shaped by the same music she listened to growing up in Mexico. While there was a norteño group that performed at the end of the wedding, for the most part, Alejandro and his wife played predominantly American pop, R & B, and rock in English (in Mexico), illustrating the internal heterogeneity of the Mexican American community through musical repertoires.

In order to elucidate the nuances of generational dissonances within Latina/o families and the pivotal role of musical selections in weddings, it is fitting to connect our surveys with a reading of Afro–Puerto Rican Amina Gautier's short story "Aguanile." A Yoruba word recited in rituals to the sea goddess Yamaya, *aguanile* refers to spiritual cleansing and exemplifies the influence of the Afro-Cuban religious practices of Santería. *Aguanile* is widely known as the title of Puerto Rican/Nuyorican Héctor Lavoe's signature Salsa song, first recorded in the 1972 Fania-produced album *El juicio*, with Willie Colón. For a famous singer of the next generation, New York–born Puerto Rican Marc Anthony, "Aguanile" became the opening song in many of his concerts. Anthony himself plays Lavoe and Jennifer Lopez portrays Lavoe's wife in the biographical film *El cantante* (2006).

Given the powerful ways that the song sonically and verbally performs the meanings of Santería in Latina/o Caribbean communities while drawing on continuous infatuation of Latina/o Americans with Lavoe (and Anthony performing the song and playing Lavoe), it is not surprising that Gautier would choose *aguanile* as the title for her story.

The young female narrator tells about her biological grandfather, who years ago abandoned her grandmother and left the family in a state of poverty. Her recollection of phone conversations with her grandfather form the canvas of the story. The grandfather was an ardent fan of the music of Héctor Lavoe, among other Salsa greats.[7] He referred to Lavoe intimately by the singer's first name and flew from Puerto Rico to New York to attend Lavoe's funeral. The grandfather called his granddaughter every time a Salsa musician passed away, mourning them as if they were family members or loved ones. "The calls had little to do with any ability on my part to appreciate the musicians he revered. He turned to me by default; none of his children shared his interest in the music."[8] The granddaughter, who has been scarred by the grandfather's abandonment of his first family, grapples with both bitterness and affection for him. And it is through salsa that both grandfather and granddaughter maintain an affective relationship that otherwise is fraught with pain and resentment.

The wedding of the grandfather's son from his second marriage, Chali, is one of the key episodes in the story. Although raised by a salsa lover, Chali embodies the hip-hop generation. Having practiced to become a DJ, and "locked behind his bedroom door" playing Run DMC and Big Daddy Kane, Chali refuses to play any music in Spanish at his wedding. Instead, he chooses a repertoire consisting of Hip-Hop and R & B and including songs by Destiny's Child—none of which his father (the narrator's grandfather) recognizes or can relate to. The grandfather confides in his granddaughter that Chali "is not going to play anything by *him*," referring to Héctor Lavoe. She describes his tone of voice as if this were a "personal affront" to him, a gesture of disdain on the part of the son he raised. The grandfather's "second set of children shunned his tastes, preferring hip-hop and Top 40 tunes."[9]

While Chali's dismissal of his father's predilection for Lavoe reveals the lack of respect for his father and his family cultural heritage, ironically it is the narrator who, learning to appreciate Lavoe from her grandfather, develops a genuine relationship with him: "When he took the time to explain the music to me, I could not hate him. With the music between us, I could almost forget that he was the man who should have been in Brooklyn with us, but had abandoned us and had a whole other family who got all of his time, care and attention."[10] Finding out that her grandfather has passed, the narrator returns to Lavoe's song, "Aguanile." Having confessed early in the story that she mistrusts men largely because of her grandfather's neglect of her grandmother and mother, at the end of her narrative she realizes that sharing Lavoe's musical affinity was her grandfather's way of making peace with her family and showing love for his granddaughter.

The story "Aguanile" reflects on the complicated family histories that inform musical selections in Latino diasporic weddings. Generational disconnect in musical tastes and preferences are further complicated by diasporic histories as well as stories within individual families. As the story suggests, and as our surveys with Latino couples propose, music in weddings ties multiple threads in the fabric of the family.

LEARNING TO SING AND DANCE:
THE SOCIAL MEANINGS OF MUSICAL GENRES

How does a little girl learn to sing and dance and love the plentitude of genres and repertoires identified with her immediate community within the larger frame of American Latina music and in the context of American global pop? Bride Vicky, whose music selection for her wedding was discussed earlier, relates cumbias with her childhood memories of "watching her family dance at just about any family event." Rancheras remind her "100% of [her] grandmother and uncles," and she associates bachata and salsa with her "college days" and with her girl-friends at the university who introduced her to these musical traditions. While for Vicky both cumbias and rancheras are situated in the past and reified as the music of the Mexican family and of the older generations, a sort of nostalgia, bachata and salsa are linked to her years as a young adult, and thus to her pres-ent, and her potential for social mobility indexed through her college education.

Unlike her Caucasian husband, who did not care about the musical selec-tions for their wedding, Vicky has strong affective investments in these musical genres. As she stated: "My husband had no perspective on wedding music. He just wanted to get married. It seemed music was much more important to my family because it has played such a big part of our lives." This heterogeneity is articulated as well in the selection of musical genres.

The novel by Mexican American writer Mary Helen Ponce *The Wedding* narrates the celebration of the marriage of two young pachucos, Cricket and Blanca, during the 1950s in Southern California. The generational divides in the Mexican American community are iconized through the contrast between the danzón and the mambo. Gato Cortez, the bandleader performing at the recep-tion, decided on playing mambo since it was a popular dance form among the youth (a connection also included in the film *My Family*). Fueled by his desire to get more gigs and to remain relevant, Gato's musical selections privileged the younger generation. In Gato's thinking, if the mambo failed to attract danc-ers to the floor, he would return, by default, to performing danzones that "ap-pealed to old folks who could barely move."[11] He refers to danzones as a "return to Mexican standards,"[12] cementing the boundaries between Mexican Amer-ican communities and Mexico proper. Even though the mambo was incredibly popular among pachuco dancers in the novel (and actually in California), the groom, Cricket, detests this music. He disavows it for racist reasons—"This ain't Africa"[13]—yet truly he rejects mambo because of his own insecurities as a dancer, a factor that threatened his public masculinity as the leader of his gang.

If Cricket is described as a "giraffe with weak knees" and "like a fly trying to take off" on the dance floor, Skippy, the blond leader of the Planchados, "was a renowned dancer." He "jitterbugged like a pro, excelled at the mambo, and danced the danzón with ease." As a strategy to mask his anxiety and to compete with Skippy, Cricket requests Gato and the band to play "slow tunes to allow him to look suave, handsome."[14] Yet he does ask Blanca to dance to the mambo music during the wedding, which she hardly believes. While the narrator describes him as having difficulty finding the beat, the women on the dance floor are portrayed as expert mambo dancers, thus constructing this intricate dance as a domain of female agency. Cricket's anxiety over dancing the mambo was not uncommon at the time. As Anthony Macías explains, Mexican Americans in Greater Los Angeles were dancing to swing bands, Latin jazz, the bolero, the mambo, and cha cha chá, among other tropical musical forms, since the late 1930s.[15] For them, these dance forms enabled them to "evoke a certain Latinidad, indulging their social aspirations while participating in an international music industry and ballroom dance culture."[16] Yet "not every Chicano went out there to dance the mambo and the cha cha chá at those clubs," as Zenda Ballroom regular Jaime Corral stated.[17] While the mambo, like many other tropical musical genres, enabled social mobility, Blanca's desire for dancing the mambo was consistent with the class anxieties that fueled her wedding plans, an aspirational desire evident in the first pages of the novel.[18]

ETHNICALLY AND RACIALLY DIVERSE
LATINAS VOICES

In both "Aguanile" and *The Wedding*, although in very different ways, the generational tension was bounded by a single nationality; in many actual weddings, there are multiple racial and ethnic factors to be negotiated. Discourses on the sounds of Latinidad are shaped by diasporic voices of different generations and ethnicities and further complicated by racially mixed Latinas/os. Susana (wedding in Berkeley, California, 2009), a Panamanian Caucasian Latina bride who married a Caucasian man from Nebraska, commented, "There are multiple generations present, multiple geographies present, multiple tastes and traditions and we want everyone to have a good time." Her words highlight the challenge for any bride and groom to identify musical genres, songs, and a repertoire with which most guests will identify. Susana and her partner chose to "crowd-source" some of the music as a strategy to encourage as many people as possible to get up and dance, asking guests in advance to name a song they'd like to hear at the wedding. This couple made sure to include the sounds important for Susana or her family (including the Gypsy Kings, Shakira, the Buena Vista Social Club) and the Beatles songs and alternative rock that her husband enjoys. The reception also featured a diverse array of selections reflective of their Bay Area community, including Bhangra, where they met in graduate school. Many interviewees pointed to the importance of honoring the elderly in the extended family and including the music that parents and grandparents love. Yet given the internal heterogeneity of the Latina/o community in the United States, the multigenerational profile of Latina/o brides and grooms since 2000, and the increasing numbers of cross-cultural and transracial couples, like Susana and her husband, this desire to please the guests is complicated.[19]

Inés (Laguna Hills, California, 2014), a Mexican American who married an African American man, shared the generational tensions that arose in her wedding despite their efforts to offer a diverse musical repertoire. They spoke to their DJ about compiling a musical selection that would please their relatives and made sure the DJ "knew about English and Spanish music," rendering the DJ a mediator of different cultural and musical tastes. Furthermore, Inés and her spouse made sure that the songs would not include any profanity because of her husband's older relatives. They also limited the number of hip-hop songs, which her relatives could not or preferred not to dance to. Despite these efforts, one of her aunts commented after the event "that she didn't really dance because she thought we mostly played our generation's type of music so she didn't really know how to dance to that."

Patricia (wedding in Pasadena, California, 2014), a third-generation, part Nicaraguan and part Irish Latina who grew up in East Los Angeles County, underlined the ways in which Latino communities are associated with sounds and auditory identities. For Patricia and her Brazilian husband from Hortolân-dia, Latino rhythms "symbolize part of who [they] are" and the rhythms they "genuinely love." Their wedding music included wide-ranging genres as diverse as samba, Brazilian popular music, the Beatles, the Strokes, the Grateful Dead, Ray Charles, Lauryn Hill, and the Beach Boys, along with Latina/o singers such as La Lupe, Carlos Vives, Santana, Shakira, the Buena Vista Social Club, and Celia Cruz. They hired an L.A.-based Filipino American DJ who loves Latino music and funk. Unlike other couples we engage with here, Patricia noted that their selections were vastly distant from the musical cultures both she and her husband grew up with at home: "Neither of us particularly love the music our parents were raised with—my husband doesn't like the Brazilian *sertanejo* music he was raised with, and I'm not nuts about some of the American pop I was raised with. So, we thought of the musical 'traditions' we've adopted as adults." This rich heterogeneity of sounds, dancing music, and musical traditions exemplifies the increasingly global experiences and aspirations of this couple and, by exten-sion, of many mixed-race and third-generation Latinas/os.

SABOR AND SENTIMIENTO /
LATINOS AS A SONIC CULTURE

Many brides and grooms reiterated the expectations that a Latino wedding cannot but include Latino sounds and musics. As Mercedes commented, "Latinos expect music to be at weddings," and the Mexican American community requires mariachis at the church and lively music at the reception. Although Mercedes would have loved to have a mariachi perform at her own religious celebration, this wasn't possible for economic reasons. Indeed, a live mariachi, or any live music band for that matter, is both an affective and monetary investment. Instead, she and her husband, reflecting on their interracial union, worked with the church's musical director to incorporate Mexican, Japanese, and American church music into the ceremony.

Mercedes, who danced with her father accompanied by "La recién casada," compared a Latina/o wedding without music to a "funeral" and reiterated how "music is very central to our everyday life." She further explained that music is essential to the affective textures of Latinidad since it inspires both joy and sorrow as it triggers memory and a "sentimiento" that reminds the community "of our roots and our perseverance."

Bárbara, who like her groom grew up in Chicago, discusses this unique quality of Latino music as undeniable. According to her, Latino sounds serve as a unifying force in events such as weddings, producing a communal space. Yet there is an essentializing and self-tropicalizing gesture[20] in her choice of the word *sabor* to refer to the effect that Latino sounds have in celebrations. While the Spanish word *sabor* means "taste or flavor" in the context of Latin food and cuisine, it has also been historically used to refer to good music among Latina/o musicians. By linking the *sabor* of music as a metaphor for taste in melody, instrumentation, and rhythms, with the communal function of music as a social equalizer and universalizing experience, Bárbara engages in a double discourse that is simultaneously oppositional as well as hegemonic. Having situated herself as a proud second-generation Mexicana who grew up in Little Village, segregated by race and class, she hails the term *sabor* as a form of "strategic essentialism" that attempts to decolonize her while reproducing some of the very dominant tenets of hegemonic tropicalizations.

The fact that Bárbara got married in Cancún (a destination wedding) also illustrates the increasing mobility and choices of the younger generations. Most significantly, Cancún is still Mexico, which suggests a recuperative act on the part of this Mexican American couple, and it is also the Caribbean, which reiterates the use of sabor within the geocultural space of Chicago, where both Mexican and Caribbean Latinos such as Puerto Ricans share an urban history.

Patricia underlined the ways in which Latino communities are associated with sounds and auditory identities. For her, even as non-Latinos have accepted the visual heterogeneity of Latino racial phenotypes—that is, that by now "Latinos can look like a lot of things"—Latinas/os are still stereotyped and homogenized as sounding outside the norm, whether it is in their spoken voice (stereotypically loud or accented), regional tone, or musical preferences. According to Patricia, measuring authenticity, belonging and discrimination are effected through two "auditory activities": speaking Spanish and listening to music, which are also used as surveillance mechanisms. A scholar on sonics, race, and politics of listening, Jennifer Stover-Ackerman writes, "Dominant groups use sound with impunity to forge 'reasonable suspicion' about the citizenship status of anyone who sounds different from them and who creates, consumes, and appreciates sounds differently from them."[21]

This homology of Latinidad and sound is extended to the expectations for Latino weddings. If fourth-generation European Americans are not generally expected to include their heritage music at weddings, all Latinos, despite their generational status, are expected to play Latino music, thus playing into notions of authenticity. Despite this critical observation, Patricia does embrace Latino music at weddings since it expresses the joy of such celebrations. Their wedding, discussed earlier, included a wide array of Latina and non-Latina pop.

SOUNDING LOVE

Indeed, the second- and third-generation US Latinas in our survey shared increasingly unorthodox musical repertoires that transcend the homologies among music, nation, and family. The high number of interracial and intercultural couples surveyed explains, in some ways, this increasing hybridity that troubles the standard expectations and representations of US Latino weddings. The stories shared in the survey exemplify the intimate details and affective family dynamics that inform these musical selections. Ultimately, for many of these couples, the musical selection for their weddings was a public expression of their love for each other. They commented on how the wedding music, and particularly the first dance, had to be a "reflection of their interests and personality" or "a reflection of them as a couple," and how they "wanted [their] own identities reflected in the mood the music created." They located and situated these specific songs or musical genres in particular moments within their affective histories as a couple. For instance, Patricia spoke about how she and her husband would "lounge around the house listening to Latino rhythms." Amalia shared how she and her husband listened daily to Spanish guitar. Inés recalled sitting in the car with her then boyfriend listening to "oldies on 92.3" and talking about life.

Mariana's (Racine, Wisconsin, 2007) choice for the first dance, Alicia Keys's "If I Ain't Got You," exemplified the sacrifices that she and her spouse endured living apart for professional development. Finally, Julia (Racine, Wisconsin, 2014) explained that their first dance was John Legend's "All of Me," a song that her husband "immediately loved and said it reminded him of [them]." They also combined this song with Marc Anthony's "Vivir mi vida," chosen for its jubilant rhythms and buoyant lyrics. After losing her husband's mother, "moving across country and relocating back to Chicago, we felt this song really struck a chord with how we felt about life and each other." In brief, "Vivir mi vida" resonated with the couple's struggles and plans for their future, the death of her husband's mother, and their homecoming to initiate a life together in the Midwest. While she added that they chose this salsa song because "they love to dance," the song also offered them a language through which they could reclaim life for themselves. The inclusion of salsa music as part of the couple's first dance expands its traditional expectation as a slow dance. That many couples now move from a slow ballad to faster rhythms during that first dance illustrates these everchanging traditions.

Like Julia, other couples' choices of the music for their first dance similarly conveyed their memories of their history and their current aspirations for the future. For Inés, whose husband is African American, the genre that was close to their heart and served as soundtrack to their early dating was "Forever Mine," a tune from 1979 by the O'Jays, a sort of retro sound that transported them back to their dating years with rhythms and melodies that are older than they are. Moreover, the fact that Inés and her husband listened to the O'Jays and selected their song for their first dance hints at a larger social history of musicking and affective interactions between African Americans and Latinas/os that remains underacknowledged in the larger context of American history.[22]

Like Inés, Guillermo also chose an oldies song, "Can't Take My Eyes Off Of You" by Frankie Valli, a song that he and his spouse sang on their first long trip. It was special because when they sang it together, it marked the moment when he realized that he "would marry [his] wife." Again, this musical selection marks a pivotal moment in the history of the couple. It serves as a vehicle for memorializing that decisive instance of committing fully to their relationship, as gendered as it may have been. Raúl and Lisette (Chicago, Illinois, 2013) also chose "Can't Take My Eyes Off Of You" but in a mariachi version, which sounded these transculturations of American pop songs through Mexican musical traditions. Many mariachis have performed this song and in the process have reproduced the original melodies with the bewildering effect of familiar mariachi sounds and instrumentation to covering classic English-language love songs. This specific transculturation exemplifies a "dissonance" that is both visual and sonic: the staging of mariachi musicians, both men and women, and the sounds emanating from the vihuela and the violins disrupt our expectations for 1950s doo-wop. For Raúl and Lisette this choice represented the merging of two cultural worlds as second-generation US Latina/os.

For some interracial and intercultural couples, the choices for the first dance included selections outside of Latino soundscapes. While Alejandro selected "How Do I Live Without You" by LeAnn Rimes, his wife chose "Bella" by Ricky Martin. As teenagers, Alejandro and his wife (who grew up in Mexico) both listened to English-language music, in which they found "refuge, peace, and pleasure." Susana and her spouse played "a handful of Frank Sinatra songs," ending with "Come Fly with Me." They wanted "a dance with some fun moves, and her spouse knows swing (given he was a competitive dancer in college)," so they narrowed it down to Sinatra. Mercedes's Japanese American spouse chose "Truly, Madly, Deeply" by Savage Garden, while she selected Rogelio Martínez's "Tú y yo," a slow-moving banda song. For Mercedes and her husband, these wedding decisions made them realize for the first time that they came "from different culture/race/and socioeconomic backgrounds" so it was important for her to uphold "certain wedding traditions that were embedded in her Mexicanness." The inclusion of the banda cut "Tú y yo" was part of the reaffirmation she needed to "stay true to [her] roots, to honor where she came from" and to assert her Mexicanidad "in her present and future."

For Amalia and James, who got married in Malta (2012), the selection of the music for the first dance was Alicia Key's "No One," a song that was released when they first met and that reaffirms James's African American and mixed-race family heritage. For the reception, they hired a local Maltese band that included a violin, a guitar, and drums/percussion and played fast-rhythm dance music in addition to the couple's request for Spanish guitar music. The fact that this wedding took place in Malta, far away from the United States, signals the ever-increasing globalized spaces for Latina/o contemporary weddings for young professional couples like them. Yet Malta also leads us to the longer history of sea and border crossings of immigrants from North Africa trying to enter Western Europe. More recent drownings and catastrophes at sea have forced European governments to address immigration policy. This scenario complicates our understanding of Latino diasporic weddings. If Malta is now fraught with immigration dilemmas, the personal trajectory of this mixed-race couple points to their own, and their parents' and grandparents', histories of displacement as second- and third-generation sons and daughters of migrants to or across the United States, as subjects of multiple diasporas.[23]

Weddings are productions where identities, rituals, and economies intersect. These family celebrations trouble notions of purity even as they uphold traditions dear to the celebrants. Many of the participants in our survey defied the classifications "Latina/o wedding" and "Latina/o music." They confirmed that these labels do not signify a particular kind of celebration or ethnicity or a specific sound. To listen to the music these (mixed) Latina/o couples chose to play at their weddings is to listen to an orchestration of both their intimate lives and globalized trajectories. In their festivities, they displayed their affective lives aurally. Their selections resulted from a series of economic, familial, and generational negotiations. For many, the curation of music entailed a consciousness-raising exercise regarding race and identity. Many of these couples suggested their own decolonial readings of Latinidad, acknowledging the impossible task of defining its sound but claiming specific sonorities as manifestations of belonging. Without privileging marriage or heterosexual relationships, these unions signal a defiant gesture in a time of continued hostility toward US Latina/os, particularly when they consciously choose to foreground their Latinidad at their weddings. When they don't, the couples defined their Latinidad beyond hegemonic representation or tropicalizations. In both instances, they countered various forms of elisions and stereotypes that limit our listening to both the dissonant and essential patterns of celebration, survival, and community.

LORENA ALVARADO is Assistant Professor in the Global Arts Studies Program at the University of California, Merced.

FRANCES R. APARICIO is Professor of Spanish and Portuguese and Director of the Latina and Latino Studies Program at Northwestern University. She is author of *Listening to Salsa: Gender, Latino Popular Music, and Puerto Rican Cultures,* and editor with Candida F. Jaquez of *Musical Migrations: Transnationalism and Cultural Hybridity in Latin/o America.*

NOTES

1. Rivera, *New York Ricans from the Hip Hop Zone,* 251.
2. Rivera, *New York Ricans,* 236.
3. All subjects included in this chapter (under the pseudonyms of Patricia, Alejandro, Guillermo, Lisette and Raúl, Inés, Bárbara, Amalia and James, Vicky, Julia, and Mercedes) responded to email surveys. They each responded in writing and we received all responses between November 2014 and March 2015. The location and year of the wedding are provided when available.

4. See Macías, *Mexican American Mojo*, 52.
5. Vargas, *Dissonant Divas in Chicana Music*, xiv.
6. For a lengthier discussion of the meanings of the term, see Aparicio, "Latinidad/es."
7. Gautier, "Aguanile," 1–15.
8. Gautier, "Aguanile,"1.
9. All quotations in this paragraph, ibid., 10.
10. Ibid., 11.
11. Ponce, *The Wedding*, 169.
12. Ibid.
13. Ibid., 170.
14. All quotations in this paragraph from ibid., 171.
15. Macías, *Mexican American Mojo*, 52.
16. Ibid., 265.
17. The Zenda Ballroom was once a whites-only dancing space in Los Angeles that, in the 1950s, was bought by businessman Joe Garcia. His initiatives helped to open the space for Mexican and other Latinos of the area. He booked the most popular Latino performers of the time, including Tito Puente and Perez Prado. Ibid., 268.
18. Ponce's *The Wedding* indeed textualizes the diverse social meanings that the mambo triggered among California Chicanos at the time. If for Blanca it represented her social aspirations, as it did for many other Chicanos (as Macías documented), for Cricket the mambo was an index of the black roots of Mexico and the Caribbean, thus racializing it and dismissing it as a primitive type of sonic tradition.
19. Demographers have documented the increasing numbers of interracial marriages among Hispanics or Latinos in the United States. Lee and Edmonston report the increasing numbers of interracial marriages among Hispanics and Asians in the United States and also argue that racial intermarriage transform the way Americans think about race and ethnicity. Their demographic analysis concludes that in 2000, 30 percent of US-born married Hispanic men and women had intermarried, and by 2000 more than two million children were Latino of mixed race. While they note the "greater acceptance of interracial romantic relationships," they also highlight the fact that in 2000 still 38 percent of white Americans "opposed their relative marrying a black person." "New Marriages, New Families," 3–36.
20. Here we use the term *tropicalization* in reference to the dominant ideologies embedded in first-world representations about Latin America and/or US Latina/os that reproduce pejorative images of these geographies and communities. As Frances R. Aparicio and Susana Chávez-Silverman define it, "To tropicalize ... means to trope, to imbue a particular space, geography, group, or nation with a set of traits, images, and values." The "hegemonic tropicalizations" are "a mythic idea of latinidad based on Anglo (or dominant) projections of fear" "intricately connected to the history of political, economic, and ideological agendas of governments and of social institutions." See Aparicio and Chávez-Silverman, introduction to *Tropicalizations*, 1–17.
21. Stover-Ackerman, "The Noise of SB1070: Or, Do I Sound Illegal to You?"
22. Scholars such as Anthony Macías, Theresa Delgadillo, and musician/scholar Marta González, lead singer for Quetzal, have each analyzed and documented the cross-racial sonic traditions of Mexico and Mexican Americans with African, African

American, and black musics. The resurgence of fandangos among Chicano/as in California, the circulation of a song such as "Angelitos negros" from Venezuela to Mexico and
African American performances in the United States, and the popularity of swing, the jitterbug, and the mambo among Mexican Americans in the 1930s and 1940s Los Angeles, all
speak to a long history of Mexican musical traditions rooted in blackness.

23.   While migrations from the Global South to the Global North are not new to European nations, the numerous crises and wars in Africa and the Middle East have led to
an increase in refugees migrating to Europe. In her article entitled "Europe's Migration
Crisis," Jeanne Park describes the Mediterranean Sea "as the world's most dangerous border crossing."

BIBLIOGRAPHY

Alarcón, Norma. "A Wedding." *Revista ChicanaRiqueña*. 1980.
Aparicio, Frances. "Latinidad/es." In *Keywords in Latina/o Studies*, edited by Lawrence
    La Fountain-Stokes, Nancy Mirabal, and Deborah Vargas, 113–117. New York: New
    York University Press, 2017.
Aparicio, Frances, and Susana Chávez-Silverman, eds. *Tropicalizations: Transcultural
    Representations of Latinidad*. Hanover: University Press of New England, 1997.
Delgadillo, Theresa. "Singing Angelitos Negros: African Diaspora Meets Mestizaje in the
    Americas." *American Quarterly* 58, no. 2 (2006): 407–30.
Gautier, Amina. "Aguanile." In *Now We Will Be Happy*, 1–15. Lincoln: University of
    Nebraska Press, 2014.
González, Martha. "Zapateado Afro-Chicana Fandango Style: Self Reflective Moments
    in Zapateado." In *Dancing across Borders: Danzas y Bailes Mexicanos*, edited by
    Norma Elia Cantu, Olga Najera-Ramirez, Brenda M. Romero, 359–378. Champaign:
    University of Illinois Press, 2009.
Lee, Sharon, and Barry Edmonston. "New Marriages, New Families: U.S. Racial and
    Hispanic Intermarriage." *Population Bulletin* 60, no. 2 (June 2005): 3–36.
Macías, Anthony. *Mexican American Mojo: Popular Music, Dance, and Urban Culture in Los
    Angeles, 1935–1968*. Durham, NC: Duke University Press, 2008.
Nava, Gregory. *My Family*. Directed by Gregory Nava. *American Playhouse* (PBS),1995.
Park, Jeanne. "Europe's Migration Crisis." Council on Foreign Relations, September 23,
    2015. http://www.cfr.org/migration/europes-migration-crisis/p32874.
Ponce, Mary Helen. *The Wedding*. Houston: Arte Público Press, 1989.
Rivera, Raquel. *New York Ricans from the Hip Hop Zone*. London: Palgrave McMillan,
    2003.
Stover-Ackerman, Jennifer. "The Noise of SB1070: Or, Do I Sound Illegal to You?"
    SoundingOut! August 19, 2010. http://soundstudiesblog.com/2010/08/19/the-noise
    -of-sb-1070.
Vargas, Deborah R. *Dissonant Divas in Chicana Music: The Limits of La Onda*.
    Minneapolis: University of Minnesota Press, 2012.

FOUR

—∿∿—

TAMBURA MUSIC, FLAGS, AND THE DETERRITORIALIZATION OF RITUALIZED VIOLENCE AT CROATIAN AMERICAN WEDDINGS

IAN MACMILLEN

DECEMBER 2009: THIS WEDDING UNITING a Croatian Canadian bride and a Croatian American groom from Pittsburgh took place in the bride's community outside of Toronto. Hundreds of guests arrived from Ontario and various midwestern US states. The groom was a semiprofessional tambura chordophone player, and many of his guests were experienced tambura musicians from Western Pennsylvania. Croats commonly view tambura as their national instrument, but the ownership of tambura is also claimed by Serbs, Roma, and other Balkan neighbors.

Before the ceremony at a Croation Catholic church, the guests gathered for a celebration hosted by the bride's family. The party was held under a large tent, where the three flags of Croatia, the United States, and Canada were exhibited alongside the hired tambura band, which would later play the three national anthems. As the tambura band began playing, the bride, groom, and others danced and enjoyed liquor and sliced Croatian sausages. Atypically, the *zastavnik* (flag standard-bearer) kept a low profile, holding the banners bundled upright and closely furled as he stood outside of the tent. Everyone's attention was directed to other traditional elements of Croatian wedding, such as the presentation of a false bride (in this instance, a teenage boy wrapped and veiled in white tulle) that the bride's family jokingly presented to the groom instead of their daughter.

Based on my experiences of weddings in Croatia and what I had learned about Croatian weddings in Canada, I was surprised by the rather subtle presentation of flags during the daylong procession, including the drive to the church,

87

when flags are typically waved vigorously. In this part of Canada, the flag often appears in noisy, public displays alongside tambura bands. I realized that the omission of flags might be intentional, because among the groom's guests from Pittsburgh including his closest friends were a number of Serbian Americans. The low visibility of the Croatian flag enabled both Croats and Serbs to celebrate their shared South Slavic traditions, such as instrumental *kolo* dances and the false bride spoof.

At this particular wedding, the visible and audible expression of Croatian nationalism transpired in the relatively private context of the preceremony photography shoot. Taking place inside a large atrium attached to the Croatian Catholic church (unlikely to be attended by Orthodox Serbs), this part of wedding was seen by few of the guests. Here three flag-bearers waved flags fervently as the photographer snapped pictures of the bride. They brought the banners to a rest as the twelve bridesmaids and twelve groomsmen assembled in lines flanking the wedding couple. All posed for photographs with the flags distributed to the ends of the lines and held low as the bearers crouched in front of their betrothed friends. Then the event took a somewhat unexpected turn. One groomsman—a Serbian American tambura player who had performed with the groom in Duquesne University's South Slavic folklore troop the Tamburitzans several years earlier—took up the Croatian flag and began to dance with it. The wedding guests laughed; the photographer continued to shoot; and the groomsman thrust himself into a pose reminiscent of early Elvis Presley. With hips held low, legs bent outward and slightly forward, and arms raised just above the head, he clutched the banner tightly and waved it around. With no music playing, his dance parodied the patriotic processions of the Croatian flag usually performed to the sounds of tambura bands, car horns, and even rifle shots. This allowed the musician to navigate with humor the tensions inherent in an ethnically mixed wedding party.

The prominence of the flag at Croatian weddings in North America symbolizes Croatia's violent secession from Yugoslavia and its largely Serbian government and military in 1991. However, both Croatian and Serbian diasporas alike uphold and share tambura music in combination with the banners' display as affectively and symbolically potent aspects of wedding rites with deep South Slavic roots. Vigorous flag waving traditionally accompanies and syncs rhythmically with fast, energetic tambura tremoloing at Croatian weddings in their homeland and elsewhere in the world. Throughout this chapter, I ponder whether there is something different about the Croatian weddings in the United States. Why has the banner's use faded into the background at ceremonies involving specifically US Croats? How is it that tambura bands' performances of the anthem of Croatia—a country independent for little more than a quarter

century—are nonetheless desirable? Do these tambura performances national-
ize and territorialize weddings attended by a multiethnic Balkan crowd?

This chapter examines the vacillating deployment of national flags in Croatian American weddings, where the banners are combined with voiced anthems
and tambura accompaniment. I situate all three elements—banner, anthem,
tambura—in relation to the affective, symbolic, and physical territoriality that
are common at South Slavic weddings and look comparatively at their significance and impacts. Gilles Deleuze and Felix Guattari, considering the respective potentials for "'fascist' danger" in music and flags, have claimed that "music
(drums, trumpets) draws people and armies into a race that can go all the way to
the abyss (much more so than banners and flags, which are paintings, means of
classification and rallying)."[1] I challenge this idea, examining the deterritorializ-
ing abandon of parading the flag at weddings and the reasons that music, rather
than flag processions, has remained a part of diasporic Croatian weddings in the
United States. I argue that tambura performance, the singing of anthems, and
traditions of the flag reterritorialize Croat-Serb relations in the diaspora along
unequal geographies of access that reverse the perceived directions of physical
wartime incursion. Paradoxically, they afford a nonterritorializing presence to
Serbian musician comrades who attend and/or play for Croatian brides, grooms,
and their families.

THE TRADITION IN CROATIA

Since most of my *tamburaši* (tambura players) interlocutors are fourth- or fifth-
generation Americans, the only sources (*izvori*) of tradition to which they have
been able to turn directly are socialist Yugoslavia and its successor states. In
Croatia, where I have also researched tamburaši at weddings and other performance occasions, many of my interlocutors who were married in the socialist
period recall having two weddings, one official and one religious. The flag of
Socialist Yugoslavia, with its blue, white, and red bars and its central red star,
was a hallmark of official buildings such as the Bastion in Osijek (eastern Croatia) and the various registries in Zagreb (the capital), and thus it was present at
weddings. It was at the second, religious wedding, however, that the flag made
its most public and loudest appearance: young male friends of the groom would
parade it in a procession incorporating the cars of the groom and his friends and
family to the house of his *kum* (best man), then on to the bride's house and to the
church, and finally to the wedding hall for the longest period of the day's celebration.[2] At each stop along the way, the tambura band would strike up music for
singing and dancing, and during the procession cars would blast tambura music
out of their windows and beep their horns loudly.

In Slavonia, the region of eastern Croatia where the tambura tradition is strongest and with which American tambura players most actively seek musical inspiration and relationships, the procession of the state or republic flag seems to have developed out of an older tradition. A *zastavnik* would take a special wedding flag (*svatovska zastava*) made of multiple strips of differently patterned, multicolored fabrics and lead the procession.[3] In both Croatian regions this procession was one of noisy celebration, marked by singing, often the playing of musicians (tamburaši in Slavonia), and the shooting of guns. In recent years, young drivers have taken to swerving wildly back and forth across the road's center divider, to encouraging passengers to hang out of windows and sun roofs, to lighting and waving multiple flares that fill the churchyard with smoke and red light, and to instigating other dangerous, noise- and light-polluting activities that have tested the patience and patriotic good will of neighbors and police. This tradition still remains a point of reference for many US Croats, especially those who have grown up performing in junior tamburitzans ensembles and received training in folklore. It throws into relief the absence of independent Croatia's (or any older) flag vis-à-vis its appearance in contemporary weddings in Canada and Croatia that many of them attend.

WEDDINGS, MUSIC, AND FLAGS IN
RECENT HISTORICAL CONTEXT

Both weddings and nonreligious tambura performances, including Croatian bands' North American tours, continue to unite Croats from Croatia and from various parts of its diaspora and its geographically proximate foreign enclaves (what collectively I have termed Croatia's "intimates").[4] In fact, the two types of occasions are closely related and tend to beget one another, fostering a strong link between tambura bands, weddings, and transnational patriotism.[5] During the last decade or so of Croatia's membership in Yugoslavia, the Matica iselje-nika Hrvatske (MIH, in English: Croatian Heritage Foundation) in Croatia and the Croatian Fraternal Union (CFU) in North America increasingly col-laborated on events that reunited Croatian families on opposites sides of the Atlantic; these resulted in many new weddings between Croatians and diaspora Croats. An initial 1979 North American tour by professional tambura band Slavonski Bećari, singer Krunoslav "Kićo" Slabinac, and the amateur orches-tra of the Slavonian Tambura Society named after Pajo Kolarić.[6] Numerous betrothals between male Croatian tamburaši and Croatian American women have resulted. Their subsequent weddings have typically involved complicated and challenging patterns of international travel in order to satisfy parties in multiple countries of the fulfillment of important ritual obligations. This frequently includes the sponsorship of additional musical travel by transnationally hired tambura bands.

In 1986, Slavonski Bećari embarked on another United States and Canada tour. With the group was Miroslav Škoro, then a little-known rock singer and songwriter from Osijek who told me that the band had invited him as much for his comedic routine and talent for introducing the band as for his ability to sing some songs and accompany himself on guitar.[7] It was on this tour that Škoro met Kim Ann Luzaich, a Croatian American resident of Pittsburgh, Pennsylvania, who had come to hear Slavonski Bećari play at the nearby White Swan Park amusement center in June 1986 and had subsequently asked to be introduced to Škoro.[8] After a brief courtship in Pittsburgh that continued in Croatia when Luzaich decided to pursue the relationship and visit her ancestors' homeland with her mother, the two became engaged and eventually wed in Osijek in 1989.[9] They then returned to Pittsburgh, where they held an additional wedding celebration and dwelt for the next few years.[10] Their first child, Ivana, was born there in 1991, and though they would later resettle in Osijek, where their son would be born in 1995, the initial result of the romance that Škoro's touring with Slavonski Bećari had made possible was the establishment of a new family in the United States.

Their courtship, however, also forged a new familial relationship between Škoro and members of Slavonski Bećari back home in Osijek. As Škoro relates in his autobiography, Branko Helajz, the tambura band's youngest member, had liked Kim Luzaich very much when they met her on tour, and he "immediately offered" that "if you marry her, I will be your *kum*."[11] The kum (pl. *kumovi*) and the female variant, *kuma* (pl. *kume*), are important figures throughout the Slavic Christian peoples of Southeast Europe. "They refer not only to the person present at the baptism of a baby," writes linguist Ronelle Alexander, "but also to the witnesses at a wedding. The *kum* and/or *kuma* are generally not blood relations, but through taking part in family ceremonies they become nearly as close as kin. The *kum* is expected to give the grandest wedding present . . . and often makes the wedding's most important toast."[12] By becoming the kum at Škoro's and Luzaich's wedding, Helajz not only took on a prominent role in the wedding ceremony's rituals and subsequent party but also became a kin-like relation of the wedding couple. His ties to the young tamburaš were sanctified through the Catholic marriage rite. It is the friends and family of the kum and groom who arrange for the music and the parading of the flag, and thus the sonic and visual performance of male bravado and camaraderie take a central position within both the wedding rituals and the new marriage even before the latter is itself sanctified in the church.

The musical cultivation of male friendship and showmanship is certainly a priority at Croatian American weddings as well. The flag's usage, however, has, in the words of a Cleveland-area semiprofessional tamburaš, been "really fragmented." The Croatian Spring's suppression in the early 1970s resulted in the political exile of many Croats who had participated in that movement for Croatian autonomy. The hijacking of TWA Flight 355 out of New York by pro-independence Croatian activists in 1976, however, is believed within the North American Croatian community to have soured the United States' receptiveness toward Croatian political immigrants. The restricting of immigration to those seeking better economic opportunities did translate into a relatively minor in-flux of Croatians in the 1970s and 1980s in comparison to the growing wave of (political and economic) migrants that Canada received during this time.[13] Canadian cities such as Vancouver, Sudbury, Toronto, and Mississauga have historically been home to strongly anti-Yugoslav Croatian communities, where rituals have typically involved Croatian flags and other nationalist symbols.[14] In comparison, flags have appeared relatively less frequently in Croatian wed-dings and other events in cities in the United States. Serbs and Croats have long performed at and attended US events together, and many Croats there either feel little attachment to a specifically Croatian separatist flag or worry that raising a patriotic banner would harm their communities' unofficial forms of South Slavic brotherhood. In the 1970s, however, cities such as Cleveland and Chicago also received waves of Croatian immigrants from parts of rural Croatia and from Bosnia and Herzegovina who have integrated far less with other South Slavic diasporic communities and have maintained flag and tambura traditions largely as they performed them on stage and in weddings back in Yugoslavia.[15] Religion and nationalism in North American Croatian contexts have thus historically signaled isolation just as much as they have bolstered forms of attachment to nation-building projects back in Croatia. This isolation is not only from main-stream American culture and Yugoslav/Serbian communities but also from more integrated Croatian enclaves.

Weddings enact the religious and familial union of two individuals but also connect them to in-laws and kumovi/kume. As events that bring together extended and displaced branches of the (national) family, weddings offer the promise of renewing this responsibility through future generations. This is felt most keenly when they incorporate guests and even participants from both Croatia and its intimates, as was the case with Škoro's weddings in Osijek and Pittsburgh. The rituals of flags and patriotic songs at Croatian weddings ac-complish more than a signification or rehearsing of common national senti-ment: they enact affective investment in the perpetuation of a core territory that shelters and cares for its people as it also demands from them its defense from outside powers. The participation of those who live in foreign lands controlled by such powers only accentuates this internalization of maternal and paternal feelings. That participation may take the form of returning to the homeland with a spouse, finding a partner there who can take advantage of new familial and economic opportunities in Croatia's intimates, or supporting its citizens by hiring them for weddings abroad.

THE TRANSNATIONAL LIFE OF THE CROATIAN FLAG

The Croatian flag's occasional absence or low visibility at Croatian American weddings is not indicative of the banner's low significance among Croats in the United States. One particularly well-known Croatian American tambura player in Cleveland shared with me that the political exiles who made it to the United States in the early 1970s brought with them the red, white, and blue bars of previous Croatian flags and the forbidden red-and-white-checkered coat of arms (which the World War II–era Independent State of Croatia and the 1971 "Croatian Spring" had used in their projects for autonomy from Yugoslavian governance). This banner achieved a prominent role in their weddings and helped to spread this flag's usage twenty years before its official adoption in Croatia and its intimates in the 1990s. He noted that his crossover rock/tambura band commonly performs Miroslav Škoro's songs on these topics in weddings, thus introducing the flag into weddings through text and as a musical referent if not in a lively, physical, embodied fashion. The particular example he gave was Škoro's "Domovina" (Homeland), a song that references the coat of arms somewhat subtly but deliberately and relates it to a need to remember and honor Croatian heroes (such as those killed or forced into exile while fighting for the homeland's independence in various twentieth-century wars and movements). The song's exegesis has become an important part of Škoro's live performances, too, in ways that reinscribe the familial relations of diasporic families to the now independent homeland.

November 20, 2009: Škoro, now one of Croatia's most successful pop/rock stars and media moguls, was holding a twentieth-anniversary concert in Zagreb, Croatia. I had recently completed a year of fieldwork among tamburaši in Pennsylvania and was at the Zagreb concert during a second yearlong stint in Croatia. The concert celebrated twenty years since Škoro's wedding to Kim Ann Lazaich and an initial, contemporaneous moment in his rise to stardom when he had been performing with tamburaši in Pittsburgh and living there with his in-laws and wife. He took time during the performance to honor two musical fruits resulting from their union, beginning with the song "Ne dirajte mi ravnicu" (Don't touch my plain). The young couple's decision to dwell initially in the house of Lazaich's parents placed him thousands of miles from his home but a short drive from the tambura virtuoso Jerry Grcevich, with whom Škoro began to collaborate as he wrote this hit song of nostalgic longing for his native fields and mother. Released in 1992 by Croatia Records with Grcevich's original 1989 tambura arrangement and recording, the song rose to popularity among a wartime Croatian public longing for its own (occupied) territories and missing family members. Škoro broadcast a video greeting from Grcevich before performing the song with three tambura bands from Osijek.[16]

Škoro next honored their teenage son, Matija, who joined his father onstage to play a solo in the middle of the latter's successful 2008 pop/rock song, "Domovina." Škoro's lyrics address Matija in the second person, stating that life is not like what's written in books. They relate stories of wars that Miroslav Škoro's father, Ivan, had witnessed, tell of Croatian nationalists' emigration following the Croatian Spring's 1971 suppression (and of their families' questions about their disappearance, which went unanswered until these émigrés started returning from North America after 1991), and request Matija's promise to relate this to his own son one day (for the homeland is *u venama*: "in [our] veins"). This promise is necessary because the "modern" trend is to dress in "cubes" (*kockasto*, i.e., the checkered coat of arms) and then put on some "peculiar music." Here Škoro suggests a disconnect between embodied patriotism, which should connect back through the veins of the patriarchal bloodline to past struggles for Croatian independence, and a musical taste that breaks with the country's own popular and traditional styles. His son obliged Škoro when he walked out onto the stage moments later in a red-and-white-checkered Croatian national football jersey and replicated David Gilmour's famous electric guitar solo from Pink Floyd's 1979 song "Another Brick in the Wall, Part Two."

The concert's opening song "Jorgovan" ("Lilac") had made a similar statement about the decline in the citizenry's patriotism, which should sustain these living embodiments of the nation's symbols. It called the Croatian flag a red, white, and blue lilac that remains unpicked and unfaded in Škogo's garden (perhaps only in his), despite the grief that he experiences when his "brothers in blood" feel ashamed of their people. One might expect, then, that the subtler appearances of flags and other paraphernalia bearing the coat of arms at Croatian American weddings similarly reflect a withering of national expression in the diaspora. Yet many patriotic Croatian musicians laud Croats in the United States for keeping national symbols alive, even as they become less popular in Croatia. Škoro wrote: "Our emigrants, especially in the U.S.A., nourish Croatian tambura music, and appeared to do so even when we all consequently were thinking that we are Beatles and Stones."[17] He continued: "They teach their children how beautiful it is to be your own and love your own, they take pride as well in tamburica.... To my question 'why are you a Croat,' Jerry Grcevich completely calmly and with deep conviction answered: 'Because I play tamburica.'"[18]

Performances at Croatian weddings across the broader network of the nation and its intimates not only strengthen friends and family members' relations and affective attachments to one another's traditions and territories. They also, particularly within Croatia, facilitate exceptionally patriotic public displays in years of waning wartime remembrance. Many Croats from the diaspora, neighboring countries, and Croatia alike come to embrace the overt (not disconnected) musical and visual coding of Croatian nationalism at weddings. In addition, they at times realize more permanent shifts in economics and constituencies when Croatian emigrants or their descendants move "back" (a term used even by Croatian Americans who have never visited).

For his part, Jerry Grcevich often spends much of the summer in Croatia. He makes prominent appearances not only at festivals for new *autorske pjesme* ("original songs") but also at weddings, marching with the flag from house to church to wedding hall at the request of his extended family, friends, and colleagues. When he determined that he would not be able to travel to one friend's wedding, he composed, recorded, and sent as a music file a new song for the event.[19] Differences in expectations, economic resources, familiarity, and geographical closeness generate a range of physical, cultural, and technological proximities. Wedding attendees negotiate these at the height of an emotional life event and its attendant, affectively charged rituals of Croatian and Croatian-diasporic music and flags.

LIMITATIONS ON MUSIC AND FLAG
TRADITIONS IN THE UNITED STATES

These rituals' more violent and dangerous aspects jeopardize participants' safety, relationships with neighbors, and standing with the police. While in Croatia weddings often remain violently patriotic events, many Croatian American weddings are rather tame affairs in terms of overt displays of national symbols. In part, this stems from the difficulties of implementing Croatian traditions in new contexts. Flares appear much less frequently in Croatian weddings in Canada and the United States, where only a small minority of Croatian residents have immigrated recently enough to have become accustomed to this practice's adoption in Croatia as a seeming replacement for the firing of guns. Gunshots, too, are relatively rare at Croatian American weddings. As a tamburaš from Milwaukee told me, the flag sometimes accompanied their processions, but the "more civilized" social customs and "stricter gun laws" found in the United States meant that they did not shoot off guns as they did in (the former)

Yugoslavia. There, he stated, it was more common in Bosnia than in his ancestors' regions of Croatia anyway.

In fact, safety precautions seem inadvertently to have afforded an alternative
of sorts: the blinking of hazard lights. At a July 2015 Cleveland-area Croatian
immigrant wedding that I observed, the groom arrived at the bride's house in a
column of cars with flashing hazard lights. He was leaning out the lead sports
car's back door, which was draped in two Croatian flags. The kum held a bottle
of *šlivovica* (plum brandy) out of the opposite door and a bridesmaid stood waving the wedding bouquet through the sunroof. They were met by the bride, her
family, and a trio of accordionist, violinist, and vocalist that accompanied dancing and drinking until the two wedding parties transferred themselves (along
with one of the flags) to a party bus limo coach to be driven to the church. The
continuity with the bus's lighting suggested that the hazard lights served an aesthetic, celebratory purpose as well as a practical, cautionary one.[20] The bus kept
its headlights on throughout the trip, and was also lit inside with bright neon
lights of green and pink (the couple's wedding colors). The bride, groom, kum,
and kuma, with their accents of green silk, stood at the back of the bus drinking, dancing, and singing a Croatian pop song along with the pink bridesmaids
and pink-accented groomsmen seated before them. The Croatian flag swayed
gently back and forth, its white checkers and white middle stripe bathed in the
party lights' pink glow.

The curtailing of the zastavnik procession among older diasporas addresses
safety concerns similar to those of Croatian police and residents who object to
the practice. If anything, the challenges to the tradition are augmented by the
much longer distances between home, church, and wedding hall typical in the
United States and Canada. Also, police forces that regulate such behavior are
relatively unfamiliar with and intolerant of such rituals. A musician from Los
Angeles commented that there the tradition of parading the Croatian flag in cars
with loudly honking horns had disappeared from weddings and been preserved
only for funerals: serious occasions that seemingly excused the disruption in
the public eye and permitted their noisy transport. When flags are carried for
weddings, their movement (subtler than in Croatia) involves mostly the holding
of the flag by the (typically male) standard-bearer *inside* the church, wedding
hall, and car. A professional musician from Pittsburgh commented that on one
exceptional occasion he and his band had played for a wedding in Astoria, New
York, where there is a fairly large community of recent Croatian immigrants.
The distances to traverse were much smaller, and they had marched down the
street playing music from the kum's house to the bride's house and then on to
the church, holding up traffic to the discontent of local residents. On most occasions, however, his group merely stood by the flag at the wedding hall in order

to perform the Croatian and the Canadian and/or United States anthems (in Canada they also sometimes played by the flag outside of the church).

SERBIAN AMERICANS: SHARED MUSIC AND TROUBLING SYMBOLS

What is not new or different in the United States, however, is the vicinity of Serbs to Croatian weddings. The decision not to exhibit the flag prominently, or at all, is in these contexts also typically read (positively or negatively) as a deliberate choice not to engage in postwar nationalism. As the mother of a prominent Seattle-area tambura pedagogue told me, she explicitly turned down requests to organize a standard-bearer for her daughter's wedding because Croats and Serbs generally get along in Seattle and she wanted her Serb friends to feel welcome at the event.

This has not always been a guiding concern, because the Yugoslav conflicts ruptured interethnic bonds in the 1990s. As Croatian American folklorist Richard March writes, "in the fall of 1991, a wedding in Chicago brought public attention to the tensions between the local Serbian and Croatian ethnic communities that had been engendered by the outbreak of the Homeland War."[21] A "Croatian American bride-to-be" found that "the *tamburaši* hired to play at her long-planned wedding to a Serbian American groom had cancelled the booking indicating that they feared they would lose business as a result of playing for the 'mixed wedding'"; he noted that other Serb and Croat musicians formed an ad hoc tambura group to play instead.[22] This testifies both to weddings' mediation of strained interethnic relations and to the strong ethnic symbolism attached to tambura music in Chicago (for wedding parties, for bands, and for Chicago's broader Croatian publics, which are infamous among Pittsburgh's tambura players for tolerating little deference to Serbs). Some fourth- and fifth-generation Croatian Americans certainly still harbor ill will against Serbian Americans or at least are unconcerned by the politics of flaunting flags before local Serbs. Yet recent decades (since roughly 2004, according to my Pittsburgh interlocutors) have seen great improvements in Croat-Serb relations and a desire to preserve them.

Many Serbian American weddings, on the other hand, still feature the Serbian flag quite prominently. Following a fall 2016 wedding at a Serbian Orthodox church that I observed, a band consisting of several tamburaši and one accordionist assembled outside the church doors just as the bridesmaids began to exit the building bearing the American and Serbian flags. While the band's playing was more continuous than the flags' waving, wedding party members lifted the latter whenever important members from their ranks exited the church. When the bride and groom emerged, the band cut short the upbeat Serbian song that it was playing and began a somewhat slower and heavier song that accompanied the waving of the banners over the couple's heads. As the band moved on to contrasting repertoire, the man now bearing the two flags continued to jerk them about intermittently to the music's pulse. As the band finished its final, instrumental piece of this celebration immediately following the wedding, playing a long, drawn-out tremolo on the final chord, the bearer shimmied the two flags vigorously with small but decisive movements of his two arms. He thus emphasized the rhythmic and physical synchronization of music with flags that historically has been a hallmark of youthful energy at both Serbian and Croatian weddings. It is just such shaking and excitement that the wild parading of the flag at some weddings in Croatia and Canada sets in motion, striking an equalization between the tamburaši's playing (which many wedding-goers characterize as "dangerous" or "aggressive") and the flag's crazed motions.

The guests were of mixed (predominantly Serbian and Croatian) ethnic backgrounds, as was the tambura band. This group was famous, in the words of an Orthodox but non-Serb accordionist who joined them that afternoon, for "riding down the middle" of Pittsburgh's once divided South Slavic milieu. In addition to accompanying the procession with the Serbian and American flags, they played a number of Serbian tambura ballads as well as folkdances and popular songs adapted for this instrumentation.

Serbian American weddings commonly feature both flag processions and tambura performances of Serbian national repertoire very prominently at weddings with Croatian guests and musicians. This begs the question of why the opposite is not true. Why have Croatians generally become accustomed to taking part in Serbian American wedding rituals involving both flags and Serbian music but been reluctant to risk distancing Serbian American friends (and intermarried kin) by parading the Croatian flag alongside performances of Croatian music on the "national" instrument? Do Croatian Americans' perceptions of Serbia as the aggressor in the Yugoslav conflicts not come to bear on these traditions' politics?

MUSICAL DETERRITORIALIZATION AND
TERRITORIES OF THE FLAG RECONSIDERED

Deleuze and Guattari have argued that "there is a territory precisely when milieu components . . . cease to be functional to become expressive. There is a territory when the rhythm has expressiveness. What defines the territory is the emergence of matters of expression (qualities)."[23] This explains the ambiguous relationship of music to territoriality: a "refrain is rhythm and melody that have been territorialized because they have become expressive," as in the case of a national anthem or a bird's territorial call.[24] Yet musicking, according to Gary Tomlinson, "affirms the becoming and change immanent in all repetition and signification"; it is "caught up in the parahuman, semiotic play of transversals that *re*territorialize as they *de*territorialize."[25] Thus while anthems clearly territorialize rituals on their nations, other aspects of musicking such as the virtuosic improvisations and rhythmic flux that characterize "dangerous" tambura playing tend to deterritorialize milieus of listening. They allow musical performance to function affectively rather than express qualities. In South Slavic weddings in the United States, most guests' limited command of Bosnian/Croatian/Serbian certainly facilitates such deterritorialized listening.

In this regard, Deleuze and Guattari are right to note the difference between music and flags: the latter clearly express qualities and territorialize by virtue of their dominant ontology as indexes of nations. Tamburas, conversely, can signify the Croatian or another nation but also function as vehicles for a diverse array of expressive and functional performances. Because Serbia was viewed as both territorial aggressor and bastion of supernational power (Belgrade was multinational Yugoslavia's state seat) in the 1990s wars, Croats' entrance into the spaces and rituals of Serbian American weddings has been somewhat normalized as a postwar act of mutual solidarity rebuilding. The flags are territorial, and perhaps territorialize Croats' participation, but they also frame territorial incursion in terms of countering perceptions of Serbian infiltration with a welcome into the ritual spaces of Serbian rather than Yugoslav family-building. The Croatian flag, however, not only territorializes but also *re*territorializes. The perception of many Croatian and Serbian Americans is that its use in weddings stakes a claim of separation, warning Serbs, as perceived aggressors, not to infringe on the territories of Croatian familial, national, and religious sovereignty. The music, in contrast, through both its "lines of flight" from territorialization[26] and the polysemy of its tremolos, improvisations, and little-understood lyrics, is *de*territorialized enough to balance its *re*territorializing capacities.

Yet Deleuze and Guattari's attribution of "fascist" danger to music rather than flags misses a key aspect of their functionality. While the latter may become expressive as "paintings," this is not an ontological fact but a product of their use and interpretation. Croatian flags still appear at Croatian American weddings, but they are made to express in ways that override their capacities for other, more forceful affective and embodied experiences. Thus in Toronto the zastavnik bore the flags but kept them still for much of the wedding's processions and ceremonies. At Serbian American weddings the Serbian flag is excited through response to the rhythms of Serbian tambura performance, and in Croatia and some weddings in Canada the same happens with the Croatian flag through tambura music but also through the sensorial stimulation of flares, car horns, and gun shots. There is in Croatian American weddings, however, a striking disconnect between flag-bearing and these other violently expressive and physically forceful modalities. Flag-bearers, too, could veer toward the abyss of embodied abandon and bring crowds along with them, as they do in Croatia. Music's special role here stems not so much from a unique danger for affective intensities beyond systems of representation as from the proximity and ready slippages between semiotics and physicality in tambura performance that allow it, more than flags, to mean just enough, and not too much.

The scene in Toronto in which the Serbian American groomsman danced with the Croatian flag showed the importance of this. It distinguished between the embodied, affective intensities of tambura musicking and the flag's subtler movements at Croatian American weddings planned for multiethnic crowds. The groomsman's humorous imitation of a zastavnik's potentially wild flag procession broke the atmosphere of patriotic and romantic devotion cultivated during the photo shoot. It cleared the air among the wedding parties and helped to prepare (even as it established an extreme point of comparison) for the flags' more public display during dancing later that night. Following the ceremony and the move to the wedding hall, the flag-bearers, pairs of bridesmaids and groomsmen, and the newlyweds themselves paraded into the banquet room to the accompaniment of a series of pop songs blaring from the speakers (tambura bands had played beforehand in the foyer and would strike up again later but at this moment were replaced by recorded music). A number of individuals, including even the newly minted couple, incorporated humorously exaggerated moves into their dancing, but the flag-bearers were notably stoic, each holding his body erect as he waved one of the flags back and forth upon entering the room (though later they began to wave them somewhat more vigorously to one side of the bride and groom as the couple began to dance).

Here the civil, patriotic demeanor of the parading of the flag remained clearly distinct (at least in terms of the embodiments of specific participants) from the wilder movements enacted by the music. The Serbian American's mock combination of the two earlier that day stood in striking contrast to the flag's stoic presentations at the start and end of the day's rituals. It served both to reterritorialize (make overt) his incorporation into a Croatian wedding in a part of Canada known for Croatian patriotism and then, through the affective break of laughter, to deterritorialize his presence as a nonaggressor. The concern (on the part of Croatian and Serbian American wedding participants alike) not to territorialize Serbs' presence as aggressors parallels their accommodation of United States laws and police enforcement. They similarly avoid confrontation with officials and neighbors by eschewing rituals that express

Croatian presence with violently infiltrating noises, lights, and moving vehicles and bodies. Weddings guests laud tambura players who perform "dangerously"; they certainly do not cultivate a tame music aesthetic. Yet nonetheless, tambura music's comparatively low volume and its shared South Slavic heritage facilitate the navigation of desires for both a sovereign home territory and a vibrant local South Slavic milieu at the moment that both are given renewed hope in the forging of marital bonds. Vital to this is its slippage between *reterritorialization* and *deterritorialization*, between expressing too much and moving bodies simply through resonance and rhythm, between refrain and musicking. For now, at such weddings the Croatian flag expresses too much to risk taking it to the abyss of motion and feeling along with the music that Serbs and Croats commonly employ to do just that.

IAN MACMILLEN is Assistant Professor of Russian and East European Studies and Director of the Oberlin Center for Russian, East European and Central Asian Studies at Oberlin College.

NOTES

1. Deleuze and Guattari, *Thousand Plateaus*, 333.
2. According to tamburaši, either the Yugoslav flag or the Socialist Republic of Croatia's flag, with bars in the reversed order (red, white, and blue) of the flag of independent Croatia.
3. Vondraček-Mesar, *Svadbeni Običaji Sesvetskog Prigorja*, 19.
4. MacMillen, "From the Center in the Middle."
5. "Patriotism" is the most common translation of the Croatian concept of *domoljublje* ("love of the homeland"). The appropriateness of its gendered, paternal connotations becomes clear in the following section on the transnational life of the flag.
6. Pajo Kolarić was a nineteenth-century Croatian composer and the founder of the first amateur tamburitza orchestra. See Šovagović, *Mostovi Preko Žica Tamburice*.
7. Škoro, personal communication.
8. Škoro, *Stoput bih isto*, 57.
9. Ibid., 63, 66.
10. Ibid., 70.
11. Ibid., 66; my translation.
12. Alexander, *Bosnian Croatian Serbian*, 356.
13. Powell, *Encyclopedia of North American Immigration*, 68.
14. Cf. Beljo, *Croatians in the Sudbury centennial*.
15. See March, *Tamburitza Tradition*, 140.
16. MacMillen, "From the Center in the Middle."
17. Škoro, *Stoput bih isto*, 12; my translation.
18. Ibid.

19. Grcevich, personal communication.
20. The Cleveland Police Department's Transit Unit informed me that no official requirements or special privileges pertain to wedding processions (as they do to funeral processions); the use of hazard lights is purely a matter of choice.
21. March, *Tamburitza Tradition*, 176.
22. Ibid.
23. Deleuze and Guattari, *Thousand Plateaus*, 315.
24. Ibid., 317.
25. Tomlinson, "Sign, Affect, and Musicking," 168.
26. Deleuze and Guattari, *Thousand Plateaus*, 423.

BIBLIOGRAPHY

Alexander, Ronelle. *Bosnian Croatian Serbian: A Textbook with Exercises and Basic Grammar*. Madison: University of Wisconsin Press, 2006.

Beljo, Ante. *Croatians in the Sudbury Centennial: Canadian-Croatian Folklore Festivals, Sudbury Centennial, 1983*. Sudbury, Ontario: National Association for the Advancement of Croatian Culture and Folklore, 1983.

Deleuze, Gilles, and Félix Guattari. *A Thousand Plateaus: Capitalism and Schizophrenia*. Translated by Brian Massumi. Minneapolis: University of Minnesota Press, 1987 .

Grcevich, Jerry. Personal communication with the author, phone interview between Pittsburgh, Pennsylvania, and Oberlin, Ohio, April 3, 2012.

MacMillen, Ian. "From the Center in the Middle: Working Tambura Bands and the Construction of the In-Between in Croatia and Its Intimates." *Current Musicology* 91 (2011): 87–122.

March, Richard. *The Tamburitza Tradition: From the Balkans to the American Midwest*. Madison: University of Wisconsin Press, 2013.

Powell, John. *Encyclopedia of North American Immigration*. New York: Facts on File, 2005.

Škoro, Miroslav. Interview with the author. Zagreb, Croatia, March 28, 2011.

———. *Stoput Bih Isto Ponovo: Autobiografija*. Zagreb: Večernji posebni proizvodi d. o. o., 2010.

Šovagović, Đuro. *Mostovi Preko Žica Tamburice (Dnevnik s puta po Sjedinjenim Američkim Državama i Kanadi)*. Osijek: Matica Iseljenika Zajednice Općina Osijek, 1981.

Tomlinson, Gary. "Sign, Affect, and Musicking before the Human." *boundary* 2 43, no. 1 (2016): 143–72.

Vitez, Zorica. *Hrvatski svadbeni običaji*. Zagreb: Golden marketing–Tehnička knjiga, 2003.

Vondraček-Mesar, Jagoda. *Svadbeni Običaji Sesvetskog Prigorja: Katalog u publikaciji*. Zagreb: Nacionalna i sveučilišna knjižnica, 2003.

FIVE

〜〰〜

LIKE AN *ERHU* PLAYER
ON THE ROOF

*Music and Multilayered Diasporic Negotiation at a
Taiwanese and Jewish American Wedding*

MEREDITH SCHWEIG

On the way from Taipei to New York, the in-flight entertainment was showing the classic film *Fiddler on the Roof*. We know the story is about love and family, destiny and courage. There is a traditional Jewish wedding scene, between [the character Tevye's] eldest daughter and the tailor. I first saw this movie when I was still a teenager. At that time, I couldn't have imagined that today I would have a lovely wife and two wonderful sons, and my eldest wouldn't even wait until he had begun his college classes to find his love. And more amazing is that today I get to participate in this *un*traditional Jewish wedding!"

—Su Chien-hsing

AT THE RECEPTION OF OUR June 2009 wedding at the Massachusetts Museum of Contemporary Art in North Adams, Massachusetts, Su Chien-hsing stood before our closest family and friends, quieted the band, and raised his glass to his son Andres and me. Engaging in the shared American and Taiwanese custom of delivering a prepared speech in honor of the bride and groom at the wedding banquet, he described the deep sense of contentment he felt in his own marriage to Yu-an, his wife of thirty years, and in the experience of raising two sons. Fortune had smiled on their family time and again, he said, but my marriage to Andres had satisfied a long-unfulfilled desire for a daughter. Andres and I had been a couple for nearly a decade by the time we walked down the aisle, but Chien-hsing's wholehearted embrace of our union on that day still surprised me. An American Jew of Ashkenazic heritage, I always wondered if Andres's parents had hoped for a Taiwanese or Taiwanese American partner for their firstborn. Although I had spent extended periods of time in Taiwan conducting research for my doctoral studies in ethnomusicology and we had become very close over the years, my future in-laws and I still sometimes labored to reconcile one another's cultural values and preferred modes of interpersonal communication. I was therefore deeply moved when Chien-hsing, incandescent with joy, described me as "a member of our family, and our beloved daughter."

The latter part of Chien-hsing's toast, transcribed in the epigraph above, expressed his delight at participating in a wedding ritual that incorporated recognizable Jewish traditions but struck him as "untraditional" because of its divergence from those portrayed in Norman Jewison's 1971 Academy Award–winning film adaptation of the 1964 Broadway musical *Fiddler on the Roof*. Based on the Jewish humorist Sholem Aleichem's 1894 collection of short stories about the dairyman Tevye and his strong-minded daughters in early twentieth-century imperial Russia, *Fiddler* follows the three eldest girls through courtship and marriage to three men who represent increasing degrees of compromise with Jewish custom.[1] Tevye gradually accepts his eldest daughters' desire to control their marital fates as signs of change in the world around him. But his youngest daughter's marriage to a Russian gentile, outside the Jewish faith, proves too much to bear, and Tevye cannot accept it.

"Tradition" is one of *Fiddler*'s most trenchant themes as well as the title of one of its most memorable songs, and Chava's choice reveals the limits of its flexibility with respect to Tevye's religious and cultural worldviews. As Chien-hsing concluded his speech, our wedding band commenced a brisk performance of "Sunrise, Sunset," another popular tune from the show. The original context for the song is the wedding of Tevye's eldest daughter, and the lyrics describe her parents' astonishment at the swift passage of time. The song, a waltz in G-minor that is played frequently at Ashkenazi Jewish weddings, provided a sweet and expedient closing accompaniment to the toast. Chien-hsing earned enthusiastic laughs from friends and family tickled by the idea that the century-old wedding depicted in *Fiddler* could serve as a point of reference for our largely secular nuptials at a contemporary art museum in the Berkshires. Yet citing the musical at the event struck me and Andres as ironic: Had our marriage—interfaith, interethnic, interracial—transpired in the world of the play, it would have challenged Tevye in new and uncomfortable ways.

In fact, the process of planning our wedding had been a strenuous exercise in self-exploration and compromise for both of our families, who hail from different diasporic communities, each with its own complex history and politics. In this chapter, I document and analyze the outcome of this experience, which merged practices citing multiple Jewish, Taiwanese, Chinese, and American sources, to explore the collision and convergence of social imaginaries inherent in mixed diasporic weddings. Marriage rituals in North America, already elaborate undertakings, can acquire additional complexity when the event formalizes the union of individuals from different backgrounds. Having chosen to marry beyond their communities of origin, a couple may be called on to demonstrate cultural affinities shared not only with one another but also with the many relatives and close family friends who form the social web in which they will embed their new home—in effect, to ensure that all participants feel included in the festivities.

While food, clothing, and decoration all carry symbolic import, music emerged, for us, as the most critical avenue for this negotiation. We invoked music to communicate our commitment to one another, our families, and our broader diasporic communities. Inherently intertextual, interdiscursive, and intermedial, music created multiple opportunities for us to comment explicitly on aspects of our individual and collective cultural identities and to sound a harmonious union among them. In this chapter, I will examine some of the alloys that emerged through the collaborative efforts we undertook with our friends, our families, and the musicians we hired, including the performance of a popular Mandarin tune by a klezmer artist, a first dance to American pianist and composer Vince Guaraldi's "The Great Pumpkin Waltz," and a *chuppah* (Jewish wedding canopy) embroidered with text from the Zhou dynasty–era *Book of Songs*.

I employ an interpretive autoethnographic methodology, "[seeking] to describe and systematically analyze (*graphy*) personal experience (*auto*) in order to understand cultural experience (*ethno*)."[2] As Tony E. Adams, Stacy Holman Jones, and Carolyn Ellis have written, "autoethnography is a *qualitative* method—it offers nuanced, complex, and specific knowledge about *particular* lives, experiences, and relationships rather than *general* information about large groups of people."[3] As weddings are among the most heavily documented of life cycle events, my memories are fortified by a personal archive of videos, photographs, emails, and other ephemera (programs, menus, ceremony notes, sheet music). In addition to these sources, I draw on new interviews conducted with family, friends, and the musicians who performed at our ceremony and reception. My use of the collective pronouns "we" and "our" reflects my intention to convey some of the ideas, feelings, and recollections Andres has shared with me about the event over the years, and I quote him directly whenever possible. The majority of the analysis presented here, however, crystallizes at the intersection of my particular identities as bride, Ashkenazi Jewish American, and ethnomusicologist.

Although I do not expect that an interpretive autoethnographic account of music at our wedding will produce generalizable conclusions about the process of identity negotiation in mixed Jewish and Taiwanese American marriages, this chapter responds to recent calls for more qualitative work on the subject. As sociologists Helen K. Kim and Noah S. Leavitt note in their work exploring the intersection of racial, ethnic, and religious identities in Jewish and Asian American couples, "few attempts have been made to understand intermarriages from an in-depth qualitative perspective. While the majority of literature incorporates quantitative methods to understand how partnerships which are mixed along dimensions such as race, ethnicity, and religion can be described and explained, we know very little about how these relationships operate and have factored in these differences over an extended period of time."[4] Composed seven years after the wedding and nearly a decade after we became engaged, this essay constitutes a focused retrospective study. Our memories and interpretations of that experience are inflected by all that has transpired since our betrothal, from the completion of our graduate studies to the survival of serious illness, to the birth of our delightful daughter. Looking—and listening—back on our wedding day, I ponder the musical statement we made about our partnership and ask: Do things sound different today?

The process of researching and writing this piece on multilayered diasporic negotiation at a past event has necessitated additional negotiations in the present. I write with a keen awareness that this chapter might be read not only by an audience of people I do not know but also by the family members and friends who attended and the musicians who performed at our wedding. It will become part of a very small quantity of narrative writing chronicling my family's history, both for members of previous generations and for my daughter, who I hope will carry it into the future. In an effort to balance the needs of both personally close and distant readers, I have made deliberate decisions about which things ought and ought not to be shared, even in the parts of this chapter that blur the line between memoir and academic text. Sometimes, research associates asked me to omit certain details; occasionally, they did not recall things transpiring as I did. Through prolonged discussion and compromise, I hoped ultimately to produce prose of an intimate, immediate, and truthful nature, appropriate to recounting an event that lives in the collective memory of our integrated family.

My discussion will proceed through four parts. The first briefly situates a conversation about mixed diasporic weddings in the adjacent discourse surrounding intermarriage in the Jewish and Asian American communities.[5] The second tells a story about my husband's and my relationship, with particular emphasis on the connection we cultivated through our shared intellectual and emotional investments in music and our desire to understand better one another's backgrounds. Then, I will discuss the imperative we felt to plan an event that celebrated our multiple identities and incorporated traditions legible to members of our communities. Finally, I will examine some of the unexpected musical sounds and objects that emerged from this act of integration.

—⁊⁊—

With the exception of Kim and Leavitt's work, there is little scholarly literature exploring the sociocultural dynamics of mixed Jewish and Asian American marriages and no work on music at the weddings that initiate them. A notable exception is Wendy Leeds-Hurwitz's *Wedding as Text: Communicating Cultural Identities through Ritual*, which examines how intercultural couples negotiate difference at, around, and through their weddings. Leeds-Hurwitz provides qualitative descriptions of marriage proceedings between a Jewish woman from New York and an atheist man originally from the People's Republic of China ("Couple 77"),[6] as well as an atheist Chinese Malaysian man raised in Canada and a Jewish American woman of Swedish and Romanian heritage ("Couple 80").[7] Both discussions focus primarily on the couples' efforts to create material objects that demonstrate a converging of their multiple identities in wedding rituals. Couple 77 describes their careful design of a wedding invitation incorporating an illustration of a chuppah vaulted over the Chinese ligature "double happiness" (*shuang xi* 囍), a symbol of celebration associated with weddings. Couple 80 worked closely with an artist to create a Jewish marriage contract (*ketubah*) intertwining the Hebrew symbol *chai*, meaning "alive" or "living," with the double happiness symbol. Although neither couple has much to say about music, both make clear the imperative to communicate to family and friends "how they were going to handle the differences in their backgrounds."[8]

The legitimacy of intermarriage in religious Judaism and its effects on Jewish continuity and survival have long preoccupied community members. It is hardly surprising that the couples profiled by Leeds-Hurwitz felt, as Andres and I did, compelled to address the matter at their weddings. Marriages between Jews and non-Jews are prohibited by Jewish law (*halacha*), as delineated in Deuteronomy 7:3–4.[9] Rabbis affiliated with the Orthodox and Conservative Jewish movements do not currently recognize the Jewish validity of intermarriage. The more progressive Reform movement, the largest denomination within American Judaism, officially discourages intermarriage but does not forbid rabbis from officiating at weddings where one partner is not a Jew because "rabbis are given autonomy in such matters and each rabbi interprets Jewish tradition according to his or her own understanding" (ReformJudaism.org).[10] Increasing numbers of Reform rabbis are choosing to recognize intermarriage, very likely in response to an irrefutable demographic reality: according to a 2013 Pew Research

Center survey, of the "non-Orthodox Jews who have gotten married since 2000, 28% have a Jewish spouse and fully 72% are intermarried."[11] The Union for Reform Judaism's "Resolution on Jewish Continuity and Growth," adopted in 1993, addresses the need for rabbis to welcome intermarried and interfaith families or else face a continued decline in synagogue membership and ritual observance and a gradual "breakdown of the Jewish family."

Although attitudes are shifting within the Jewish community, couples considering intermarriage remain in many cases uncertain about how to, as Leeds-Hurwitz put it, "handle the differences in their backgrounds." Organizations like InterfaithFamily, a nonprofit organization dedicated to "supporting interfaith couples exploring Jewish life and inclusive Jewish communities," publishes advice online on how to cope with the feelings of ostracism that can attend intermarriage. When I became engaged to Andres in 2007, interfaithfamily .com was one of a very small number of resources that offered practical guidance for wedding planning, such as a free referral service to rabbis and cantors who officiate at intermarriages, and a guide to designing inclusive wedding ceremonies. I was relieved to discover this kind of support, not only because it helped streamline the wedding planning process, but also because it provided validation that did not emerge as readily from institutional sources.

The discourse about the significance of intermarriage among Taiwanese Americans is comparatively less robust, likely reflecting the absence of a halacha-like code influencing community conduct as well as the community's recent vintage. Taiwanese migration to the United States was limited prior to the 1960s, when students from elite families began leaving the island in search of greater educational and economic opportunities as well as, in some cases, freedom from martial law and political repression.[12] The Immigration and Nationality Act of 1965 created pathways for those who had begun putting down roots in the United States to become naturalized citizens. When the United States broke official diplomatic relations with Taiwan in favor of rapprochement with the People's Republic of China in 1979,[13] heightened uncertainty about the island's future inspired many Taiwanese to seek greater economic and political stability abroad. The number of Taiwan-born immigrants to the United States more than tripled between 1980 and 1990, from 75,353 to 253,719, and reached approximately 358,000 by 2010.[14] About half settled in California, not in Chinatowns but in predominantly non-coethnic, middle- and upper-middle-class neighborhoods in the Los Angeles area. Historically, first-generation immigrants from Taiwan and their children have tended toward high levels of educational attainment and declared professional or managerial occupations at higher rates compared to immigrants from China or Hong Kong.

There is no data available on Taiwanese American rates of intermarriage, but rates of intermarriage for Asian Americans—here defined as marriage across racial or ethnic lines—are high.[15] Among Asian Americans born in the United States in 1965 and after, approximately 55 percent were intermarried in 2009, the year Andres and I were wed.[16] Among those who have non-Asian partners, a majority marry whites from similar socioeconomic backgrounds.[17] There is recent evidence, however, that this pattern may be changing: the percentage of Asian Americans marrying interracially declined from 30.5 percent in 2008 to 27.7 percent in 2010.[18] These statistics are useful in understanding large-scale trends, but they communicate little about the lived experiences of Taiwanese Americans who marry outside the community. Among approximately two dozen Taiwanese American friends I interviewed informally while writing this chapter, most reported that their parents had often shared hopes that they would find a Taiwanese or Taiwanese American spouse. Most of these friends ultimately intermarried, but they went to great lengths during the betrothal and wedding processes to reassure their parents of an ongoing commitment to their Taiwanese heritage.

To some extent, Andres and I were born into already mixed families, so our relationship was not without precedent. My maternal grandfather, Paul, a lapsed Catholic from Minnesota with German and Scandinavian heritage, met my maternal grandmother, Ency, a first-generation Ashkenazi Jewish American whose family had emigrated from Russia, while serving in the military during the Second World War. Despite their divergent backgrounds, they forged a bond in part over their love of music. My grandfather's affection for country singers like Hank Williams mystified my grandmother, but she reminisced often about their raucous dancing to songs by the Glen Miller Orchestra. They were married for nearly five decades, until my grandfather's death from a stroke in 1991.

Paul never converted to Judaism, but he participated in Jewish life alongside my grandmother as they raised five children in Chelsea, Massachusetts, observing the high holidays and celebrating as my uncles became bar mitzvahs. Although they remained close to my grandmother's side of the family, Paul and Ency did not have as much contact with Paul's relatives in Minnesota. As my mother, Ellyn, told me:

> They would come to visit us every four years or so around Christmastime. We had a Christmas tree because my mother wanted them to feel at home. I think my [paternal] aunts and uncles liked my mother—they wouldn't have come if they didn't. When I was about twelve years old, we made our very first trip to Minnesota to see my dad's family—his aunts, uncles, and cousins. It was obvious they had no idea we were Jewish from certain comments they made about their

dream that we would all kiss the pope's ring someday. I am not sure they would have known what it meant to be Jewish.[19]

My grandparents did not consciously conceal their different backgrounds, but they came together at a time when intermarriage was not something to be celebrated in the context of a wedding. I do not know how any of my great-grandparents felt about their union, but I do know that my mother grew up in what she felt was a loving home and that she and her siblings emerged with resolutely Jewish identities.

Andres's parents entered into their own mixed marriage in the late 1970s. Chien-hsing has both Hoklo and Hakka ethnicity and is descended from a family that migrated to Taipei from Fujian sometime between the seventeenth and nineteenth centuries, while Yu-an was born to a family that migrated to Taipei from Shanghai after World War II. In Taiwan, such pairings are sometimes referred to as "taro and sweet potato" marriages (與子配番薯 yuzi pei fanshu), the taro a symbolic representation of post–World War II migrants from China and the sweet potato of prewar ethnic Hoklo and Hakka peoples. These two groups have historically had an acrimonious relationship, as the Chinese arrival in Taiwan heralded decades of political oppression and subjugation for the Hoklo, Hakka, and indigenous peoples.[20]

Chien-hsing and Yu-an met in college, and their relationship developed through their membership in an American-style rock band called Cactus, which they founded with friends in 1972. Chien-hsing played guitar and organ, and Yu-an, who also performed in the university choir, sang. By the time they became engaged eight years later, Chien-hsing told me that his parents did not protest: "They had accepted it—Yu-an came to our house all the time. I think my parents were open-minded, but in those days it was very difficult for some families."[21] He speculated that previous mixture between Hoklo and Hakka ethnicities in his own family line helped soften their perspectives. Chien-hsing recalled the moment that he knew his family embraced Yu-an, when he began serving his mandatory military service in 1978: "After college we needed to go to the army, and, unfortunately, I was deployed to the island of Matsu. Taiwan was still in the middle of the Cold War with mainland China, so I remember I needed to take the ship from Keelung to Matsu, and it was dangerous because bombs were still falling. My father and second-eldest brother went with Yu-an to Keelung to say goodbye to me, so I think at that time they accepted us."[22]

They married in December 1979, and following local custom, Chien-hsing's parents planned the wedding banquet, which was held in a Cantonese restaurant the family owned. Afterward, the couple shared an apartment in the old Wanhua district of Taipei with two of Chien-hsing's brothers and their wives.

Yu-an remembers this as a period of cultural adjustment: "It was totally differ-ent, food, language, and even religion—I didn't even know how to pray like his family did."[23] In time, they remember their differences fading. Decades after they performed together in Cactus, my mother-in-law still loves to sing as my father-in-law strums along on his guitar, and they held their thirtieth anniver-sary party in Taipei at a live music venue. Although the band did not reunite for the occasion, everyone in our family was invited to perform a song or two in honor of the happy couple.

—ɯ—

Similarly, music is a cornerstone of my relationship with Andres. One of the first things I learned about him over lunch on the first day of college in 1999 was that his parents had named him after Andrés Segovia, the famed Spanish guitarist. We had both enrolled at Harvard University in the hopes of pursu-ing studies in music, and in that initial conversation I discovered that Andres played piano, loved Bill Evans, and wanted to write poetry. He was quiet and gentle, and funny in a fantastically offbeat way. He shared that he had been born in New York City, but that the family had moved several times—first to Los Angeles, then to Melbourne, Australia—before returning to Taiwan. Although Andres matriculated to a public middle school in Taipei, his lack of fluency in Mandarin hindered his ability to adjust both socially and academically, so Chien-hsing and Yu-an enrolled him at the Taipei American School for the ninth through twelfth grades. There, he blossomed among a community of Tai-wanese Americans whose families had returned to Taiwan after years abroad. More comfortable in that English-language learning environment, he began to write poetry and short stories. Taipei inspired him, its sounds, smells, and de-crepit beauty a constant source of surprise and joy. In addition to participating as a solo pianist in high school music competitions, Andres also played cello in the orchestra and performed as a vocalist and pianist with a small jazz combo called the Lone Iguanas. His parents eagerly supported these endeavors, and they were delighted for him to explore his interests in creative writing, music theory, and composition at Harvard.

I was born in the United States but had likewise lived overseas with my parents and two siblings for several years after my father, an electrical engineer who worked for a telecommunications company, was dispatched to Amsterdam. I began singing and writing songs at a young age and commenced studies in voice, piano, guitar, and later double bass when we moved back to New Jersey for my teenage years. I was very fortunate to attend a public school with a strong arts program and, like Andres, took advantage of every music-related activity available, including choirs, the orchestra, string quartets, and jazz bands. I also studied Jewish liturgical music and filled in for the cantor at my family's syna-gogue when she went on maternity leave after the births of each of her three children. In the Netherlands, we had belonged to an Orthodox synagogue where women did not play central roles in worship, so my tenure as substitute cantor at this Reform congregation in New Jersey provided a welcome opportunity to connect with Judaism on my own terms, through music. Several years later, I ac-cepted an offer of admission to Harvard. My parents were thrilled. They would have supported my decision to attend any college, but having grown up in the poorest working-class neighborhoods of Boston, they considered Harvard a once-in-a-lifetime opportunity. They encouraged me at every turn to continue engaging my passion for music and hoped I would take advantage of the rich culture on offer in Cambridge.

Andres and I became fast friends and subsequently expended most of our ex-tracurricular energies on performing as a voice-and-piano duo, playing together in pit orchestras, and collaborating on music direction for campus theater. In our first week on campus, we worked with several classmates to write and per-form a sentimental ballad about a love affair between two large puppets. (We unabashedly reprised this piece at our rehearsal dinner the night before our wedding.) Falling in love, we spent our idle hours listening to music, huddled close around a boom box in my dorm room and poring over liner notes. I de-clared my intention to pursue a joint major in music and East Asian Studies prior to meeting Andres, a decision that grew out of a travel experience to China with my father in the early 1990s. Andres introduced me to his favorite Mandopop artists and helped me to navigate the complex cultural landscape of Taipei when I conducted my senior thesis research there. Likewise, I was excited to introduce him to American popular music that had not crossed the Pacific during his teen-age years, as well as the Jewish folk and liturgical musics that so captivated me. Cassettes and CDs flew back and forth between us like passenger pigeons. They communicated complex messages through the works of Faye Wong, Morrissey, David Bowie, Cui Jian, Otis Redding, Maurice Ravel, The Clash, Samingad, Stephen Sondheim, Keith Jarrett, and Sarah Vaughan.

We moved in together after graduation in 2003 but did not become engaged until 2007 at the end of a season spent apart for work and study. By then a gradu-ate student at Harvard in ethnomusicology, I spent the summer months in Taipei conducting dissertation research while living with Andres's parents. Meanwhile, Andres remained in Massachusetts, working at a nonprofit by day and under-taking by night postbaccalaureate studies in hopes of attending medical school. After his classes ended in August, he traveled to Taiwan in the middle of a ty-phoon, walked with me through the wind and rain to a restaurant in the Far

Eastern Hotel, and asked me if I would marry him. I said yes without hesitation, and after dinner, naturally, we celebrated by singing karaoke.

—∿—

Committing to spending our lives together was easy. Wedding planning, on the other hand, was anything but. We were uncertain of whether to marry privately or with others, before a judge or clergyperson, in the United States or in Taiwan. In the American tradition, the bride's parents typically pay for the wedding, while in the Taiwanese tradition the groom's parents do—yet neither of us felt comfortable asking our parents to foot the bill for what we realized might prove to be a very expensive day. After so many years together as an unmarried couple, we also grappled with the question of why exactly we should alter our marital status. We felt no particular social pressure to marry, and while we were not naive to the many legal advantages conferred on married couples in the United States, we already lived together and shared costs, and remained undecided about if or when we would ever have children. Ultimately, we concluded that we wanted to marry because we were eager to join our two families—our histories and communities—in a formal way and to engage in a ritual celebrating that union.

We settled on holding our event in a geographic location between Boston and New York, the two cities around which the vast majority of our family and friends in the United States resided, at the Massachusetts Museum of Contemporary Art (Mass MoCA) in North Adams.[24] Located in the former Sprague Electric Factory, Mass MoCA has high ceilings and large multipaned windows that frame views of the Berkshire mountains. The galleries felt to us as close to a sanctuary as any place in the world. We had visited several times together previously and always delighted in the museum's dedication to showing the work of Chinese and Taiwanese diaspora artists and to staging innovative music programs. The idea of supporting the institution with our rental payment also appealed to us, as did working with local vendors and bringing visitors to an area hit hard by the recession. Mass MoCA invited us to be the first to wed in newly finished galleries dedicated entirely to installations by recently deceased artist Sol LeWitt (1928–2007). LeWitt was himself Ashkenazic, born to a Russian immigrant family, and celebrated in the Jewish community.

My parents and I were disappointed to learn that the rabbi we knew so well from our congregation in New Jersey, now living nearby in Massachusetts, would not officiate at an intermarriage. It was of course his prerogative, but the refusal still stung. Uncomfortable seeking out a rabbi whom we did not know, we contemplated independently the best ways to incorporate cultural and religious symbols into our ceremony that held personal meaning for us and adequately reflected the mutual transformations in our identities that had transpired over our ten years as a couple. As Andres put it:

> For the purposes of our wedding, I didn't want our relationship to Taiwanese or Chinese cultures to seem less complex than it is. I am both from and not from Taiwan. Also, Meredith has a different and significant relationship to Taiwan. It would be inaccurate for me to say that I am the sole representative of Taiwan culture in our relationship, or that our connection to Jewish culture and rituals is significant only to her. At the time of our wedding, I was several years into having shared holiday meals with her family. I had been privy to her struggles with the nature of her Jewish identity. I had participated in a conversation with her childhood rabbi who counseled us prior to the wedding, but who ultimately did not officiate because of his personal beliefs and practice. I helped Meredith deal with that disappointment, and we moved on to request that a close family friend officiate instead. I wanted our wedding somehow to demonstrate that the union of our cultures and selves had started the day we met, that it developed thrillingly, haphazardly over years, and that our relationships to our cultures, while complex and frequently ambivalent, are very real.[25]

Andres felt strongly that our wedding should still have "a Jewish structure and scaffolding," that he should wear a yarmulke, and that we should stand under a chuppah and sign a ketubah. We would recite the Seven Blessings and interpret them for our Jewish and non-Jewish guests who did not speak Hebrew. Andres wanted to ensure that, even without a rabbi present, the ceremony would still feel Jewish in ways that mattered to both of us and to my family.

Identifying Taiwanese and Chinese cultural traditions to incorporate into our celebration posed additional challenges. Modern wedding receptions in Taipei take place in hotels, restaurants, or banquet halls, and neither Andres's parents nor his grandparents on either side had had any ceremony that anyone could recall. Great symbolic importance is attached to food at wedding banquets in Taiwan, but key dishes would have featured emphatically non-kosher ingredients like pork and shellfish, and we could not find a local caterer in Massachusetts capable of preparing wedding staples like glutinous rice balls (*tangyuan* 湯圓). We looked to academic sources for information on Taiwanese wedding traditions but found many to be the province of rural communities and religious households, completely alien to Andres's urban-dwelling, secular parents. We explored the possibility of inviting the Gund Kwok Asian Women Lion and Dragon Dance Troupe, a fixture of many Boston Chinatown events, to perform at our reception. Chien-hsing and Yu-an, however, had never cultivated a close relationship to an American Chinatown community and found the notion totally befuddling—they associated lion and dragon dances with Lunar New Year celebrations and business openings more than weddings. For them, marriages are consummated through the distribution of locally made engagement cakes to family and friends, the display of Taiwan-style engagement photographs, and the presence of perfectly prepared banquet foods, none of which were readily available in western Massachusetts.[26] Frustrated at this state of affairs, Yu-an cried out at one point over the phone that she feared she would not recognize our wedding as a wedding at all. She was understandably adamant that her son's identity, and his family's heritage, should not be subsumed beneath the weight of so many Jewish cultural symbols.

It was at this point that we turned our attention back to music, a resource that we trusted to communicate the complexity of our intertwined diasporic lives in ways that other things could not. Music has historically played diverse roles in Jewish, American, Taiwanese, and Chinese weddings, but we did not in this case feel an obligation to cleave to any particular notion of tradition. On the contrary, as lifelong musicians from music-loving families, surrounded by musical friends, we looked forward to thinking creatively about how to sound a harmonious union between us and our communities, to perform in a meaningful way "how we were going to handle the differences in our backgrounds."

—◆◇◆—

Our first idea was to have a Beatles tribute band perform at our reception. I recall my mother and father, who offered to cover the cost of musicians at the wedding, knitting their brows in confusion at this proposal. I explained that we knew the Beatles had meant something to both our family and Andres's family, and hoped they would induce delight and nostalgia in all our guests. The Fab Four have been a favorite among Taiwanese audiences since the 1960s. Cactus had performed their tunes alongside a seemingly endless roster of local cover bands. Chien-hsing often speaks of his affection for George Harrison and has spent many evening hours playing the 1968 song "While My Guitar Gently Weeps" on his Gibson acoustic in the family television room in Taipei. My mother and her siblings had all been huge fans as well, riveted to their television screen when the Beatles debuted on the Ed Sullivan Show in 1964 and purchasing albums in every available format—vinyl, 8-track, cassette, and CD—during each subsequent decade. Andres and I, who had grown up devotees of the 1968 animated film *Yellow Submarine*, thrilled at the idea of having a concert in miniature at our reception and imagined members of both of our families drawn inexorably to the dance floor at the opening riffs of "Twist and Shout" and "Paperback Writer." As my mother considered it, she grew more and more enthusiastic at the prospect of encountering a John Lennon lookalike hovering around the wedding cake. My father, however, proved intractable. He loved the Beatles but simply could not countenance the idea of Liverpudlian accents on the Israeli folk song "Hava Nagilah," which would accompany our dancing of the hora and which he considered a cultural imperative.

Disappointed at my father's resistance to our admittedly eccentric plan, I scoured online forums for alternatives. A friend who lived in Brooklyn recalled having heard at her friend's wedding what she described as a "klezmer punk rock explosion," a local group of six musicians who impressed her for their mastery of not only Jewish repertoire but also Euro-American pop music.[27] After some sleuthing, she discovered that the band's name was Golem, a reference to a creature from Jewish folklore, usually fashioned from stone or clay, that comes to life through magic in order to serve a master. They were signed to JDub Records, a label that kindled a renaissance in Jewish popular music in New York in the early 2000s, and they performed frequently at weddings. I sent off an inquiry and heard back from bandleader, accordionist, and vocalist Annette Ezekiel Kogan almost immediately. She agreed to the date and venue and assured me that they had extensive experience playing at intermarriages.

Annette describes her identity as itself "mixed"—she grew up as a Jewish American in Massachusetts, but her father is Mizrahi from Baghdad and her mother's side are Ashkenazim from Austria-Hungary. She shared with me that her dedication to performing for diverse crowds at weddings is rooted in part in the stories her parents told her about their own wedding, wherein the Ashkenazim looked on in shock as the Mizrahim ululated at the appearance of the bride and groom. Ululation was an unfamiliar practice to the Ashkenazim present, and their expressions begged the desperate question, as Annette's mother put it: "Are they *really* Jewish?!"[28] Golem, which Annette cofounded with her high school friend, vocalist Aaron Diskin, describes itself on its official website, golemrocks.com, as "a leading re-interpreter and innovator of Yiddish and Eastern European music, pushing tradition forward into the 21st century.... Golem is known for its virtuosic musicianship, theatricality, humor and fearless wild energy, combined with a boundless love of tradition. Golem is clearly 'not your grandparents' klezmer' (NPR)." The group has played at hundreds of weddings since it coalesced in 2000, and Annette estimates that fully 30 to 40 percent of those have been intermarriages, uniting couples from even more disparate communities than her parents'.

When one side of the family is Jewish and the other side non-Jewish, Annette told me that she views Golem as serving a particularly vital role in the marriage proceedings: "With intermarriages, you can have two crowds sitting on opposite sides of the room talking among themselves. But there needs to be a new community around this couple, around this new family. They're coming together, like it or not, so you have to create a sense of community for them." She accomplishes this through a variety of means, including playing a strict ratio

Figure 5.1. Golem performing at the wedding reception. *Photo by Heather Waraksa.*

of one Jewish song to every three non-Jewish songs, and "sneaking the Jewish songs in when people are already dancing and they're open to something new and can think, 'Hey, I like this!'" She also makes a concerted effort to explain dances like the hora to non-Jewish attendees and, if the crowd simply cannot muster enthusiasm to participate, will jump off stage and "grab people to get it going—when there's a lot of non-Jews it usually dies down pretty quickly otherwise!"

My parents embraced the idea of hiring Golem to perform at our wedding. Contra NPR's description of the group above, Golem struck them as very much "my grandparents' klezmer"! They were thrilled to hear one of Annette's signature songs, the Yiddish swing tune "Shayn Vi Di Levone" ("Beautiful as the Moon"), which my mother described as "the kind of thing my grandmother and her elder sisters—who spoke Yiddish as their first language—used to dance to in the kitchen when we were kids."[29] Likewise, my father *kvelled* when he listened to the MP3 Annette had emailed me of a *niggun*—a tune typically sung using vocables like "dai-dai-dai" or "bim-bim-bam"—associated with the Hasidic Bobov community. Golem typically perform this for the bride's procession to the chuppah; although he did not grow up Hasidic, my father heard in that song traces of the *niggunim* he remembered from Shabbat services as a child. Andres and I were equally delighted that Golem was fluent in punk, rock, soul, funk, and new wave, artful interpreters of repertoire from

Rick James's "Superfreak" to the Clash's "Rock the Casbah," to the B-52s's "Rock Lobster."

—⁓—

Golem agreed to learn one new piece for our ceremony, to be performed after the traditional Jewish blessings over wine. We settled on an interpretation of the song "See the Chimney Smoke Rise Again" 又見炊煙, made famous throughout the Sinophone world by Taiwan-born pop icon Teresa Teng 鄧麗君 (1953–1995). Teng rose to stardom in East and Southeast Asia as a gifted interpreter of folk tunes and romantic ballads, revered for her power to reach audiences across deeply entrenched linguistic, cultural, and geopolitical divides. Her recording of "See the Chimney Smoke Rise Again," released in 1978, was a version of the Japanese song "Autumn in the Village" 里の秋, a setting of a children's nursery rhyme originally performed by Kawada Masako. Teng released her version, with Mandarin lyrics by her frequent collaborator Zhuang Nu 莊奴, at the end of a long period spent developing a recording career in Japan. I was passionate about Teng's music and had written extensively about her in my scholarship, and she was also beloved by Andres's parents, who came of age at the height of her fame. Andres was familiar with a version of "See the Chimney Smoke Rise Again" by his favorite singer, Beijing-born Faye Wong, from a 1995 album of Teresa Teng cover songs called *The Decadent Sound of Faye* 菲靡靡之音. This was one of the cassettes we enjoyed sharing during our first years in college—we practically wore it out through repeated listening.

Andres and I recognized in Teng's life and work a penchant for syncretism and a desire to enact her own multilayered diasporic negotiations in songs merging Chinese, Taiwanese, Japanese, and American influences. Born in Taiwan to parents who had emigrated from China, and living much of her adult life in diaspora, Teng moved constantly among places, peoples, and languages, never quite settling down. "See the Chimney Smoke Rise" describes memories of love evoked by the sight of chimney smoke curling into the evening air, dissipating, and blowing away. We heard in it an opportunity to sound a bridge between the multiple communities to which we belong and to meditate on the geographic and cultural movement that has always characterized our lives together. We collaborated on a translation of Zhuang's lyrics, the first and fourth verses of which are excerpted here:

See the chimney smoke rise again, as twilight covers the land.
I have a mind to ask the smoke, where are you going?
A poem may spring from the setting sun, a painting from the dusk.
Yes, there is beauty in all these things, but in my heart, there is only you.

[....]

Today, as yesterday, the chimney smoke rises. My memories stir.
I search the blossoming skies, my dreams,
the twilit poems, the painted dusk, all for a glimpse
Of this beauty that lives only where you are, in my heart.

Although these words are melancholy, pointing to love lost or in retreat from
the song's narrator, the image of chimney smoke suggested to us the fundamen-
tal presence of a hearth and a home. This association echoed the significance
of the chuppah, itself a representation of a Jewish home in the context of the
wedding ceremony.

Andres's childhood friend Nellie recited the lyrics to the piece, alternating
verses in Mandarin and English translation over Golem's quiet accompaniment. The violinist played Teng's vocal melody with minimal embellishment,
supported by plucked double bass. This duo had minutes earlier performed
the "Bobover Niggun" that accompanied my walk to the chuppah. Identical
instrumentation, similar tessituras, and a common andante tempo suggested
continuity between East Asian and Eastern European soundworlds. It seems
appropriate that the central instrument of *Fiddler on the Roof* should supply the
melodies underpinning our ceremony, with the goal of blurring boundaries and
spanning divides. The recitation of the lyrics in English and Mandarin provided
legibility to different constituencies in our gathering, and our work on the
translation together gave us an opportunity to express our unity as partners.

Our chuppah, a gift from Andres's parents, has somewhat different significance as a material object rather than a sounded musical performance. In retrospect, however, we recognize it as eminently musical. Months before our
wedding, Yu-an contacted Du Zhiwei 杜之韋, a calligraphy artist from Shanghai
whom she knew through a mutual friend, and commissioned from him a rendering on paper of the poem "Peach Tree" 桃夭 from the Zhou dynasty–era *Book
of Songs*. With the painting in hand, she traveled to Suzhou, a city famous for its
tradition of embroidery, to seek needlework artists capable of creating a ritual
object symbolic of our mixed diasporic identities. On a rectangle of cream-
colored silk, the artists recreated the calligraphy in spectacular detail, capturing
the faintest trailing brushstrokes in wisps of black thread.

The poems inscribed in the *Book of Songs*—also known as *The Book of Odes*,
The Classic of Poetry, or *Shijing* 詩經—were once performed musically, but their
original melodies have been lost. Nevertheless, the poems are traditionally referred to as "songs," and contemporary composers such as Zhou Long 周龍 have
set works from this period like "Peach Tree" to new music.[30] For the purposes
of our ceremony, Andres, who does not have any formal training in translation,

Figure 5.2. The bride and groom stand under the chuppah, made of cream-colored silk embroidered in black thread with the text of "Peach Tree," a poem from the Zhou Dynasty–era *Book of Songs. Photo by Heather Waraksa.*

worked with his mother to write an English interpretation to accompany the classical Chinese in our program:

桃之夭夭 灼灼其華
之子于歸 宜其室家
The peach tree flushes
in every bloom.
Married, this bride
completes her groom.

桃之夭夭 有蕡其實
之子于歸 宜其家室
The peach tree bears
the fruit of the loam.
Married, this bride
begins her home.

桃之夭夭 其葉蓁蓁
之子于歸 宜其家人
This year, the tree's

new leaves come in.
Married, this bride
blesses her kin.

Andres recalls writing the translation of "The Trees" by British poet Philip
Larkin, which he had read in a college poetry course. In doing so, he drew a connection between a twentieth-century English poem about the life cycle events
of birth and death, and a Zhou dynasty Chinese poem about the life cycle event
of marriage. Reflecting on the multiple layers of creativity, craftsmanship, and
interpretation that generated the chuppah and its translation, Andres told me:

> The chuppah struck me as a real gesture, a clear sign of my parents' desire both to
> honor the Jewish traditions into which I was marrying, and to imprint their own
> cultural identity on our ceremony. In particular, the choice of a classical Chinese
> poem spoke to my mother's background as an amateur calligrapher herself, a stu-
> dent of Chinese literature in college, and a descendant of a Shanghainese family.
> I had perhaps resisted in the past attributing my own interest in English literature
> to any parental influence, but the apple doesn't fall far from the tree. Moreover,
> the effort that my parents and multiple artists had put into this project seemed
> to demand some equivalent effort from me as well, to make the poem legible to
> our audience, and to do so using skills and knowledge I had acquired through
> schooling that my parents had helped make possible.[31]

While the location of this text within a tradition of performed art would not
have been evident to most of our guests, the chuppah over our heads provided a
striking visual connection to the traditions with which Andres's mother identified most strongly.

Following the ceremony and Golem's exuberant rendition of "Hava Nagilah"
at the opening of our reception, we partook in the American tradition of the first
dance. Of all the musical selections, this was perhaps the most challenging, as
we struggled to identify a piece that reflected our understanding of ourselves as
a couple. Our choice, "The Great Pumpkin Waltz," was written and recorded by
the Vince Guaraldi Trio as part of the soundtrack for the 1966 animated film *It's
the Great Pumpkin, Charlie Brown*. Both of us had loved the Peanuts cartoons as
children, and Andres in particular developed a deeper affection for the music as
an aspiring jazz pianist in high school and college. On the original recording,
trumpet, flute, guitar, and piano trade off on a plaintive melody over bass and
drums, and a melancholy harmonic progression predominantly in a minor key
is tempered by a brisk tempo and a resolution in the relative major. The wordless
simplicity of the piece and its suitability for an improvised slow-dance appealed
to us. We invited our close friends, performer-composers Danny Mekonnen,
Jacob Richman, and Kirsten Volness, to reinterpret the song on alto saxophone,

double bass, and keyboard. They slowed the tempo down, and Danny improvised long, languorous phrases. I remember the feeling of time decelerating as Andres and I moved together.

More than any other music performed that evening at Mass MoCA, "The Great Pumpkin Waltz" represents a cultural touchstone from our American childhoods, something that we share in spite of having grown up in different contexts. Following Andres's years living in Taipei, the Peanuts cartoons and their music generated for him a certain nostalgia for an American suburban reality that he had left behind, and that his parents no longer inhabited. Moreover, our friends' reimagining of the piece as a slow dance at our wedding reconciled musically our childhood with our adult selves, the people we were before we met with the people we had become together.

—⁓—

By remembering and recounting the series of negotiations that yielded, in the end, one of the most joyful days of our shared lives, I have come to appreciate anew the complexity of planning an event that included all participants and demonstrated the viability of our mixed partnership. Through engaging in the diasporic ritual of the wedding, we sought to legitimize our identities as Jewish and Taiwanese Americans even as we broke with tradition by marrying outside our communities. Music also highlighted our areas of overlap—the ways in which Andres has come to identify with diasporic Jewishness, I have come to identify with diasporic Taiwaneseness, and we both identify as Americans. Music wove together otherwise separate threads of traditional culture, popular culture, and personal memory, teasing out and making audible (and visible) the disparate strands within our respective cultural identities. In addition to serving as a document of our particular wedding ritual for readers who are friends, family, and strangers, this exercise in autoethnography demonstrates how diasporic identity may be constituted through music and musicians, as well as through stories transmitted between generations before, during, and after the ritual.

I composed this chapter on the eve of our seventh anniversary and am grateful for the opportunity to contemplate how our union sounds today. Remembering our wedding elicits feelings of tremendous warmth. We were fortunate that our families ultimately joined hands with us in a circle and danced to our future. The experience of planning that celebration has informed subsequent attempts at multilayered diasporic negotiation and empowered us to think creatively about how we continue to expand the limits of "tradition" in our lives.

Today, a used upright piano is the musical centerpiece of our small apartment in New York City and the physical resting place of our menorah, two small wooden charms from Taiwan representing our zodiac signs, and a large canvas upon which my artist uncle printed the text of our ketubah. The piano is our most cherished possession—it is the hearth in our home, and the sounds it makes are the chimney smoke that rises. One evening not long ago, our three-year-old daughter sat next to Andres at the keyboard and sang along confidently as he first played "Twinkle, Twinkle, Little Star" and then "Sunrise, Sunset" from *Fiddler on the Roof.* Andres's performance, a melodramatic response to our daughter's seemingly overnight transformation from helpless infant to capable kid, made me laugh. As Andres played on, she began to sing a different melody on top of his accompaniment, a Chinese children's tune called "Butterfly" (蝴蝶 *Hudie*), which describes the sight of a golden butterfly dancing among flowers. The convergence of "Sunrise, Sunset" and "Butterfly" in that moment was not harmonious in the traditional sense of harmony, but it sounded beautiful to us, and we were incandescent with joy.

MEREDITH SCHWEIG is Assistant Professor of Ethnomusicology at Emory University.

NOTES

1. Aleichem, *Tevye the Dairyman.*
2. Ellis, Adams, and Bochner, "Autoethnography," 1.
3. Adams, Jones, and Ellis, *Autoethnography,* 21.
4. Kim and Leavitt, "Newest Jews?," 138. Kim and Leavitt note that most research focuses on "partnerships between Ashkenazi Jewish Americans and their non-Jewish spouses who are both, for the most part, racially White" (136), and "[more] specifically, the literature on intermarriage for Asian Americans does not account for religious difference, at the same time that the literature on intermarriage for Jewish Americans does not consider racial difference" (147).
5. I follow Kim and Leavitt's definition of intermarriage as "marriage between individuals of different racial, ethnic, and religious backgrounds." "Newest Jews?," 135.
6. Ibid., 124–28
7. Ibid., 162–68.
8. Ibid., 124.
9. The Talmud (Yevamot 23a) also includes commentary prohibiting intermarriage.
10. See Central Conference of American Rabbis, "American Reform Responsa 149. The Reconstructionist movement is slightly more permissive of intermarriage. See Jewish Reconstructionist Communities in Association with the Reconstructionist Rabbinical College's "FAQs on Reconstructionist Approaches to Jewish Ideas and Practices."
11. Smith and Cooperman, "What Happens When Jews Intermarry?"
12. On the martial law period (1949–87) in Taiwan, see Lin, *Representing Atrocity in Taiwan.*

13. On Taiwanese immigration history, see Lee, "Taiwanese and Taiwanese Americans, 1940-Present," 1331–40.

14. Tseng, "Beyond 'Little Taipei,'" 39; McCabe, "Taiwanese Immigrants in the United States."

15. Taiwanese Americans are rarely disaggregated from categories like "Asian American" and "Chinese American" in either data collected by the US Census Bureau or in the scholarly studies of intermarriage. Min and Kim's article, for example, have Taiwanese folded into the category "Other Asian," which also includes Bangladeshis, Cambodians, Hmongs, Indonesians, Laotians, Malaysians, Pakistanis, Sri Lankans, and Thais. The source of that data is Flood, King, Ruggles, and Warren, *Integrated Public Use Microdata Series*. See also Min and Kim, "Patterns of Intermarriages," 447–70.

16. McCabe, "Taiwanese Immigrants in the United States."

17. Ibid. There is little scholarship exploring the prevalence of Asian-white intermarriage. The model minority myth has served as a wedge between Asian Americans and African Americans discouraging Asian-black intermarriage. See Lee, *Orientals*. On skin-tone discrimination and colorism in Asian and Asian American communities, see Rondilla and Spickard, *Is Lighter Better?* and Jones, "The Significance of Skin Color."

18. Wang, "Rise of Intermarriage." This statistic regards the rate of interracial, not interethnic marriage, for Asian Americans. The data also suggests differences along gender lines—Asian American women in 2010 were more likely to marry non-Asians than Asian American men.

19. Author's interview with her mother, New York, May 10, 2016.

20. On interethnic politics in Taiwan, see Brown, *Is Taiwan Chinese?*

21. Interview, Taipei, June 18, 2016.

22. Interview, Taipei, June 18, 2016.

23. Interview, Taipei, June 18, 2016. Women have traditionally been said to "marry out" of their natal families in Taiwan, which is why Chien-hsing and Yu-an went to live with his family after they wed. See Lee, "Between Filial Daughter and Loyal Sister."

24. We wanted to marry in Massachusetts because same-sex marriage had been legal in the state since 2004.

25. Interview, June 3, 2016, New York.

26. We procured engagement cakes from Taiwan. Made with honey, they were sent to family and friends in the United States before the holiday of Rosh Hashana, when honey-flavored foods are traditionally eaten to celebrate Jewish New Year.

27. Emily Atwood. Email correspondence, July 9, 2008.

28. Interview, New York, June 7, 2016.

29. Author's interview with her mother, New York, May 10, 2016.

30. Scholars maintain that the poems included in the *Book of Songs* were sung. Victor Mair notes that the "305 poems—more properly, songs, since they were lyrics accompanied by tunes now lost—date approximately from the Western Chou to the middle of the Spring and Autumn period (c. 840–620 B.C.E.), although they appear to have undergone substantial editing and regularization in the following centuries." Mair, *Columbia Anthology of Traditional Chinese Literature*, 61.

31. Interview, New York, June 3, 2016.

DISCOGRAPHY

Teng, Teresa 鄧麗君. Vocal performance of "You jian chui yan" 又見炊煙 [See the chimney smoke rise again], music by Nobuo Saito 斎藤信夫, lyrics by Zhuang Nu 莊奴. *You jian chui yan* 又見炊煙 [See the chimney smoke rise again]. Taiwan Kolin Denon Entertainment Inc., 1978, LP record.

Kawada Masako 川田正子. Vocal performance of "Sato no aki" 里の秋 [Autumn in the village], music by Nobuo Saito 斎藤信夫, lyrics by Uminuma Minoru 海沼實. Nippon Columbia, 1948, SP record.

Wong, Faye 王菲. Vocal performance of "You jian chui yan" 又見炊煙 [See the chimney smoke rise again], music by Nobuo Saito斎藤信夫, lyrics by Zhuang Nu 莊奴. *Fei mimi zhiyin* 菲靡靡之音 [The decadent sound of Faye], Cinepoly, 1995, cassette.

BIBLIOGRAPHY

Adams, Tony E., Stacy Holman Jones, and Carolyn Ellis. *Autoethnography: Understanding Qualitative Research*. New York: Oxford University Press, 2015.

Adrian, Bonnie. *Framing the Bride: Globalizing Beauty and Romance in Taiwan's Bridal Industry*. Berkeley: University of California Press, 2003.

Aleichem, Sholem. *Tevye the Dairyman and Motl the Cantor's Son*. Translated by Aliza Shevrin. New York: Penguin Books, 2009.

Brown, Melissa. *Is Taiwan Chinese?: The Impact of Culture, Power, and Migration on Changing Identities*. Berkeley: University of California Press, 2004.

Central Conference of American Rabbis. "American Reform Responsa 149: Rabbis Officiating at a Mixed Marriage." 1982. https://ccarnet.org/responsa/arr-467-470.

Ellis, Carolyn, Tony E. Adams, and Arthur P. Bochner. "Autoethnography: An Overview." *Forum Qualitative Sozialforschung/Forum: Qualitative Social Research* 12, no. 1 (2010): Art. 10. http://www.qualitative-research.net/index.php/fqs/article/view/1589/3096.

Flood, Sarah, Miriam King, Steven Ruggles, and J. Robert Warren. *Integrated Public Use Microdata Series, Current Population Survey: Version 4/0* [Machine-readable database]. Minneapolis: University of Minnesota, 2015.

Golem. "About Golem." Accessed September 21, 2016. http://golemrocks.com/.

InterfaithFamily. "About InterfaithFamily." Accessed September 21, 2016. http://www.interfaithfamily.com/about_us_advocacy/about_us_advocacy.shtml.

Jewish Reconstructionist Communities in Association with the Reconstructionist Rabbinical College. "FAQs on Reconstructionist Approaches to Jewish Ideas and Practices." Accessed September 21, 2016. https://jewishrecon.org/resource/faqs-reconstructionist-approaches-jewish-ideas-and-practices.

Jones, Trina. "The Significance of Skin Color in Asian and Asian-American Communities: Initial Reflections." *U.C. Irvine Law Review* 3 (2013): 1105–23.

Kim, Helen K., and Noah S. Leavitt. "The Newest Jews? Understanding Jewish American and Asian American Marriages." *Contemporary Jewry* 32, no. 2 (July 2012): 135–66.

Lee, Anru. "Between Filial Daughter and Loyal Sister: Global Economy and Family Politics in Taiwan." In *Women in the New Taiwan: Gender Roles and Gender Consciousness in a Changing Society*, edited by Catherine S.P. Farris, Anru Lee, and Murray Rubinstein, 101–19. Armonk, NY: M. E. Sharpe, 2004.

Lee, Jonathan H. X. "Taiwanese and Taiwanese Americans, 1940–Present." In *Immigrants in American History: Arrival, Adaptation, and Integration*, edited by Elliott Robert Barkan, 1331–40. Santa Barbara, CA: ABC-CLIO, 2013.

Lee, Robert G. *Orientals: Asian Americans in Popular Culture.* Philadelphia: Temple University Press, 1999.

Leeds-Hurwitz, Wendy. *Wedding as Text: Communicating Cultural Identities through Ritual.* Mahwah, NJ: Lawrence Erlbaum Associates, 2002.

Lin, Sylvia Li-chun. *Representing Atrocity in Taiwan: The 2/28 Incident and White Terror in Fiction and Film.* New York: Columbia University Press, 2007.

Mair, Victor. *The Columbia Anthology of Traditional Chinese Literature.* New York: Columbia University Press, 1994.

McCabe, Kristen. "Taiwanese Immigrants in the United States." Migration Policy Institute. January 31, 2012. http://www.migrationpolicy.org/article/taiwanese -immigrants-united-states.

Min, Pyong Gap, and Chigon Kim. "Patterns of Intermarriages and Cross-Generational In-Marriages among Native-Born Asian Americans." *International Migration Review* 43, no. 3 (Fall 2009): 447–70.

ReformJudaism.org. "What is the reform position on officiating at the wedding of a Jew to a non-Jew?" Accessed September 21, 2016. http://www.reformjudaism.org/practice /ask-rabbi/what-reform-position-officiating-wedding-jew-non-jew-my-fianc%C3 %A9e-not-jewish-and-doesnt-want-convert.

Rondilla, Joanne L., and Paul Spickard. *Is Lighter Better? Skin-Tone Discrimination Among Asian Americans.* Lanham, MD: Rowman & Littlefield, 2007.

Smith, Gregory A., and Alan Cooperman. "What Happens When Jews Intermarry?" Pew Research Center. November 12, 2013. http://www.pewresearch.org/fact-tank/2013 /11/12/what-happens-when-jews-intermarry.

Tseng, Yen-Fen. "Beyond 'Little Taipei': The Development of Taiwanese Immigrant Businesses in Los Angeles." *International Migration Review* 29, no. 1 (Spring 1995): 33–58.

Union for Reform Judaism. "Resolution on Jewish Continuity and Growth." Accessed September 21, 2016. http://www.urj.org/what-we-believe/resolutions/resolution -jewish-continuity-and-growth.

Wang, Wendy. "The Rise of Intermarriage, Chapter 1: Overview." Pew Research Center. February 16, 2012. http://www.pewsocialtrends.org/2012/02/16/chapter-1-overview.

SIX

—◆—

SONG, *SEVDAH*, AND CEREMONY

An Autoethnographic Exploration of Music and
Community Cohesion in Bosnian American Weddings

TANYA MERCHANT

MY FUTURE HUSBAND, ALEN, AND I sat across the breakfast table from one another on a late summer morning in 2011 and decided that we should get married before I gave birth to our first child (due the following spring). At that moment, I had no idea of the complex amalgam of cultural issues, refugee memories, family ties, class standards, and necessary hybridity I would confront in the process of pulling together a small, family-focused, bicultural Bosnian American wedding. Having attended more Bosnian weddings now, I understand that *small* and *modest* are difficult concepts to incorporate into the framework of a Bosnian wedding. However, with a pregnancy and a full-time job involved, I was determined not to allow our wedding to become overwhelming in size or logistics. In hindsight, I understand that by standing firm with that decision, I kept our family from creating an event that would help maintain the increasingly fleeting sense of community unity in the Bay Area's aging and assimilating Bosnian refugee community. The following autoethnographic examination of our bicultural wedding focuses on circumstances and processes that led to the event and the moments that embodied explicitly Bosnian identity. I focus on music as an important practice for the creation of Bosnian space in the diaspora and consider the events of this wedding in the context of other Bosnian weddings in the San Francisco Bay Area,[1] searching for a sense of the underlying sentiments, desires, and beliefs that occur as musical participation and aesthetic appreciation bind the community together.

This wedding was far from the first complex compromise that Alen and I had made. Although he grew up in a major Yugoslavian urban center, while my Vermont-rooted family followed my father's Coast Guard career to Alaska and elsewhere across the United States, Alen and I discovered many shared values: honesty, filial piety, lifelong learning, progressive/secular religious practice, and financial responsibility. Despite differences in culture, creed (Protestant Christianity vs. Islam), and class (my family traversed the range of the American middle class as my father was promoted up the ranks, while Alen's family could trace their ancestry to Ottoman nobility and included members of local leadership), we managed to successfully navigate cohabitation, the purchase of a house, and the decision to have children. The wedding, however, represented something public and forward-looking—a statement to our families and our communities about who we were going to be together and how we would connect to those larger groups. The norms for weddings from my childhood and early adulthood varied significantly from those Alen and his relatives remember in the former Yugoslavia and its postwar diaspora. Size was one major difference—most of the weddings I attended and my mother and father (Bruce and Martha) remembered included fewer than one hundred participants. Alen and his family remember a range of events from small home weddings to large weddings in banquet halls or hotels that involved hundreds of guests, often crowded into the space. The presence of music is another difference in norms—my parents remember that many of the wedding receptions of their youth didn't involve music or dancing at all; church hymns and organ pieces were the only music involved in sealing a marriage. Alen's mother (Sadija) and aunt (Subhija) fondly remembered music and dancing as a feature of wedding receptions, whether to live or mediated music. Commonalities in our experiences of weddings included the presence of family, expressions of goodwill and hope for the new couple, and an overabundance of food.

Throughout this chapter, I will put our experience creating a wedding that combined American and Bosnian cultures in conversation with other wedding celebrations taking place in the Bosnian American community, paying specific attention to how music supports a sense of family and/or community cohesion and aesthetic enjoyment. Beginning by unpacking recent methodological writing on autoethnography and considering what the technique can offer ethnomusicological inquiry, which is already steeped in self-reflexivity, I move on to a discussion of wedding music throughout the Balkans. Then I briefly trace Bosnia's history, including a description of my in-laws' journey to California as part of the influx of thousands Bosnian refugees to the United States in the 1990s. I focus on exploring songs and wedding celebrations Alen's family remembered from the Yugoslavian era. Finally, I locate my nuptials and music performed there within the larger amalgamation of Bosnian American weddings in the San Francisco Bay Area. The personal reflections that result from autoethnographic methods connect with larger ideas about how communities persevere after relocation, how individual aesthetics intersect with group identity, and how music has the power to transform space, evoke memory, and render time more flexible.

WHY AUTOETHNOGRAPHY?
ISN'T SELF-REFLEXIVITY ENOUGH?

Weddings and their music are deeply personal, and it is impossible to discuss such events in one's own family and community without including oneself in the narrative. Through autoethnographic method, it is possible to analyze and discuss oneself as a research subject, as well as the person engaged in the act of research. The inclusion of the ethnographer in one's scholarly narrative has been an established practice since the 1980s in ethnomusicology. Thomas Turino lists reflexivity among other methodological strategies as "academic tactics of the decade."[2] Since the 1990s, reflexivity has become a common practice for ethnomusicologists today.[3] Gregory Barz and Timothy Cooley's influential volume that considers fieldwork and its challenges from a variety of perspectives includes many essays that both incorporate and examine reflexive methods.[4]

The SAGE Encyclopedia of Quantitative Research Methods provides definitions of both autoethnography and reflexivity, which provide a sense of how the two concepts overlap and fit together. Epistemologist Maura Dowling defines reflexivity as "qualitative researchers' engagements of continuous examination and explanation of how they have influenced a research project."[5] Sociologist Carolyn S. Ellis defines the latter term, explaining, "autoethnography refers to ethnographic research, writing, story, and method that connect the autobiographical and personal to the cultural, social, and political. In autoethnography, the life of the researcher becomes a conscious part of what is studied."[6] She goes on to discuss different kinds of autoethnographic writing, and mentions the concept of reflexive narrative as a kind of autoethnography: "*Reflexive or narrative ethnographies* focus primarily on another culture or subculture, while authors use their own experiences in the culture reflexively to bend back on self and look more deeply at self-other interactions."[7] Both reflexivity and autoethnography imply the inclusion of the scholar's perspective in her/his inquiry and writing—illustrating explicitly how our selves as researchers shape the work that we are able to accomplish. Autoethnographies generally go further than reflexivity along this track, making the researcher her or himself a subject of scholarly inquiry.

As it has embraced the self-reflexive project over the past two decades, ethnomusicology has tended to enact some amount of an autoethnographic turn, whether named or not. My previous work on wedding music, which was drawn from fieldwork in Tashkent, Uzbekistan, from 2002 to 2009, referenced my participation as an observer/guest at the wedding or member/guest of the wedding band.[8] Although I included myself in narratives about these events and tried to illustrate the relationships I had with musicians there, I never focused the ethnographic lens on myself. Self-reflexivity demanded that I provide an account of my participation and try to make my methods, roles, and biases clear within my ethnography; it didn't demand that I consider myself worthy of research. This contrasts with my current project, in which I also wish to remain appropriately reflexive to clearly illustrate my current methods, roles, and biases. However, I am moving further along the continuum of autoethnography, entering the less clearly defined area where self and family are the focus of my ethnographic inquiry.

In my life and ethnomusicological work with the Bosnian American community in California, I am continually forced to consider how my research affects my friends and family. Married into this community, I cannot avoid negotiating issues of cultural crossing and/or compromise. Ethnographer Norman K. Denzin reminds us that regardless of methodological strategies for reflexivity or autoethnography, the target of research is the stories, the "fictions," that we fashion for ourselves to provide meaning in our lives. "Lives are biographical properties. They belong not just to persons, but also to larger social collectivities, including societies, corporations, and, for some, the world-system."[9] This chapter seeks to explore the stories that my family tells about weddings, in order to understand how my affinal, insider/outsider role fits within the larger challenge that Bosnian Americans face—to find a way to express a sense of self that is true to their sense of Bosnian-ness and American-ness, that brings the various places and histories and memories together to form a sense of cohesive identity that both adapts and holds true to Balkan sensibilities.

WEDDING MUSIC AS CULTURAL EXPRESSION AND STAPLE OF THE MUSIC ECONOMY IN THE BALKANS

Weddings and their music have been documented around the world as one of the major rites of passage. Large and small, weddings usually require music and dancing as part of their celebration. While wedding music is especially well documented in parts of the Balkans, such as Bulgaria, Macedonia, and Albania, where wedding music provided an important alternative to music produced in various state-controlled venues during the communist period in the latter half of the twentieth century. Truly, it seems to be nearly impossible to write about music in parts of the Balkans (especially Bulgaria) without discussing wedding music. Donna Buchanan, Timothy Rice, and Carol Silverman have documented both sides of the situation in communist and postcommunist

Bulgaria, showing how many musicians who had prestigious positions in state ensembles and were associated with the state-run radio station still made a significant portion of their living playing weddings in the late communist period (as well as those who eschewed the state ensembles completely). After communism, these same musicians found increasingly creative ways to continue to make a living as capitalism upset their economic situations and as weddings became more modest, even as Bulgarian music simultaneously gained international recognition.[10] Donna Buchanan emphasizes the complex nature of the rise and denouement of Bulgarian wedding music as it intersects with a number of factors, including the transition from communism to capitalism and the complexity of how nationalism affects ethnic minorities, as well as more local and regional concerns. Her 1996 article highlights the challenges that wedding musicians faced in Bulgaria: "Largely because of their association with minority cultures, performers of *svatbarska muzika* (wedding music) became targets of harassment and discrimination by cultural, political, and juridical authorities during the 1980s. At the same time, wedding music was by far the most popular musical genre in the country, despite the fact that it developed and flourished without state patronage."[11]

Indeed, aside from Sugarman's focus on Prespa Albanian practices,[12] most scholarship on wedding music in the Balkans focuses on Romani musicians and the various communities they perform for.[13] Carol Silverman's book on Roma music across the Balkans and the diaspora especially illustrates the importance of wedding music within Roma communities. She notes, "By far weddings are the most frequent celebratory event and the focus of community attention . . . weddings and circumcisions often involve hundreds of guests, numerous meals, and lavish presents."[14] Her account provides a clear image of the size, scope, and influence that weddings have as life cycle events within the community and as livelihood for musicians.

Despite its prominence in the region, wedding music never gained the kind of notoriety or popularity in Bosnia that it did in Bulgaria, and it never ascended to the status of a separate genre or a significant alternative to state-sponsored musical careers. The situation in Bosnia was distinctive within the former Yugoslavian republics, because of its plurality (as opposed to a clear majority) of ethnicities and religious affiliations.[15] This meant that musicians need to have fluency in the musical practices of various ethnic groups. Furthermore, individuals often participated in life cycle events with exogamous friends and family, so even non-musicians regularly experienced ritual and folk music from a range of ethnic groups.

This holds true for musical scholarship in Bosnia as well; Svanibor Pettan described how Bosnia bucked the Yugoslavian trend with regard to folk music research, saying "the approach [that pushed for research on the dominant ethnic group within former Yugoslavian territories] was different in Bosnia-Herzegovina where researchers, at least partly due to the absence of one dominant ethnic group and linguistic boundaries, considered cross-ethnic research."[16] However, while heterogenous research was the norm, a strong urban-rural divide and attenuating class differences resulted in rural folk music's neglect as a research topic until Ankica Petrović's paradigm-shifting work on the *ganga* rural vocal genre.[17]

This urban-rural divide in Bosnia has strongly influenced musical aesthetics and listening practices. Both my affinal family and the refugee community in the Bay Area that I focus on hail from the city of Banja Luka, and thus the focus of my research, both in America and as remembered in Yugoslavia, is entrenched in urban sensibilities. Generally, the music and dance featured at urban weddings includes mediated music, whether played by a family friend from their iPod, CD, cassette, or record collection; or a professional DJ; or a band that performs popular songs live. Wedding music, since it lacks its own specialist term, is often described and remembered as "popular music" (*zabavna muzika*), and dancing is described as simply being "dance" (*ples*) with *kolo* (circle dancing, a term used widely among Slavs) as a highlighted activity.[18] Although weddings in this community are important affairs, they seem to have more range in terms of size, scope, and musical repertoire than the enormous gatherings that Silverman describes from the 1980s. Weddings often occurred in the groom's home and didn't always feature a live band, and especially in the diaspora, they might include a range of pop music in Bosnian and English.[19]

BOSNIAN HISTORY AS POLITICAL AND PERSONAL

Bosnian identity is complex and contested, even without the additional complications of the diaspora. The area now known as the nation of Bosnia and Herzegovina (which itself has a partition between the Federation of Bosnia and Hezegovina and Republika Srpska) has spent the large majority of the past centuries controlled by larger empires or entities (the Ottoman Empire, the Austro-Hungarian Empire, Yugoslavia). During the Yugoslavian era, in 1970, "Bosnian" became officially recognized as the ethnonational category, though certainly the area east of Dalmatia and west of the Drina River has been referred to as Bosnia for centuries.[20] The term also describes the ethnoreligious category, Bosnian Muslim (or Bosniak).[21] Historian Cathie Carmichael notes that the Western Balkans are remarkably linguistically unified through the Bosnian-Croatian-Serbian language complex (BCS), which is spoken by a vast majority in the region.[22] She also notes the strong cultural division between urban and rural populations: "for centuries, the primary political, cultural and religious divide in the Western Balkans [usually, present-day Bosnia, Croatia, and Slovenia] was between the towns and the mountains."[23] This unification of community beyond national lines, yet division along urban/rural (and, often class) lines, persists even in the diaspora where the "mountains" and "towns" no longer physically separate the refugee communities. Even with the melting pot of the diaspora, maintaining the appearance of sophistication and urban sensibilities was important in Bay Area Bosnian American weddings—all that I attended were elegant cosmopolitan affairs, not reimaginings or revivals of village weddings.

The history of Bosnia under the Ottoman Empire (1463–1878) has been especially noteworthy to many of my friends, family members, and contacts (as well as the scholarly community and Bosnia's current national project). The Ottoman Empire brought Islam to the region and established a class system that was largely divided along religious lines.[24] Members of my affinal family and community continue to underscore this system, as they trace their lineage back to a *beg* or *aga* (members of the Bosnian Ottoman nobility). Following the Ottoman period, Bosnia fell under Hapsburg rule and the Austro-Hungarian Empire (1878–1918). During the interwar period, it became part of the Kingdom of Yugoslavia, which unified an area roughly equivalent to present-day Bosnia and Herzegovina (BiH), Croatia, Kosovo, Macedonia, Montenegro, Serbia, and Slovenia. Following World War II, under the leadership of Josip Broz Tito (1892–1980), it became the Socialist Federal Republic of Yugoslavia (1945–1992), which endured until the war in the Balkans during the 1990s.

A power vacuum, economic unease, and continued urban-rural divisions combined with memories of previous tensions were the conditions that brought about the nationalist movements that ignited the Balkan war (1992–1995). This, combined with continued tensions over land redistribution that occurred throughout the twentieth century, rendered Yugoslavia ripe for a rise in toxic nationalism. Carmichael provides useful context on how resentments from World War II and before added to the growing hostility.[25] The dissolution of Yugoslavia in 1992 resulted in a great deal of uncertainty in Bosnia. Coupled with the Serb nationalist revival the country was set up for tragic conflict and genocide. Though all sides took civilian and military casualties, the systemic expulsion and execution of non-Serb populations from areas in northern and eastern Bosnia caused the refugee crisis of the 1990s. Surrounding countries like Croatia and Austria absorbed much of the primary wave of refugees, but many continued on to settle in other nations through secondary migrations. The formerly tight-knit community of Banja Lukan Bosnians, including my affinal family, were scattered across the globe and currently reside in Germany,

Sweden, Croatia, Australia, Canada, South Africa, the United States, and elsewhere.

Although the Bay Area community largely came to the United States as a result of the war and genocide in the 1990s, Bosnians had been immigrating to the United States in much smaller numbers since the late nineteenth century. During the war, Europe absorbed much of the first wave of migration as Bosniaks and Croats who lived in eastern and northern Bosnia scrambled to find safe havens. The United States has become an especially important site of secondary migration and hosts significant communities of Bosnian refugees. The largest of the communities reside in St. Louis, Missouri, where 70,000 Bosnians have now revived the south city. Journalist A. Cogo, citing the US State Department's Office of Immigration Statistics 2010 report, concludes that 127,800 Bosnians obtained permanent residency in the United States from the beginning of the war until 2010, including both primary and secondary migration to the United States.[26] He notes that most refugee programs aimed at refugees from the war ended by the early years of the twenty-first century, which (along with the end of hostilities) contributes to the constant decrease in the numbers of newly declared permanent residents.

My husband, Alen, and mother-in-law, Sadija, followed a typical trajectory as refugees fleeing the Bosnian Serb Army's occupation of Banja Luka (a strategically important trade city) to stay with family in the Croatian capital Zagreb. The conflict would eventually displace approximately sixty thousand Bosniak and Croat residents of the city. Alen was sent away first in 1992 on what was one of the last flights out of Banja Luka. Sadija remained in Banja Luka for another year and a half, even after the historic Ferhadija Mosque (an Ottoman landmark from the sixteenth century and UNESCO heritage site) was destroyed—an event that signaled to many Bosniaks and Croats that it was time to flee the city.[27] Sadija remained steadfast in her desire to remain in Banja Luka until the White Eagles, a Serb paramilitary organization, forcibly removed her from her apartment. After joining a refugee caravan over the border to Croatia, Sadija joined Alen and other relatives in Zagreb, and the International Rescue Committee facilitated the family's resettlement in California's Silicon Valley in 1995. This was also the year that the ceasefire was declared and the Dayton Accords signed, which divided Bosnia into two administrative zones, the Federation of Bosnia and Herzegovina, and Republika Srpska, of which Banja Luka is now the administrative capital.

REMEMBERING BOSNIAN WEDDINGS IN YUGOSLAVIA

Although weddings and wedding music were hardly homogenous in Yugoslavia, they bear inclusion here. Both family and community members remembered the weddings that they participated in from that time period, and these provide a helpful illustration of how wedding celebrations have maintained consistency in some ways and changed greatly in others. The earliest wedding I heard about was that of Alen's aunt Subhija in 1952, when she was living in the family's village, Vrbanjci (now located in Republika Srpska, BiH, near Banja Luka). As she described it, "for me, it was all about Banja Luka, so I agreed to marry Asim if we could make our way to Banja Luka." She described how her marriage first was officiated by a *hodža* (a local imam or other Muslim leader) and afterward was registered in the city record with a magistrate. Hers was the only wedding described to me from the early Yugoslavian period. Most of the memories I heard from later years (mainly the 1970s and '80s) involved only the official wedding with the magistrate, even though the individuals identify as Muslims. Alen's aunt emphasized that she "didn't have a real wedding," in the sense that her wedding reception occurred at home with close family, rather than a large gathering in a hall.[28] When asked about the music, she remembered an accordionist who performed and recordings played on a gramophone. This memory touches on two key aspects of Bosnian and Bosnian American musical practices—the accordion and recorded music. The accordion has been used to accompany the voice throughout the twentieth century. Accordions also play a prominent part in larger folk orchestral performances of *sevdah* and are featured in many pop-style versions of *sevdalinka* as well. Beyond the instrumentation, dancing is also a key mechanism for celebrating a wedding and enacting community unity. Aunt Subhija remembered guests dancing kolo with the accordionist playing while surrounded by the dancing line. Although individual songs were tough to recall, she specifically mentioned "Mujo Kuje," which she described as "an old song" that was popular at the time.[29] It is included within the sevdalinka repertoire (known interchangeably as sevdah [a term from Arabic meaning love and/ or ecstasy], an urban folksong genre in Bosnia and Herzegovia that traces back to the Ottoman era).[30] "Mujo Kuje" remains one of the more popular tunes and is included in many anthologies. This tune makes a sweet choice for wedding music, since it depicts a man preparing his horse to visit his beloved, dismissing his mother's concerns that he's saddling his horse at night and not in the daytime under the sun. But Mujo is so eager:

"Mujo Kuje" (Mujo Saddles His Horse)

Mujo kuje konja po mjesecu,
Mujo kuje, a majka ga kune:
—Sine Mujo, živ ti bio majci,
Ne kuju se konji po mjesecu,
Već po danu i žarkome suncu.
—Ne kuni me, moja mila majko,

Jer kad meni na um pa'ne draga,
Ja ne gledam sunca, nit' mjeseca
Ni moj doro mraka nit oblaka
Već pod pendžer dragoj!

Mujo is saddling his horse under the moonlight,
He saddles and his mother scolds;
—Son Mujo, listen to your mother,
Don't saddle your horse under the moonlight,
Do it in the daytime under the hot sun.
—Don't scold me, dear mother,
Because when my mind is on my dearest,
I don't look at the sun or moon,
My horse takes no notice of the darkness or clouds,
Already my dearest is at the window![31]

Although, in her framing, weddings at home weren't presented as worthy of much attention, at least in Bay Area circles and Banja Lukan memories, having a reception at home after a previous civil and/or religious ceremony is fairly common. The more intimate context of a reception at home alters community members' expectations about music and entertainment, since a large production with a band is not usually feasible in a home setting. As a result, I was curious how our wedding overlapped with what my affinal family was accustomed to within Bosnian and Bosnian American wedding practices. Sitting down at the kitchen table with my recorder, one day, I asked my husband and mother-in-law about the weddings that they remembered from Banja Luka before the war. A few themes arose, the most prominent that it is hard to remember specifics about events that occurred more than twenty years ago. Over the course of the conversation, we discussed Sadija's sisters' weddings, and the weddings of her nephew and niece. Another topic that became important was that receptions weren't typically held in large wedding venues.

Both Alen and Sadija emphasized that there was an old tradition of fetching the bride (escorting her from her family home to the wedding [not bridal kidnapping, in this case]) and that even weddings in the Yugoslavian period embraced that practice, having a "big line of cars" go and fetch the bride to bring her to city hall, then another "huge crowd of cars" to transport everyone home for the party. The other comment that resurfaced regularly was food (not unexpectedly). Indeed, although the specifics of food in Yugoslavian era weddings eluded their memories, both Alen and Sadija distinctly remembered large amounts of food and big feasts (gozbe). At one point, Alen commented that "I can't remember what we ate, but I remember being very full afterward."[32] The other memory was the crowds and the noise, especially in the weddings that were at home and not in a hall. Although they weren't able to articulate the specifics of the Banja Lukan wedding soundscape, both made it clear that weddings in Banja Luka sounded different than their American counterparts. Neither Alen nor Sadija had very musical memories from these weddings in the 1970s and '80s, except to note that often home weddings didn't involve musical professionals; usually a friend played recorded music for people to listen and dance to. This may connect to issues of class and the size of the gatherings. Many weddings occurred in people's houses with guests crowded in and someone playing albums on a record player.[33] This reliance on recorded music for entertainment at receptions occurred in my natal family as well for weddings in the 1960s and '70s, before middle-class American weddings commonly featured DJs. My mother fondly remembered sitting with her mother selecting albums to play during her reception. (Burt Bacharach was deemed appropriate, but due to an oversight, the music was never turned on during her reception.)[34] Although wedding receptions at home with record players are events that our family histories have in common, one major difference is that my natal family's weddings didn't feature dancing before the age of the DJ. This could reflect my natal family's Puritan ancestry, as well as the prohibitive cost of live music for members of the middle class. Both Alen and Sadija remember dancing along with the music in pre-Balkan war home weddings. When asked what kind of dancing, Sadija replied, "Dancing of all kinds."[35] The people were mostly listening to *zabavna muzika*, but they would also do line dancing and kolo. This blend of individual dancing in groups with occasional forays into kolo lines was common in the weddings that I attended since joining the family and community in 2008.

WEDDINGS AND THEIR MUSIC IN
THE BAY AREA DIASPORA

When I began attending Bosnian American events in the Bay Area, I was struck by the culture shock and the cognitive dissonance involved in traversing the insider-outsider continuum that I found typical of my fieldwork endeavors even though I wasn't framing my forays in to this community as fieldwork but rather attempting to get to know my partner's friends and extended family. Much like my early days in Uzbekistan and Russia, I had the experience of grasping only one or two words in a sentence until someone benevolently switched the conversation into English, which then made me uncomfortable and grateful, since I'd forced my language into events in which the ability for community members to speak their native tongue was a major feature. I always felt more comfortable at these events once singing and music making happened. My lack of language skills didn't affect my ability to carry a tune or hold my own on the dance floor.

In the summer of 2011, I was invited to a Bosnian American wedding with two hundred to three hundred attendees (this was the largest wedding I had ever attended as a guest or researcher).[36] My language skills had improved significantly by this time, and I had begun to understand the order of events and priorities of these kinds of large gatherings. This huge event followed much of what I'd expected from my previous experience with other Bosnian events and their focus on food, coffee, conversation, and song and from my expectations from American weddings. The event was held in a large conference hotel, with a lovely outdoor area for a short civil ceremony. When I asked about religious aspects of the wedding, I was told that the family is fairly observant, so a Muslim ceremony probably happened previously. The bride wore a long and elaborate white dress and veil, with attendants in yellow; the groom and his attendants wore suits of varying shades of gray and beige. The ceremony was short and soon after it concluded, we were ushered into a cavernous ballroom where a stage and speakers were set up in front of a dance floor, which was in view of more than a dozen large round tables and a buffet off to the side. On stage, the all-male band set up, with a synthesizer and vocals and drum machine. They sang mostly popular music in Bosnian from the 1980s and beyond. Tunes included those popularized by Eurovision artists like pop megastar Dino Merlin and more recent songs from the *turbofolk* genre that combines Western Balkan folk instruments and melodic elements with pop instruments, techno beats, synthesizers, and harmonies. Turbofolk vocals include a wide vibrato and lyrics with light, love-centered folky themes. Native listeners often characterize turbofolk as Bosnian, former-Yugoslavian, or "our" (*naša*) country music.[37] Sonically, it is reminiscent of *čalgia* (popfolk) in Bulgaria and Macedonia and grew out of the earlier Yugoslavian pop hybrid known as "newly composed folk music."[38]

Throughout the evening, people enjoyed themselves on the dance floor in between trips to the buffet filled with roast lamb, salmon, *pita* (filo pies), and eventually baklava and wedding cake. The dancing is what I've found to be a typical mix of individual dancing, some couple dances to slower songs, and occasional lines of kolo. Hours into the reception, however, the band shifted styles to perform a well-known sevdalinka, "Moj Dilbere". Whereas pop songs brought handfuls of people to the floor, as the first strains of "Moj Dilbere" sounded through the hall people streamed to the dance floor, filling it and forming long kolo lines, singing along and dancing.

"Moj Dilbere" (My Dearheart)

Moj dilbere, kud se šećeš,
Što i mene ne povedeš?
Povedi me u čaršiju,

Pa me prodaj bazarđanu
Uzmi za me oku zlata,
Pa pozlati dvoru vrata.
Ko god prođe neka pita:
—Čija li su ono vrata?
—To su vrata moga zlata.

Where are you going, my dearheart,
Why don't you take me with you?
Take me downtown
And sell me to a merchant
For my price, take a ration of gold,
To gild the door of your courtyard.
Whoever walks by might ask:
—Whose is that door?
—That is the door of my treasure (lit: my gold).[39]

The crowd sang along with the band, who also provided a harmonic accompaniment on synthesizer and accordion. Sevdalinke, at their roots, are courting songs, so the genre sets up expectations for themes around romantic love. Although this text could be interpreted as a rebuke to one's beloved who values gold more than love, my affinal family describes it as simply a love song. Alen interprets it as a teaching song, warning men not to neglect those they love. There are nuances and implications that are complicated to unpack; Alen has often remarked that "what is not said in Sevdalinka is more important than what is said." With that in mind, one can also read "Moj Dilbere" as including a challenge to those who value gold more than love, and an underscoring of the connection between love and sacrifice. Emotionally and musically, this was the climax of the event, sealing a new marriage, celebrating the unification of two families, and manifesting—physically, kinetically, and musically—a joyful and lasting sense of Bosnian identity.

THROWING A BICULTURAL BOSNIAN AMERICAN WEDDING

Preparations for our wedding were exciting and challenging, since they involved confronting the many differences in cultural, class, and familial expectations that Alen and I brought to our relationship. Our small wedding included mostly family, twenty-four people total. This meant omitting most members of the Bay Area Bosnian community who supported Alen and Sadija as they came to the country and who provided crucial ties to Bosnian culture, practices, and identity. We didn't throw one of the large weddings that I've attended at other times, and thus missed an opportunity to bring the whole community together. Our bicultural wedding failed that mission, rendering it and us less connected to the refugee community and to memories of weddings in hotels or banquet halls, such as those that Aunt Subhija contrasted against her own home wedding (and what caused her to declare her wedding "not real"). Remembering our wedding nearly five years later in the context of other community events (Eid gatherings, New Year's celebrations, and large picnic parties), I see how twenty years in the United States has filled families' lives with other obligations, loosening some community ties and resulting in fewer gatherings every year. By feeling too busy and overwhelmed to host a large wedding, we contributed to that trend and lost opportunities to frame ourselves as hosts. Attending allows one to participate in the community, but hosting actively constitutes the community.

Another challenge we faced was the issue of religion and how to create an acceptable expression of our union that upheld our values and backgrounds, yet maintained a level of comfort for all participants and guests. It was important to me to have the pastor of the Methodist church I attended in Los Angeles officiate, yet I didn't want to have an overtly Christian wedding that could alienate members of both sides of our family. My pastor was happy to come up to Santa Cruz and officiate a bireligious, yet primarily secular, wedding for us. Both Alen and I wanted to incorporate his Islamic heritage into the service but didn't have a personal relationship with an appropriate religious leader. Though we hoped to find a progressive imam who would stand up with my pastor and declare us married in a largely secular fashion, we never found someone. Part of this issue connects to the ways that my in-laws identify as cultural or secular Muslims. Elders in the family may be religious, but everyone sublimated religious practices during the communist period. And Alen's generation was not raised to be religious. Add this to the ethno-religious persecution of the 1990s and the current prevalence of Islamophobia in the United States, and the result is a reticence to perform Islamic identity, even though we observe and celebrate the religious holidays in our homes. Home celebrations in private fit very well within a communist Yugoslavian framework—religion was personal, not public. Furthermore, for a century or more, it was typical to have two marriage ceremonies, one with a hodža or imam and a separate civil ceremony to record one's marriage "in the book."

Here in the diaspora, most wedding celebrations are receptions, with the ceremony having happened previously and privately. The real work of a wedding, in this case, is the celebration, the music, dancing, and feasting. This may connect to a broader Balkan sensibility, as Charles and Angeliki Vellou Keil noticed a similar phenomenon in Greek Macedonia, with what they frame as the "indoor liturgy" of the church and marriage ceremony and the "outdoor liturgy" of the reception: "the outdoor liturgy where the sound is made dance lasts longer, has more energy, and allows full involvement and expression of all participants, and one is tempted to proclaim: This is it! This is the *real* wedding. This is the Balkans of the body, of bodily poetry beyond words, beyond ideologies."[40]

In practice, we reversed the indoor/outdoor dichotomy that Keil and Keil set up, holding our ceremony in the garden of a local Afghan-owned restaurant (so that the food would be "right," that is, they wouldn't serve pork and would definitely have lamb and other offerings that would appeal to the Bosnian palate). The wedding ceremony was sweet, small, and ecumenical, with the pastor declaring us married "in the name of love." We curated a playlist for the restaurant to play that included Bosnian popular music, some sevdalinke, some American folk music, and some alt-country songs, with some Afghan tunes thrown in for good measure. Despite the care and many debates we put into the creation of that musical experience, it was barely audible in the garden and hardly remarkable. Following the ceremony and restaurant-catered dinner, we returned to our house for a reception with Bosnian coffee, baklava, *hurmašica* ("little date" butter cookies), and wedding cake.

The party at home was most people's favorite and most memorable part, from both sides of the family. It was also the only time that music took a central role. Once we had made coffee, put out the Bosnian sweets, poured champagne, and cut the cake, everyone settled in to food and conversation. As the drone of chewing and conversation spread across our living room, Sadija grabbed Alen, her sister, and me, and said that we should sing her sister's favorite sevdalinka, "Put Putuje Latif-Aga":

"Put Putuje Latif-aga" (Lord Latif Takes to the Road)
Sa jaranom Sulejmanom

Moj jarane Sulejmane
Je l' ti žao Banje Luke

Banjalučkih teferiča
Kraj Vrbasa, Akšamluka?

Lord Latif takes to the road
With his friend Sulejman

My friend Sulejman,
Do you miss Banja Luka,

Banja Lukan picnics, and
Evenings by the Vrbas river?[41]

The melody repeats as I've transcribed it for each couplet, with vocalists often adding ornamental melisma and vibrato. When singing together with others, ornaments tend to be less pointed and less common than when performing solo. The melody, especially the first phrase, spends a great deal of time exploring the *hijaz* tetrachord with its distinctive augmented second. This augmented second is often a locus for extra turns and ornaments; often vocalists will reach back for those pitches when the melody pauses on a nearby note. Vocal melisma and wide vibrato are typical of current performance practice of the genre, by renowned vocalists and those who strive to imitate them. The text focuses on the historical figures, Latif-aga Tetarić (1884–1957), a local merchant, and his friend Sulejman. It is written from the perspective of the Austro-Hungarian era, after the Ottoman Empire receded. This was a time when many Ottoman Bosnians migrated to present-day Turkey, and Sulejman was one of those migrants. The song presents Latif-aga traveling and meeting his friend on the road, asking him if he misses Banja Luka. The song is especially important to Alen's aunt and to our family as a whole, because it underscores their own yearning for a return to the Banja Luka of their prewar memories. It also connects to their family history, since members of their family also attempted to migrate to Turkey during the Austro-Hungarian period, but returned to Banja Luka after being waylaid in Macedonia.

This song is the strongest memory I have of our wedding, being enveloped into the arms of my new family, singing a song about someone who left their Banja Luka and remembers it so fondly. As we sang, the room fell quiet as most other guests listened and a few more Bosnian guests got up to join the line and the song. I remember the sensation of building the arcing melodic contour up in volume and intensity, eventually singing in a full-throated style. As we sang, I felt our unborn son start to kick—I wish I could say it was in rhythm, but alas no. The bodily sensation of having rhythmically random kicks in the abdomen while singing in sync with a handful of family members was intense, challenging, and joyful. Four months later, we would name our son Sulejman. Though it is a family name, it was that experience of song and celebration that solidified our naming decision—after our reception we never mentioned any of the other contenders.

There are many versions of this song, all of which center around Latif's pleasant reminisces about the city. The version that my family sings is currently very common—it is a fairly short version, easily singable, and commonly recorded. In the case of my family, recordings and radio may have entered the oral tradition, since sevdalinka albums get repeated listenings in our households, and the text I have translated is almost identical to the texts sung by some of the most famous sevdalinka singers, such as Safet Isović (1979) and Hanka Paldum (n.d.). This version, however, is not as specific to Banja Luka as those contained in scholarly collections of sevdalinke, which often include more verses that refer to specific neighborhoods and families. What follows is a text provided by Vehid Gunić, which he cited as one of the oldest versions of this popular sevdalinka.[42]

"Put Putuje Latif-aga"
Sa jaranom Sulejmanom.
Progovara Latif-aga:
"Moj jarane Sulejmane,
Je l' ti žao Banje Luke
Banjalučkih teferiča
I tekije Hadž' kadića.
I jalije Tetarića
Kul-mahale Dervišića,
Akšamluka kraj Vrbasa?"

Lord Latif takes to the road
With his friend Sulejman
Lord Latif says:
"My friend Sulejman,
Do you miss Banja Luka,
Banja Lukan picnics,
And Haji Kadić's tekije (*khanqah*, sufi house),
And Tetarić's beachfront
And the servant's neighborhood of Dervišić,
And evenings by the Vrbas river?"[43]

This older text is marked by the specific references to the "kul-mahala" or servant's neighborhood where both Muslim and Romani populations lived, the Tetarić holdings on the shores of the Vrbas River, and a sufi gathering house overseen by Haji Kadić (*haji* is a title given to those who complete the hajj pilgrimage).[44] After finding this more detailed version of the song, I inquired why my family knew and sang the more abridged version. They noted that the historical landmarks and neighborhood names in the older version were not commonly used in their lifetimes. It's possible that the less detailed version would allow for easier radio play; even with instrumental breaks between couplets it could still fall within a three to four minute time frame. In addition, it eliminates "Turkicisms" (*Turcizmi*) that were not in favor during the Yugoslavian era and often carried associations with backwardness. The shorter text has the benefit of near constant repetition in my family and community circles, as it is has been sung at gatherings and holidays before and since my wedding.

After "Put Putuje Latif-aga" wound down to a close, everyone clapped and someone asked for a translation, which those of us singing collectively cobbled together. We went on to sing a few other beloved sevdalinke, though no one in my family remembers exactly which ones. "Moj Dilbere" and "Snijeg Pade Na Behar Na Voće" (Snow falls on the blossoms and on the fruit) are the most probable ones, according to my, Alen's, and Sadija's foggy memories. In our 2016 interview, it struck me that this song continued to be the most powerful memory of our wedding for Alen and Sadija as well, though it was charged with different sensations and concerns. Although everyone mentioned how they enjoyed singing and what a memorable moment it was, my memories focused on feeling embraced by my new family members and feeling a deep sense of inclusion. Alen, on the other hand, remembers being concerned about the non-Bosnian-speaking guests. He remembered not wanting to sing too much, because not everyone understood and might become uncomfortable.[45] This concern is understandable but was unfounded. When interviewed, my parents remembered wanting to understand sung and spoken Bosnian but also understanding the celebratory nature of the songs and occasion. My father discussed the singing, not something typical of celebrations he was accustomed to, saying, "Here's a different way that this family celebrates. It's not the way my family did it, but it's a celebration, and that came through."[46] Even though they enjoyed the singing and understood it as a joyous moment, the language barrier was a challenge, but not an insurmountable one. My mother commented, "Even though there's a language barrier and cultural barriers, customs that are so different and strange, [there are] feelings of—wow, we are all here to celebrate this wonderful occasion and that happiness transcends all the awkwardness."[47] Despite differences in cultural practices and mutual concerns over communication, we forged a sense of family unity through song and celebration. Thus this powerful musical moment, performing a song that memorializes a different diasporic moment from Alen and Sadija's city, connected to a range of tropes in the Bosnian American experience. As I reveled in the joy of fitting into the musical practices of my new family, Alen worried about the aesthetic sensibilities and comfort of his new American family members, and those American family members enjoyed the song and wondered about the meaning. Sometimes compromises occur without discussion or clear decisions, yet they manifest the delicate negotiations involved in blending cultural, familial, and individual sensibilities.

CONCLUSION: WHAT DOES SEVDALINKA SIGNIFY IN THESE CONTEXTS?

Clearly sevdalinka doesn't sound in every Bosnian American wedding, but when it does, it seems to be doing very specific work for those who hear it, sing it, and dance along. Part of this has to do with its history—sevdalinka is a genre that began as an Ottoman courting genre, sung by women and men in those contexts, and has been continually remade throughout the many changes of empire, era, and regime in Bosnia. Sevdalinka began as unaccompanied song, sometimes sung with percussive accompaniment and eventually the *saz*, then the accordion came into common usage and eventually the larger folk ensembles of the Yugoslavian era. In the postwar era, there is an effort to create the "new sevdah" by artists such as Damir Imamovic, Amira Medujanin, Božo Vrećo, and the group Divanhana, which includes some roots exploration involving Turkish and Arabic instrumentation and melodic inflection, as well as hybridization with pop and jazz idioms.

In each diaspora wedding I've attended that included sevdalinka, there was a palpable increase of emotion and intensity that other music didn't provide for participants. It is well-loved and much heard in Bosnia proper, but there is an intensity to its appreciation in the Bay Area diaspora and in my family. Alen reflected on how sevdalinka is connected to his refugee experience, saying, "I didn't really listen to sevdalinka until I got to Croatia and [my cousin] played me a Himzo Polovina album."[48] He went on to clarify that he certainly heard sevdalinke through his childhood, but didn't pay it much attention—it was his time in Croatia during the war that solidified his fandom. Part of sevdalinka's power to evoke emotion and Bosnian group identity may have to do with personal histories that connect with the song and with the longer history of the genre. Sevdalinka is inherently urban and associated with Ottoman and thus Muslim history in the region. It is connected with the upper classes in urban centers who converted to Islam, which layers with panethnic folk sensibilities gained as it was performed and recorded (by Bosniaks and others) through the communist period. The living memories of many participants link sevdalinka to favorite performances and artists from the Yugoslavian era. Furthermore, sevdalinka seems to have gained a further and, perhaps deeper, symbolic and emotive power in refugee communities. While it has long been part of the Bosnian soundscape, its perseverance as a genre, with continuous performance practice through the Ottoman and Austro-Hungarian empires, through the monarchic period, the communist period, beyond war and conflict, it persists. Instruments may be added, texts might change, but its musical dissemination is a sonic representation of the community's ability to endure.

TANYA MERCHANT is Associate Professor of Music at the University of California, Santa Cruz. She is author of *From Courtyard to Conservatory: Women Musicians of Tashkent.*

NOTES

1. The Bosnian refugee community in and around San Francisco is diverse. The section that I concentrate on includes Bosniak and Croat refugees from the city of Banja Luka and its surrounding villages and towns.

2. Turino, "Structure, Context, and Strategy in Musical Ethnography," 410.

3. Ethnomusicologist and dance scholar Ruth Hellier-Tinoco's article on relationships and responsibility in ethnomusicological fieldwork provides a useful overview of the development of reflexive methods in the field of ethnomusicology and the social sciences as a whole. Hellier-Tinoco, "Experiencing People," 19–34.

4. Barz and Cooley, *Shadows in the Field.*

5. Dowling, "Reflexivity," 748.

6. Ellis, "Autoethnography," 49.

7. Ibid., 50.

8. For an example of how I engage reflexivity in my previous research on Uzbek weddings, see Merchant, *Women Musicians of Uzbekistan,* 156–69.

9. Denzin, *Interpretive Biography,* 29.

10. Buchanan, "Wedding Musicians, Political Transition, and National Consciousness in Bulgaria"; Buchanan, *Performing Democracy;* Rice, *May It Fill Your Soul;* and Silverman, *Romani Routes.*

11. Buchanan, "Wedding Musicians, Political Transition, and National Consciousness in Bulgaria," 664.

12. Sugarman, *Engendering Song.*

13. For example, Keil and Keil, *Bright Balkan Morning,* and Silverman, *Romani Routes.*

14. Silverman, *Romani Routes,* 84.

15. Of course, there are many similarities between the music cultures in Bosnia and those in Bulgaria and elsewhere in the Balkans—for example, there is a similar instrumentarium, and kolo dance can be found throughout the region. Romani musicians are an important part of the musical landscape in Bosnia, as well as its diaspora, even though they don't feature prominently in the music of the community that I work with.

16. Pettan, "Encounter with 'The Others from Within,'" 121.

17. Petrović, "Perceptions of 'ganga,'" 60–71.

18. In this context, kolo is danced as an open circle, with the line leader on the far right leading the circle in a generally right-ward direction as s/he pulls the line of dances around (and often follows a shape that is not terribly circular). This kind of line or circle dancing is common throughout the Mediterranean and is the primary dance form found in International Folk Dance (IFD) and Balkan dance groups, who perform similar dances from Greece, Turkey, Bulgaria, and the former Yugoslavian states. Mirjana Laušević discusses this dance form and its popularity with American dance enthusiasts extensively in her book, *Balkan Fascination.*

19. In this case, I am using *Bosnian* to describe both the language spoken by the community and heard when consuming pop music. However, it is important to note the complexity and political tensions that can arise when labeling this language, especially in ethnically mixed groups. Community members usually employ the simple solution

of calling the mutually understandable language complex of Bosnian, Croatian, and Serbian *aš jezik* (our language). It is a wonderfully inclusive turn of phrase, which erases ethnonational divisions and brings all who speak into the concept of "us." Academically, there are a variety of strategies. I follow Carmichael's approach of simply calling it Bosnian since the community I work with hail from what is now the nation of Bosnia and Herzegovina. Historically, the language was known as Serbo-Croatian, which seems inappropriate, given the very explicit current project to differentiate the three languages, and others opt for the more unwieldy Bosnia-Croatian-Serbian, or BCS, which I use when discussing the language complex as a whole rather than the specific language spoken in country and in refugee communities.

20. Carmichael traces the first reference to the territory of Bosnia (or, in this case, "Bosona") to a treatise by Emperor Constantine VII (Carmichael, *Concise History of Bosnia*, 11).

21. Carmichael describes this as Bosnia's "'soft' borders with its neighbours in terms of religion, language, and family connections, which often confound nationalism" (*Concise History of Bosnia*, 4).

22. Ibid., 16.

23. Ibid., 43.

24. Malcom, *Bosnia*.

25. Carmichael, *Concise History of Bosnia*, 91–136.

26. Cogo, "Close to 130,000 Bosnian Received Permanent Residency in USA."

27. After its destruction, the mosque's rubble was carted away to various unknown locations and the site was paved over into a parking lot. This rendered the postwar reconstruction project (which began in 2001) especially challenging, but it eventually succeeded, and Ferhadija opened again on May 7, 2016. Coward, *Urbicide*, 8.

28. Spahić, personal interview.

29. Ibid.

30. The term *sevdalinka* comes from a Turkic word for love, *sevda*, which hearkens to its roots as a courting genre. It is often called *sevdah* these days, especially when including newly composed works in the style of sevdalinka, such as those in the "new sevdah" genre.

31. As with most songs transmitted via oral tradition, there are many small variations of "Mujo Kuje" and the other sevdalinke mentioned in this chapter. Most variations hold true to the central narrative of the story, and the variation can often be explained by changing language use throughout history, as well as the differences between contemporary Bosnian, Croatian, and Serbian (singers of many ethnicities perform sevdalinke, though it is generally acknowledged as an urban Bosnian phenomenon). This version of the text for Mujo Kuje comes from Gunić, *Sevdalinke* 1:275 (translation by author).

32. Alen Pličanić, personal interview.

33. Ibid.

34. Martha Merchant, personal interview.

35. Sadija Pličanić, personal interview.

36. The norm for weddings that I've attended as a guest was approximate 75 to 100 guests, with any more than 100 being considered a very large wedding. This is true of previous generations, since during an interview, my parents remembered that weddings in both of their families usually involved around 100 people. They purposely held their wedding

in another state so that they "wouldn't have to invite the whole town" and only had around 50 guests at their wedding in 1970 (Bruce and Martha Merchant, personal interviews). As a researcher, I attended Uzbek weddings in Tashkent and the surrounding areas that probably included many more than 200 guests, but they would be spread out between many events over the course of three days, never 200 or more in one place at one time. Other weddings I've attended in the Bay Area Bosnian community included 100 to 150 guests and weren't held in hotel ballrooms, so the 2011 event was impressive in size and scope.

37. Turbofolk had some associations with Serbian nationalism during the war but nonetheless had continued popularity in Bosnia and its diaspora. Art and design scholar Uroš Čvoro noted, "In Bosnia, as in the other ex-Yugoslav republics, turbo-folk was a direct outgrowth of the immensely popular [newly composed folk music], and still exists as a major part of the popular music scene. . . . The popularity of turbo-folk continued to grow during the war in the nineties, seemingly despite its association with Serb nationalism, albeit as a lowly and trashy music" (Čvoro, *Turbo-folk Music and Cultural Representations of National Identity in Former Yugoslavia*, 90). For further discussion of Bosnian and Serbian turbofolk, see Rasmussen, "Bosnian and Serbian Popular Music in the 1990s."

38. Čvoro, *Turbo-Folk Music*, 90.

39. Text, Gunić, *Sevdalinke* 1:269 (translation by author).

40. Keil and Keil, *Bright Balkan Morning*, 270.

41. Text as sung on November 19, 2011 (translation by author).

42. Gunić, *Sevdalinke* 2:56.

43. Text, Gunić, *Sevdalinke* 2:56 (translation by author). Muhamed Žero presents an identical version in his volume. Žero, *Sevdah Bošnjaka*, 299.

44. The tekije is where the daily ritual prayers required by the Muslim faith would be held and where they would perform *zikr* devotional practices.

45. Alen Pličanić, personal interview.

46. Bruce Merchant, personal interview.

47. Martha Merchant, personal interview.

48. Alen Pličanić, personal interview.

BIBLIOGRAPHY

Barz, Gregory F., and Timothy Cooley, eds. *Shadows in the Field: New Perspectives for Fieldwork in Ethnomusicology*. New York: Oxford University Press, 1997.

Buchanan, Donna A. *Performing Democracy: Bulgarian Music and Musicians in Transition*. Chicago: University of Chicago Press, 2006.

———. "Wedding Musicians, Political Transition, and National Consciousness in Bulgaria." In *Retuning Culture: Musical Changes in Central and Eastern Europe*, ed. Mark Slobin, 200–230. Durham, NC: Duke University Press, 1996.

Carmichael, Cathie. *A Concise History of Bosnia*. Cambridge: Cambridge University Press, 2015.

Cogo, A. "Close to 130,000 Bosnian Received Permanent Residency in USA." *St. Louis Bosnian*, September 10, 2012. http://www.stlbosnians.com/close-to-130000-bosnians -received-permanent-residency-in-usa.

Coward, Martin. *Urbicide: The Politics of Urban Destruction*. New York: Routledge, 2008.

Čvoro, Uroš. *Turbo-Folk Music and Cultural Representations of National Identity in Former Yugoslavia*. New York: Routledge, 2016.

Denzin, Norman K. *Interpretive Biography*. Thousand Oaks, CA: SAGE Publications, 1989.

Dowling, Maura. "Reflexivity." In *The SAGE Encyclopedia of Qualitative Research Methods*, edited by Lisa M. Given, 748. Thousand Oaks, CA: SAGE Publications, 2008.

Ellis, Carolyn S. "Autoethnography." In *The SAGE Encyclopedia of Qualitative Research Methods*, edited by Lisa M. Given, 49–51. Thousand Oaks, CA: SAGE Publications, 2008.

Gunić, Vehid. *Sevdalinke 1 i 2*. vols. 1 and 2. Sarajevo: Planjax, 2003.

Hellier-Tinoco, Ruth. "Experiencing People: Relationships, Responsibility and Reciprocity." *British Journal of Ethnomusicology* 12, no. 1 (2003): 19–34.

Isovic, Safet. "Put Putuje Latif-aga" [Lord Latif takes to the road]. 1979. Accessed September 30, 2016. https://www.youtube.com/watch?v=EtN5QNBH4os.

Keil, Charles, and Angeliki Vellou Keil. *Bright Balkan Morning: Romani Lives and the Power of Music in Greek Macedonia*. Middleton, CT: Wesleyan University Press, 2002.

Laušević, Mirjana. *Balkan Fascination: Creating an Alternative Music Culture in America*. New York: Oxford University Press, 2007.

Malcom, Noel. *Bosnia: A Short History*. London: Pan Books, 2002.

Merchant, Bruce. Personal interview with the author, September 27, 2016.

Merchant, Martha. Personal interview with the author, September 27, 2016.

Merchant, Tanya. *Women Musicians of Uzbekistan: From Courtyard to Conservatory*. Urbana: University of Illinois Press, 2015.

Orahovac, Sait. *Sevdalinke, Balade i Romanse Bosne i Hercegovine* [Sevdalinkas, ballads, and romances of Bosnia and Herzegonia]. Sarajevo: Svjetlost, 1968.

Paldum, Hanka. "Put Putuje Latif-aga" [Lord Latif takes to the road]. Accessed September 30, 2016. https://www.youtube.com/watch?v=WGJ7-Ago9Kw.

Petrović, Ankica. "Perceptions of 'ganga.'" *World of Music* 37, no. 2 (1995): 60–71.

Pettan, Svanibor. "Encounter with 'The Others from Within': The Case of Gypsy Musicians in Former Yugoslavia." *World of Music* 43, nos. 2–3 (2001): 119–37.

Plićanić, Alen. Personal interview with the author, August 7, 2016.

———. Personal interview with the author, August 24, 2016.

Plićanić, Sadija. Personal interview with the author, August 7, 2016.

Rasmussen, Ljerka Vidić. "Bosnian and Serbian Popular Music in the 1990s: Divergent Paths, Conflicting Meanings, and Shared Sentiment." In *Balkan Popular Culture and the Ottoman Ecumene: Music, Image, and Regional Political Discourse*, edited by Donna A. Buchanan, 57–94. Lanham, MD: Scarecrow Press, 2007.

Rice, Timothy. 1984. *May It Fill Your Soul: Experiencing Bulgarian Music*. Chicago: University of Chicago Press.

Silverman, Carol. *Romani Routes: Cultural Politics & Balkan Music in Diaspora*. New York: Oxford University Press, 2012.

Spahić, Subhija. Personal interview with the author, August 21, 2016.

Sugarman, Jane C. *Engendering Song: Singing and Subjectivity at Prespa Albanian Weddings*. Chicago: University of Chicago Press, 1997.

Turino, Thomas. "Structure, Context, and Strategy in Musical Ethnography." *Ethnomusicology* 34, no. 3 (1997): 399–412.

Žero, Muhamed. *Sevdah Bošnjaka: 430 Sevdalinki sa Notnim Zapisom, drugo izdanje.* [The Sevdah of the Bosniaks: 430 Sevdalinkas with Staff Notation, 2nd edition]. Sarajevo: Ljiljan (Biblioteka Sehara), 2002.

SEVEN

—ᴍ—

SOULFUL SAME-SEX WEDDING, ARETHA FRANKLIN, LOVE, AND THE POLITICS OF (UN)FREEDOM

NINA C. ÖHMAN

SOON AFTER NEW YORK GOVERNOR Andrew Cuomo signed the state's same-sex marriage bill on June 24, 2011, Bill White and Bryan Eure started planning their nuptials.[1] They were just one among the several thousand LGBTQ couples who would enter into a legally recognized marriage in the upcoming months.[2] Their wedding celebration was held on October 23, 2011, and, like many past same-sex commitment ceremonies and marriages in other states, was expressly politicized.[3] This elaborate gathering was organized for over six hundred of the couple's friends and family members at the Four Seasons Restaurant in Manhattan; White told the press invited to cover the event that although the aim of the occasion was to celebrate their own marriage, they also sought to advocate for marriage equality nationwide.[4] In keeping with their intentions, the patriotic wedding theme projected a clear message: when it comes to affairs of the heart, politics matter. As an official highlight, White and Eure proclaimed their lawful marriage by exchanging vows and signing a wedding certificate, but the spectacularity of their nuptials arose in large part from music that was deployed to encourage reflection on social justice. Music's instrumental role culminated in the performance of Aretha Franklin, an American cultural icon, whose singing presence configured this as a wedding in which the nation and its plurality could be imagined through songs about romantic relationships. On that account, the political force of her love songs drew on the diasporic consciousness that resonated at various registers in her expression.

Aretha Franklin, the majestic wedding singer, represented a sight and sound that American audiences recognize as a distinct thread in the nation's cultural

Figure 7.1. Aretha Franklin performing for the couple and the audience at the wedding ceremony of Bill White and Bryan Eure, New York, 2011. This image accompanied an article by Sarah Maslin Nir, "The Wedding as Spectacle, Bearing a Message," which appeared in the *New York Times* (Print Edition), October 24, 2011, page A17. *Photo credit: Robert Stolarik/ New York Times / Redux. Used with permission.*

fabric,[5] not simply because of Franklin's numerous historic performances but also, as Farah Jasmine Griffin points out, because she belongs in a vocal tradition associated with African American women that has played a specific role in the cultural processes shaping American race relations. In this regard, Griffin argues compellingly how the singing presence of Marian Anderson, Mahalia Jackson, and other renowned African American women has often served two functions at national events: providing a unifying voice for America and serving as a symbol of African American diaspora. Tracing the ways in which this binary construct has formed in literature, imagery, and music over a century, Griffin shows its connectedness to original conceptualizations of the black woman's singing voice as the mystical "other" embodied in foreign vocal qualities, such as the perceived tonal "darkness" ascribed to marginalized minorities. She notes that concurrently, especially black writers have interpreted the audibility of the body in this sound aesthetic as a form of social critique stemming from the black bodies' and psyches' dismemberment in slavery. In the memories of this trauma, the singing voice has also been a source of comfort and healing. Furthermore,

Griffin refers to countless writings that describe how this soothing quality has served in lullabies sung by black women for both white and black children. More than that, through this vocal tradition generations of individuals and listeners in African American communities have been able to temporarily experience a sense of "home" and "freedom."[6]

These different cultural strands form a discursive frame through which what Griffin calls "the spectacle of the singing black woman" has become a medium for a collective engagement with ideas about national identity and belonging.[7] Following Griffin's work, I will explore how Franklin's singing presence at White and Eure's wedding conveyed the remarkable history of African Americans' strength and resilience in multiple musical styles and traditions, and thus constructed through a long and painful diasporic experience a musical landscape where America could be reimagined. After contextualizing Franklin's performance within pertinent musical and social histories, I will return to the relevance of my inquiry to the issue of diaspora.

THE WEDDING

White and Eure, business leaders embedded in the social elite of New York, organized their wedding as a black-tie affair for friends and family members who included powerful and wealthy political figures, media personalities, and entertainers.[8] Following private nuptials on the island of Maldives, the couple's wedding ceremony in New York provided an opportunity to exchange vows in front of their guests and, through press coverage, the public.[9] If not a typical white wedding spectacle featuring a bride in a formal white wedding gown, this "lavish gala" was, in many ways, an American wedding in which the grooms celebrated their love for one another as they expressed their love for the United States using several patriotic symbols within the event.[10] While the presumed assimilationist goals and heteronormative effects of same-sex marriage divide opinions within sexual minority communities, the devout allegiance to the United States declared by this gay wedding seemed to assert that legalization of same-sex marriage carries the social meaning of full citizenship.[11] The thematic decor was described by the press in detail: bowls on restaurant tables were filled with American flag lapel pins; outside of the building, red, white, and blue roaming spotlights trumpeted the occasion; and three carpets of the same colors, flanked by forty uniformed Naval ROTC members, led guests to the entrance. At the coat check, the New York City Gay Men's Chorus sang popular hits.[12] Opening the formal ceremonies, Ronan Tynan, one of the Irish Tenors, sang his signature tune "God Bless America." The eminent lawyer David Boies, who had secured the couple's marriage license, officiated the proceedings.[13]

According to White, the couple planned the nuptials based on the traditional wedding format but eliminated aspects that "two guys don't really care
about," namely, dresses, flowers, diamonds, and cakes.[14] Instead, they chose to
concentrate on "great music, great food, and of course great friends."[15] Different
from the typical fairy tale wedding with a "princess" bride evoking patriarchal
and heterosexual gender order, White and Eure's black-tie wedding was a "tremendous, very masculine party" in which the "Queen of Soul" represented
the legacy established by Bessie Smith, Dinah Washington, and other "Black
Queens" whose mastery of musical subversion has brought them iconic status
in LGBTQ communities.[16] That being so, as the wedding was held in New York
where the Stonewall Inn riots in June 1969 constituted a watershed moment for
the gay rights movement, it echoed the sounds of this historical site as the only
bar where gay men could dance together "unmolested" to the jukebox tunes that
among other popular songs at the time included the music of Aretha Franklin.[17]

The next day, a *New York Times* report of the wedding featured a large image
of Franklin backed with a full orchestra, singing in front of an excited audience
and the restaurant's decorative pool displaying the couple's initials, "B&B."[18] In
contrast to the dark suit-and-tie dress code followed by several guests, Franklin
exuded a regal aura in an olive color kaftan-style gown decorated with extensive
gold embroidery. Her classic long pearl necklace and earrings were similar to
those she had worn the previous week at the Martin Luther King Jr. Memorial
dedication. Furthermore, with elegantly styled short curly hair, Franklin represented an African American beauty ideal that stood apart from the mainstream constructions of long straight hair as a marker of feminine allure.[19] More
than a dazzling entertainer, Franklin projected cultural authority and dignified
self-awareness.

FRANKLIN'S PERFORMANCE

The historical light that Griffin sheds on black women's vocal traditions helps
view Franklin's performance at this same-sex wedding within the frame of national politics. On one hand, her symbolic presence could be read as a way to
produce an image of national belonging in which sexual orientation, like race,
was an embraced form of difference.[20] On the other hand, because Franklin's
music has been used to advance the political agendas of civil rights and feminist
movements, its oppositional meanings could be translated to the continued
fight for equality for all. It is on this slippery terrain that one can probe further
on the communicative possibilities of her performance.

An extraordinarily gifted vocalist, Aretha Franklin is a master of musical expression that features African American stylistic elements identified by the late

musicologist Samuel Floyd: calls, cries, hollers, hums, declamations, rhythmic alterations, blue notes, various timbral inflections, and call-and-response devices, among others.[21] It is well known that Franklin first learned to sing African American gospel music as a soloist in the choir of the church pastored by her famous father, Rev. C. L. Franklin, and on his Gospel Caravan tours. Nonetheless, because her father's friends included many star entertainers, Franklin grew up surrounded by the sounds of jazz, blues, and other styles that provided the cultural sources she used to craft a vocal style that later became emblematic of the idea "soul."[22] Mindful of this musical background, I will next examine a song that Franklin performed at the wedding of White and Eure.

ARETHA FRANKLIN PERFORMS HER SONG "THINK"

According to White, for this occasion Franklin chose songs about love and civil rights from her repertoire.[23] Reportedly, her set included "Respect," "I Say a Little Prayer," "I Will Always Love You" (Dolly Parton), and lesser-known selections from her latest album. She also sang her hit song "Think." A publicly available video recording provides a glimpse of the sonic space that she constructed through this song.[24]

Written by Franklin with her former husband, Ted White, "Think" is an up-tempo song that expresses one party's demands for consideration in a romantic relationship beset by problems. After its release on Atlantic Records in May 1968, the song gained popularity at various markets. While it climbed up the *Billboard* Top 100 chart, the predominantly African American readers of *Jet Magazine* voted "Think" as the second-best tune in the "Soul Brothers Top 20" behind James Brown's "I Got That Feelin'."[25] Propelled by its commercial success, the song also became a powerful protest song in the turmoil that followed the assassination of Martin Luther King Jr. in April 1968. More than a decade later, Franklin sang an updated version of "Think" in the *Blues Brothers* film (1980). Her role was that of Mrs. Murphy, the owner of a diner, who demands her husband to "think" before leaving her and their family business to tour with the Blues Brothers Band.[26]

Franklin's "Think" at White and Eure's wedding inspired enthusiastic audience participation through the song's multilayered approximation of the "soul" sound of the original version. In the late 1960s, Franklin's music commonly featured no-holds-barred vocals and mesmeric piano together with the interlocking rhythms created by a driving rhythm section, piercing horns, and female background singers' infectious call-and-response patterns. At this wedding, an orchestra with a brass section, background singers, a tambourine player, and a conga player re-created her familiar "soul" sound. Furthermore, Franklin and her mixed-gender background singers together with the dynamic instrumenta-tion, created the song's catchy feel that compelled the audience to experience the music through singing and dancing.

Franklin and her orchestra produce the basis for their musical interaction with the audience by both, infusing the original "Think" with spontaneous en-ergy and conveying its familiar core elements. Throughout the song, Franklin improvises on the melody within the overall texture established by features adopted from the original recording, its *Blues Brothers* remake, and some of her live performances from the late 1960s to the present. Based on a modified basic verse-chorus popular song structure, this performance, adapted from Franklin's performance in the *Blues Brothers* film, progresses through the following form: [intro][27] chorus-verse-chorus-bridge-verse-chorus-verse-chorus-bridge-vamp-conclusion. Markedly, "Think" features two bridges as the song's emotional focal points.

As the most infectious feature of "Think," the call-and-response patterns between Franklin and her background singers are foundational for the song's community-creating potential. Most observably the calls "Think!" and "Free-dom!" elicit audiences to sing along. Moreover, the singers' insistent vocals set the straight-talking tone between the song's protagonist and the imagined wrongdoer. Certainly, the song's capability to articulate the voice of the op-pressed was harnessed by many African Americans and women in the past who used it for advancing their movements for social justice.

Although Franklin masterfully leads the song, its collective spirit issues from the unfolding of the music's contrapuntal fabric. As much as the vocal lines speak to and with each other, the background singers pack a punch that engages anybody in the audience to join in the parts that are mainly one-liners sung on a single pitch. At the same time, the instrumentation pushes the song forward with infectious energy; entwined with the vocals, the brass section's piercing sounds highlight the message of the lyrics, like sonic exclamation points. More-over, the song's vigorous feel is created by the lead guitarist's funk strumming patterns featuring fretted and muted chord notes with incidental riffs, along with the bass groove, which when played double time through the last chord cycle produces a particularly electrifying effect evidenced by Franklin and the bass player himself, who noticeably "get into it." Clearly they do not perform this song simply to entertain guests; this music-making provides pleasure and a medium of self-expression for all.

Central to the song's appeal is Franklin's vocal approach, which draws on the depth of narrative devices supplied by African American musical idioms. Singing in the B♭ key of the original recording, Franklin works the blues-based melody around her middle range in a way that seemingly avoids some of the higher notes of the original. Nonetheless, she adroitly inverts the melodic progression by using alternative B♭ blues scale notes mostly within an octave. Her melody, here as in the original version, can be situated within a conceptual approach common to blues and its derivative traditions in which a blues scale is applied on top of a major (usually dominant seventh) chord structure to create a sense of tension against a bright major scale mood. To this end, she also colors the music with blue notes, including, for instance, those that delineate the opening line along a descending B♭ scale. Some of the other ways in which Franklin constructs the assertive tone of the melody include a bent note on "you *better* think" (emphasis added) in the first verse, an interjected "you!" before "think about it" at midsong, then a half-step modulation to the B-major key, and interjections like "yeah!" to add emphasis. At times, she underscores the dialogical mode of the couplets by using rhythmic inflections and coloring some of the speaking tones with nasal sounds. It is difficult to say for a fact that she is using rap aesthetic for creating a rhetorical effect of "straight talk," but she did use somewhat similar timbral colorings when confronting her on-screen *Blues Brothers* husband, which was released when rap was emerging as the new popular music.

After the verse-chorus parts in which Franklin utilizes frequent eye contact and choreographed gestures toward the wedding guests and press, she shifts into a noticeably more reflective mode of singing at the bridge. Facing the audience at center stage, right arm gradually rising, and eyes squinted, Franklin calls, "Freedom!" She sings "flat footed" in a position that gospel music audiences know very well. Mellonee Burnim explains that in the ritual context of gospel music, this position signals a personally and spatially transformative moment during which the singer communicates with both God and the congregation.[28] As Franklin takes her audience "to church," she fosters excitement and a sense of unity among the many who cheer and sing along.

At this pinnacle moment, Franklin engages her listeners in an intellectual discourse about the nature of freedom—for whom? What is it, and what could it be? The first time around, she sings, "Freedom!" straight on the pitch B♭4; then she intensifies the statement by repeating it on gradually ascending pitches D♭5 and E♭5, as in the original version, but leaves the singing of "Freedom!" on the final F5 for the background singers and the audience. Instead, she joins the brass section in a jazzy riff and scats vocables "te-de-tat-tadaa," which to some ears might signal that, as unspoken and undeclared, freedom is an open question. The second time around, she sings "Free-dom!" on B♭4, placing both syllables on two even beats, as in steady march rhythm, rather than the syncopated style she used in the first part. Next, she alters "Freedom!" with a melismatic figure from F5, adopted from the original version. In doing so she employs a solo technique known as "worrying the line" used in both the blues and gospel music genres, which is historically rooted in oral transmission of music also known as "Dr. Watts hymn singing" that congregational leaders used to teach hymn singing to slaves.[29] Lastly, she creates textual interpolations typical of gospel and soul styles, which through the last repeats of "Freedom!" are particularly thought-provoking. On the third repeat, she replaces "Freedom!" with "yea-yea" on another descending melisma pitched lower than the previous one, and eventually, she replaces the last "Freedom!" with a contemplative "well, well" on A♭4 and B♭4 while background singers sing the F5 note of the underlying chord. The fact that she did not sing the top notes as she did in the original song might cause some audience members to speculate that she was simply saving her voice. Others, tuned into her nonverbal stylings might hear her endless vocal creativity and sonic commentary on (un)freedom.[30]

When examined together, the first bridge that calls for "Freedom!" and the second bridge that states "You need me and I need you, without each other there's nothing either can do" present a paradox. Is this song about independence, or is it about being in a relationship? The answer seems to lie somewhere in between: freedom is a collective effort.

It is important to recognize that Franklin's swaying, dancing, and orchestrated gestures throughout the song reference an African-derived conceptual approach to music-making in which movement is intrinsic to the musical process.[31] Occasionally she points her index finger around the audience as a gesture adopted from the *Blues Brother* movie. Some in the crowd mimic this gesture. Her final and most provocative use of it comes at the song's finale. At the end of the cadence, Franklin seemingly breaks out of her narrative role to summon the audience. After singing "you just better stop and think about it!" she turns to face the audience and then points her right index finger toward them the same way she pointed at her "husband" in the *Blues Brothers* movie.

A BLUE(S) WEDDING

Using blues conventions, Franklin places "Think" within a musical tradition that is regarded as an in-group communication system capable of preserving and transmitting textually and musically codified African American cultural knowledge.[32] Historically, elements of this knowledge were encoded in work songs, field hollers, spirituals, and other sound materials in the slaves' environments; as such they provided the foundations of music that became known as the blues. Generations that followed creatively transformed Euro American musical sources with sounds that carried African heritage into a music form that articulated working-class African American lifeworlds.[33] When blues performance eventually became a popular form of entertainment, the glamorous stage presence of the genre's torchbearers, Bessie Smith and other Blues Queens were sights to behold. Dressed in sequined satin gowns, feathers, glittering gold jewelry, and pearls, they made a resounding statement about self-pride, success, and show business savvy.

Glamorous and magnetic on the stage of the Four Seasons Restaurant, Franklin projected every bit of her stylistic predecessors' royal glory as well as their use of the blues as a particularly productive site of female creativity and community building.[34] To this end, Bessie Smith's "Thinking Blues," apropos, presents a case in point. In an exploration of Smith's recording of the song, Susan McClary points out how Smith interacted with her band and used the lyrics together with blues conventions to fashion a multidimensional and empowered female subjectivity, and how she stressed the verb "to think" as a way to subvert commonly held beliefs about passive female suffering.[35] Over the course of the song, Smith's tone intensified from reflection to demanding through a set of blues stylings to which her instrumentalists responded in kind. Thus, using blues-based delivery, McClary argues, Smith conveyed a relatable subjective expression, which effectuated a temporary community through music. Particularly, the instrumentalists' audible commentary served to enforce this communal conceptualization of the sentiments expressed by the song.[36]

Like Smith's "Thinking Blues," Franklin's "Think" can be placed within a blues-based tradition of love songs that emerged after the 1920s with a markedly different thematic approach from the American popular music that was circulating in the dominant society. Lawrence Levine compellingly argues that because popular music written for white audiences was invested in maintaining several myths and fantasies of the dominant society, as a separate sphere, African American songs developed a distinct thematic tradition. Levine writes that "in the blues, love seldom resembled the ethereal, ideal relationship so often pictured in popular songs. Love was depicted as a fragile, often ambivalent human relationship between imperfect beings."[37] To this one can add that as such, the blues also provided a medium for presenting varied countercultural perspectives like those of Ma Rainey and Bessie Smith, who contested mainstream heteronormative gender politics through their own lived experiences and songs that expressed same-sex romantic relationships.[38]

JOURNEYS FROM THE CIVIL RIGHTS MOVEMENT TO THE SEXUAL MINORITY RIGHTS MOVEMENT

While Franklin uses the rhetorical devices provided by the subversive art form of the blues, her gospel music stylings gesture toward the crucial role that

African American churches played in the civil rights movement. Specifically, through her work as a gospel vocalist, Franklin carries on the family legacy of fighting for social justice that her father, C. L. Franklin, established as a civic-minded and trailblazing religious leader. Since the early 1950s, Rev. Franklin became known for his exceptional oratorical skills and rousing singing that nourished the souls, minds, and sense of self-worth of his predominantly African American audiences who gathered in New Bethel and listened to his radio ministry and highly popular recorded sermons.[39] A capstone achievement in Rev. Franklin's distinguished career was organizing the Great March to Freedom in Detroit on June 23, 1963. The march, reportedly attended by over a hundred thousand people, was at the time the largest demonstration against segregation. Historic pictures of the march show Rev. Franklin next to his friend and fellow Baptist minister Martin Luther King Jr. as they led the protestors down Woodward Avenue to Cobo Hall, where Rev. King delivered parts of the "I Have a Dream Speech," which he would deliver in full two months later at the March on Washington. When Aretha Franklin sang "Think" at White and Eure's wedding and applied the even beat march tempo on one iteration of "Freedom!," ears carefully tuned to Franklin's family history could decipher this aural code as a homage to her father and his pioneering contributions to the civil rights movement.[40]

Insofar as Franklin's singing presence at the wedding bridged the present-day movement to legalize same-sex marriage and the civil rights movement that was prominently advanced by religious leadership, one cannot overlook the long-standing uneasiness of the black church toward homosexuality and public debates surrounding the commensurability of LGBTQ rights and African American civil rights. Perhaps in an effort to avoid this point of tension, many press reports from the wedding made no mention of Franklin's church background. Readers' comments in online articles, however, speculated about Franklin's attitude toward marriage equality. Skeptics pointed out that previously she had not shown visible support for the gay community and made references to her "past religious views," while the most enthusiastic identified her as a "gay icon" who might have sung at the wedding gratis.[41]

To what degree Franklin's performance projected her personal views on homosexuality may never be known. Be that as it may, this performance reveals her music's enduring reverberations among different listener communities, among which LGBTQ audiences constitute a strong base of supporters. Aretha Franklin's gospel tunes (presumably recordings) had already been played in a high-profile same-sex wedding in which Marc Jacobs president Robert Duffy married Alex Cespedes in 2010.[42] In 2014, an *Advocate Magazine* article called the successful LGBTQ rights lawyer Roberta Kaplan "the Aretha Franklin of marriage arguments in Mississippi."[43]

Importantly, Franklin also has audiences among African American sexual minority communities whose appreciation for her music is shaped by their struggle to come to terms with black churches that oppose homosexuality. It needs to be mentioned that this religious position, according to Elijah Ward, derives not only from common scriptural interpretation but also from the struggle to construct a convincing form of masculinity over the course of social history in which black sexuality has been both feared and exploited within the dominant society.[44] In an article titled after Franklin's song "Spirit in the Dark," E. Patrick Johnson elucidates the complex relationship of the black church to sexuality and notes that Franklin's music offers a medium for alternative forms of identity construction because it derives from the many African American expressive forms that blur the sacred/secular division.[45] Johnson demonstrates how this musical feature has enabled gay men to create spiritual spaces—for instance, in night clubs where "black gay men transform the supposedly solely wholly sinful, utterly perverse club into a space where the ideas of American, homosexual, and Christian no longer compete."[46]

Broadly speaking, Franklin's music from the era of the civil rights movement evokes the path to democracy that formed when sexual minorities turned to African Americans' social justice strategies for achieving full citizenship. Michael J. Klarman notes that although the first gay rights organizations were established in the 1950s, many older gay members who feared harassment and prosecution by authorities chose to remain "in the closet" until the 1960s.[47] Nonetheless, when younger gay rights activists recognized the African American strong push for civil rights, they decided to pursue direct action. Many younger activists had participated in the African American civil rights movement, from which they adopted various tactics for their quest for equality, such as an attitude of assertiveness or the celebration of difference.[48] From a legal standpoint, as John Skrentny argues, the civil rights movement established the paradigm for policy makers' understandings of "minority status" and the need for remedial treatment from the government based on past injustice, equal rights, and protection.[49] Skrentny remarks that while some groups successfully analogized their struggles with the oppressions African Americans experienced, others, including sexual minorities, had more difficulties in convincing political authorities of the legitimacy and burden of their suffering.[50] Through sounds associated with African American heritage, Franklin's music at the wedding of White and Eure carried this sustained undertone of the civil rights movement. As such it also signaled the progress that sexual minorities had finally made toward legal recognition and the sense of freedom that they have envisioned for themselves.

DIASPORIC ENTANGLEMENTS

The ways in which Franklin's singing presence at this wedding represents the imagined and actual intersections between the experiences of American sexual minorities and African Americans is intricately connected to the diasporic conceptualization of the histories of both, partially intersecting groups. One way to understand the appeal of Franklin's music for these different audiences is to locate musical meaning-makings in communication processes that characterize African diasporic music. Accordingly, musical repetition, which is a key signifying device in African diasporic music, sheds light on how Franklin's performance might create a space in which various collectives hear themselves as they hear each other in the music. Veit Erlmann shows that the use of this device in African diasporic music does not simply serve as a marker of racial difference but also produces metacommunicative signifiers of sameness and difference that interconnect cultural communities. For that reason, according to Erlmann, the "shared experience of style" ensues from the primacy of communication, which provides for engagement in what he calls "endotrophic listening." [51] Although his discussion is concerned with musical constructions of black diasporic identity, Franklin's performance at this wedding reveals how music might articulate cultural divergences and convergences among interdiasporic listener communities.

It is from this standpoint that Franklin's music can be heard as an expression that speaks to, with, and for her African American and sexual minority audiences. While African Americans are considered a diasporic population not unlike the old Jewish, Armenian, and Greek peoples that can claim determinable "origins" and processes of dispersions, defining LGBTQ identities in diasporic terms brings attention to the sense of exile within a nation. [52] Accordingly, some queer theorists have chosen to conceptualize diaspora from the perspective of "home," and its geographical and imagined constructions as a site of belonging. [53] Simon Watley explains the sense of "internal exile" as follows:

> It is not so much external exile that we experience, but more often a form of internal exile, more strictly akin to legal and cultural quarantine, or to the state of "inner emigration" described in different circumstances by Hannah Arendt. [54] The actual Jewish diaspora may attract anti-Semitism because, as Zygmunt Bauman points out, Jews may be regarded as "foreigners inside" the nation, thus producing projective anxiety and hostility on the part of those who seek to define and defend

narrowly rigid boundaries of language, custom, culture, and so on. For diasporas always imply a blurring of such boundaries, a porousness of social categories, and a tragic awareness of involuntary migrations.[55]

Furthermore, Watley somewhat skeptically identifies same-sex marriage as a political strategy for sexual minorities homecoming by observing that "for while we are all national subjects, our sexuality intersects in often unpredictable ways with our contingent national identities. One powerful strand of lesbian and gay politics has long sought to remove such anomalies, by recourse to civil rights legislation."[56] In light of Watley's views, the patriotism that White and Eure's wedding conveyed can be seen as pride in a new sense of belonging in the United States, made possible by the legalization of same-sex marriage.

CONCLUSION

When a reporter asked music magnate and wedding guest Clive Davis, a friend the couple credits with arranging Franklin's performance, whether it was particularly appropriate for Aretha Franklin "to usher in the first same-sex marriage performed in the Four Seasons," he succinctly responded: "It's a wedding, isn't it?"[57] The reporter interpreted Davis's answer as an affirmation of David Boies's earlier view on this wedding as a precursor to many that would eventually normalize same-sex weddings. While Davis's ambiguous reply intently unsettles the heterosexual presumption of marriage, it prods the readers to "think" about the significance of Franklin's singing presence at White and Eure's nuptials. As the record executive behind the careers of many American musical legends, Davis is an influential behind-the-scenes architect of the American musical landscape who undoubtedly understands the transformative influence of music in the society.[58] In retrospect, one can speculate that Davis's reply captures a nod to Franklin's unparalleled ability to express love songs. Still, his theoretical question, "Isn't it?" complicates the matter, and with the help of Griffin's theoretical framework, it can be seen as a dualization of the interpretive possibilities that Franklin's singing represents between affirming the democratic vision projected by this wedding and the voicing of a demand for its realization.[59]

In conclusion, Franklin's performance at White and Eure's wedding constructs the seemingly innocent subject of love as a sonic space for experientially engaging with meanings of nation and belonging that, ultimately, are inherently connected to the idea of humanity. In locating liberating ideologies in discourses surrounding love, Elisabeth Povinelli argues that if the humanity of a person is not fully recognized, he or she is not free.[60] Povinelli makes a case for a duality of contemporary discursive spheres—individual freedom and social constraint—as constituents of the governance of love through which social orders and distribution of wealth and power are determined in a space of boundary-less circulation of liberal ideologies in what she calls "liberal diaspora."[61] It is between these two discourses that Franklin's performance offers a counter-experience of freedom. In her performance of "Think," one can locate this interface of individuality and social consciousness on many levels: romantic relationships, music itself, and the interlocking histories of African American diaspora and sexual minorities' rights movements.

The Supreme Court legalization of same-sex marriage in 2015 brings American society a step closer to ensuring that the nation provides the same rights and options for all its constituents. Yet the ongoing social turmoil about police brutality, urgently protested today by the Black Lives Matter movement, and the horrendous homophobic hate crime in the Pulse nightclub in Orlando demonstrate that work remains to be done to bring about a secure sense of national belonging to all. As Franklin's performance at this wedding demonstrates, the fight for the recognition of humanity is a process in which music can continue to play an instrumental role as a medium for envisioning freedom to live and to love.

NINA C. ÖHMAN is Teaching and Research Fellow at the Department of Music, University of Pennsylvania, and Visiting Lecturer in North American Studies at the University of Helsinki.

NOTES

1. Boncompagni, "Free to Say 'I Do,' but Where?"
2. De Silver, "How Many Same-Sex Marriages in the U.S.?"
3. Dunak, *As Long as We Both Shall Love*, 135.
4. Lipke, "Bill White and Bryan Eure's Big, Fat Gay Wedding"; Nir, "Wedding as Spectacle."
5. Griffin, "When Malindy Sings," 102–25.
6. Ibid, 110–11.
7. Ibid, 104.
8. Woletz, "Bill White and Bryan Eure"; Knutsen, "Prominent New Yorkers Celebrate Nuptials, Marriage Equality at the Four Seasons"; see also Nir, "Wedding as Spectacle."
9. Vilensky, "Behind the Scenes of a Wedding Party."
10. On "white weddings," see Ingraham, *White Weddings*.
11. See Stacey and Davenport, "Queer Families Quack Back," 359–63; Heaphy, Smart, and Einarsdottir, *Same Sex Marriages*; Dorf, "Same-Sex Marriage, Second-Class Citizenship, and Law's Social Meanings."

12. Nir, "Wedding as Spectacle."

13. White with Eure, "One Couple Looks Back."

14. Seim, "My Big Fab Gay Wedding"; White with Eure, "One Couple Looks Back." Apart from the actual wedding ceremony, the couple reportedly cut the cake at an after party that was held at Harry Cipriani at the Sherry-Netherland Hotel on Fifth Avenue. See *Page Six*, "Aretha Sings Overtime."

15. White and Eure, "One Couple Looks Back."

16. Ingraham, *White Weddings*, 141. Quoted in Glapka, *Reading Bridal Magazines from a Critical Discursive Perspective*, 63; Otnes and Pleck, *Cinderella Dreams*, 31; Johnson, "Spirit Is Willing and So Is the Flesh," 166; Seim, "My Big Fab Gay Wedding."

17. Schiavi, *Celluloid Activist*, 61–62.

18. Nir, "Wedding as Spectacle."

19. Banks, *Hair Matters*, 35–37.

20. Griffin, "When Malindy Sings," 103–4.

21. Floyd, *Power of Black*, 6. Here I would like to thank Guthrie P. Ramsey Jr., whose analysis demonstrates the ways in which Karen Clark Sheard uses these devices masterfully in her gospel music performance. Ramsey, "When the Master Is a Woman."

22. Franklin and Ritz, *From These Roots*, 39–43.

23. White with Eure, "One Couple Looks Back."

24. "Aretha Franklin Singing 'Think' at Bill & Bryan's Wedding," YouTube.

25. "Soul Brothers Top 20," *Jet Magazine*, June, 27, 1968, 65.

26. Further demonstrating how the direct tone of "Think" lends itself to advocacy, Franklin made a version for the campaign of Mother's Against Drunk Driving in the late 1980s.

27. Absent in *Blues Brothers*, there is a short intro in Franklin's other performances of "Think."

28. Burnim, "Performance of Black Gospel Music as Transformation," 54–55.

29. Dargan, *Lining Out the Word*.

30. I have adopted this expression from Povinelli, "What's Love Got to Do with It?," 179.

31. Wilson, "Association of Movement and Music as a Manifestation of a Black Conceptual Approach to Music-Making," 9–23.

32. Floyd, *Power of Black Music*, 78–79; Lawrence Levine, *Black Culture and Black Consciousness*, 278–79; Ramsey, *Race Music, Black Cultures from Bebop to Hip-Hop*, 44–75.

33. McClary, *Conventional Wisdom*, 334.

34. McClary, *Conventional Wisdom*; Harrison, *Black Pearls, Blues Queens of the 1920s*; Davis, *Blues Legacies and Black Feminism*.

35. McClary, *Conventional Wisdom*, 45–49

36. Ibid., 42–49.

37. Levine, *Black Culture and Black Consciousness*, 276–77.

38. Ibid. As Levine correctly points out, although the African American song has sometimes provided an outlet for protest, it needs to be viewed more broadly as a rich repository and commentary on different facets of life. Davis, *Blues Legacies and Black Feminism*.

39. Ibid.; Titon, "Reverend C. L. Franklin: Black American Preacher-Poet," 86–101; Salvatore, *Singing in a Strange Land.*

40. To this end, Matt Dobkin has noticed that Franklin makes musical references that possibly express devotion to her father. See Dobkin, *I Never Loved a Man the Way I Love You,* 9–10.

41. According Anthony Heilbut, Aretha Franklin's performance at the wedding constituted a tacit approval of homosexuality (Heilbut, *Fan Who Knew Too Much,* 155–56).

42. Foley, "Marc Jacobs President to Marry: Here Come the Grooms."

43. Baume, "Roberta Kaplan Is 'Aretha Franklin' of Marriage Arguments in Mississippi." Reportedly Franklin's "Respect" was played over a few days at an Ann Arbor courtyard since the Supreme Court issued its decision on same-sex marriage (Conlin and Bouchard, "Michigan Plaintiffs Say Suit Was a Way to Protect Their Family").

44. Ward, "Homophobia, Hypermasculinity and the US Black Church," 493–504.

45. Johnson, "Feeling the Spirit in the Dark," 399–416.

46. Ibid, 413.

47. Klarman, *From the Closet to the Altar.*

48. Ibid.

49. Skrentny, *Minority Rights Revolution.*

50. Ibid., 290.

51. Erlmann, "Communities of Style," 83–101.

52. See Atkins, *Gay Seattle.*

53. Fortier "Queer Diasporas," 190.

54. Arendt, "On Humanity in Dark Times," 22.

55. Watney, *Imagine Hope,* 123.

56. Ibid. Another strand of scholarship about queer diasporic identities concerns transnational movements of people (Manalansan, *Global Divas;* Patton and Sanchez-Eppler, *Queer Diasporas*).

57. Sledge, "David Boies Calls Progress on Prop 8 Lawsuit 'Frustratingly Slow.'"

58. See Davis with DeCurtis, *Soundtrack of My Life.*

59. Griffin, "When Malindy Sings," 104.

60. Povinelli, *Empire of Love,* 191.

61. Ibid; Povinelli, "What's Love Got to Do With It"; Povinelli, "Disturbing Sexuality," 565–76. Povinelli defines this term as "an origin-less or origin-obscuring process of transformation in circulation that retroactively constitutes its beginning and center" (Povinelli, *Empire of Love,* 18).

BIBLIOGRAPHY

"Aretha Franklin Singing 'Think' at Bill & Bryan's Wedding." YouTube. Accessed November 1, 2016. https://www.youtube.com/watch?v=IRjzPnRLdYw.

"Aretha Sings Overtime." Page Six, October 25, 2011. http://pagesix.com/2011/10/25/aretha-sings-overtime/.

Arendt, Hannah. *Men in Dark Times.* San Diego: Harcourt Brace Jovanovich, 1968.

Argyle, Michael. *The Psychology of Social Class*. London: Routlege, 1994.

Atkins, Gary. *Gay Seattle: Stories of Exile and Belonging*. Rev. ed. Seattle: University of Washington Press, 2013.

Banks, Ingrid. *Hair Matters: Beauty, Power, and Black Women's Consciousness*. New York: New York University Press, 2000.

Baume, Matt. "Roberta Kaplan Is 'Aretha Franklin' of Marriage Arguments in Mississippi." *Advocate*, November 13, 2014. Accessed November 1, 2016. http:// www.advocate.com/politics/marriage-equality/2014/11/13/roberta-kaplan-aretha -franklin-marriage-arguments-mississippi.

Boncompagni, Tatiana. "Free to Say 'I Do,' but Where?" *New York Times*, July 3, 2011, ST1.

Braber, Natalie. "Sociolinguistics." In *Exploring Language and Linguistics*, edited by Natalie Braber and Louise Cummings, 274–98. Cambridge: Cambridge University Press, 2015.

Burnim, Mellonee. "The Performance of Black Gospel Music as Transformation." In *Music and the Experience of God*, edited by David Power, Mary Collins, and Mellonee Burnim, 52–61. Edinburgh: T&T Clark LTD, 1989.

Carbado, Devon W., and Rachel F. Moran. "Race Law Cases in the American Story." In *Civil Rights in American Law, History, and Politics*, edited by Austin Sarat, 16–52. New York: Cambridge University Press, 2014.

Clifford, James. "Diasporas." *Cultural Anthropology* 9, no. 3 (1994): 302–38.

Clifford, James. *Routes: Travel and Translation in the Late Twentieth Century*. Cambridge: Harvard University Press, 1997.

Conlin, Jennifer, and Mikayla Bouchard. "Michigan Plaintiffs Say Suit Was a Way to Protect Their Family." *New York Times*, June 26, 2015. http://www.nytimes.com/live /supreme-court-rulings/michigan-plaintiffs-say-suit-was-a-way-to-protect-their -family/.

Dargan, William D. *Lining Out the Word: Dr. Watts Hymn Singing in the Music of Black Americans*. Berkley: University of California Press, 2006.

Davis, Angela Y. *Blues Legacies and Black Feminism: Gertrude "Ma" Rainey, Bessie Smith, and Billie Holiday*. New York: Vintage Books, 1999.

Davis, Clive, and Anthony DeCurtis. *The Soundtrack of My Life*. New York: Simon & Schuster, 2012.

de Silver, Drew. "How Many Same-Sex Marriages in the U.S.? At Least 71,165, Probably More." *Pew Research Center*, June 26, 2013. http://www.pewresearch.org/fact-tank /2013/06/26/how-many-same-sex-marriages-in-the-u-s-at-least-71165-probably-more/.

Dobkin, Matt. *I Never Loved a Man the Way I Love You: Aretha Franklin, Respect, and the Making of a Soul Music Masterpiece*. New York: St. Martin's Griffin, 2006.

Dorf, Michael C. "Same-Sex Marriage, Second-Class Citizenship, and Law's Social Meanings." Paper 443, *Cornell Law Faculty Publications*, 2011. Accessed November 1, 2016. http://scholarship.law.cornell.edu/cgi/viewcontent.cgi?article=1879 &context=facpub.

Dunak, Karen M. *As Long as We Both Shall Love: The White Wedding in Postwar America*. New York: New York University Press, 2013.

Erlmann, Veit. "Communities of Style: Musical Figures of Black Dasporic Identity." In *The African Diaspora: A Musical Perspective*, edited by Ingrid Monson, 83–101. New York: Routledge, 2003.

Floyd, Samuel A., Jr. *The Power of Black Music, Interpreting Its History from Africa to the United States*. New York: Oxford University Press, 1996.

Foley, Bridget. "Marc Jacobs President to Marry: Here Come the Grooms." *Women's Wear Daily*, April 14, 2010. http://wwd.com/fashion-news/fashion-scoops/marc-jacobs-president-to-marry-here-come-the-grooms-3038045/.

Fortier, Anne Marie. "Queer Diasporas." In *Handbook of Lesbian and Gay Studies*, edited by Diane Richardson and Steven Seidman, 183–98. New York: Sage Publishing, 2002.

Franklin, Aretha, and David Ritz. *From These Roots, Aretha Franklin*. New York: Villard Publishing, 1999.

Glapka, Ewa. *Reading Bridal Magazines from a Critical Discursive Perspective*. New York: Palgrave Macmillan, 2014.

Griffin, Farah Jasmine. "When Malindy Sings: A Meditation on Black Women's Vocality." In *Uptown Conversation, The New Jazz Studies*, edited by Robert G. O'Meally, Brent Hayes Edwards, and Farah Jasmine Griffin, 102–25. New York: Columbia University Press, 2004.

Harrison, Daphne Duval. *Black Pearls, Blues Queens of the 1920s*. 4th paperback printing. New Brunswick: Rutgers University Press, 2000.

Heaphy, Brian, Carol Smart, and Anna Einarsdottir. *Same Sex Marriages: New Generations, New Relationships*. London: Palgrame Macmillan, 2013.

Heilbut, Anthony. *The Fan Who Knew Too Much, Aretha Franklin, the Rise of the Soap Opera, Children of the Gospel Church, and Other Mediations*. New York: Alfred A. Knopf, 2012.

Ingraham, Chrys. *White Weddings: Romancing Heterosexuality in Popular Culture*. 2nd ed. New York: Routledge, 2008.

Johnson, E. Patrick. "Feeling the Spirit in the Dark: Expanding Notions of the Sacred in the African-American Gay Community." *Callaloo* 21, no. 2 (1998): 399–416.

Johnson, Leola A. "The Spirit Is Willing and So Is the Flesh: The Queen in Hip Hop Qulture." In *Noise and Spirit: The Religious and Spiritual Sensibilities of Rap Music*, edited by Anthony B. Pinn, 157–70. New York: New York University Press, 2003.

Klarman, Michael J. *From the Closet to the Altar: Courts, Backlash, and the Struggle for Same-Sex Marriage*. New York: Oxford University Press, 2013.

Knutsen, Elise. "Prominent New Yorkers Celebrate Nuptials, Marriage Equality at the Four Seasons." *Observer*, October 24, 2011. http://observer.com/2011/10/prominent-new-yorkers-celebrate-nuptuals-marriage-equality-at-the-four-seasons/.

Levine, Lawrence. *Black Culture and Black Consciousness, Afro-American Folk Thought from Slavery to Freedom*. 30th anniversary ed. New York: Oxford University press, 2007.

Lipke, David. "Bill White and Bryan Eure's Big, Fat Gay Wedding." *Women's Wear Daily*, October 24, 2011. http://wwd.com/eye/parties/a-big-fat-gay-wedding-5330922/.

Manalansan, Martin F., IV. *Global Divas: Filipino Gay Men in the Diaspora*. Durham: Duke University Press, 2003.

McClary, Susan. *Conventional Wisdom: The Content of Musical Form*. Berkeley: University of California Press, 2000.

Nir, Sarah Maslin. "The Wedding as Spectacle, Bearing a Message." *New York Times,* October 24, 2011, A17. Also available online October 23, 2011. http://www.nytimes .com/2011/10/24/nyregion/wedding-of-bill-white-and-bryan-eure-is-extravagant .html?_r=0.

Otnes, Cele C., and Elizabeth Pleck. *Cinderella Dreams: The Allure of the Lavish Wedding.* Berkeley: University of California Press, 2003.

Page Six. "Aretha Sings Overtime." October 25, 2011. https://pagesix.com/2011/10/25 /aretha-sings-overtime/.

Patton, Cindy, and Benigno Sanchez-Eppler, eds. *Queer Diasporas.* Durham: Duke University Press, 2000.

Povinelli, Elizabeth A. "Disturbing Sexuality." *South Atlantic Quarterly* 106, no. 3 (2007): 565–76

———. *The Empire of Love: Toward a Theory of Intimacy, Genealogy, and Carnality.* Durham: Duke University Press, 2006.

———. "What's Love Got to Do with It? The Race of Freedom and the Drag of Descent." *Social Analysis: The International Journal of Social and Cultural Practice* 49, no. 2 (2005): 173–81.

Ramsey, Guthrie P., Jr. "When the Master Is a Woman: Rhetoric and Device in Karen Clark Sheard's Will to Blend." *Musiqology,* June 20, 2011. http://musiqology.com /blog/2011/06/20/when-the-master-is-a-woman-rhetoric-and-device-in-karen-clark -sheards-will-to-blend/.

———. *Race Music, Black Cultures from Bebop to Hip-Hop.* Berkeley: University of California Press, 2004.

Salvatore, Nick. *Singing in a Strange Land: C. L. Franklin, the Black Church, and the Transformation of America.* New York: Little Brown and Company, 2005.

Schiavi, Michael. *Celluloid Activist: The Life and Times of Vito Russo.* Madison: University of Wisconsin Press, 2011.

Seim, Carrie. "My Big Fab Gay Wedding." *New York Post,* July 19, 2011. http://nypost.com /2011/07/19/my-big-fab-gay-wedding/.

Skrentny, John D. *The Minority Rights Revolution.* Cambridge: Belknap Press of Harvard University Press, 2002.

Sledge, Matt. "David Boies Calls Progress on Prop 8 Lawsuit 'Frustratingly Slow.'" *Huffington Post,* October 25, 2011. http://www.huffingtonpost.com/entry/bill-white -bryan-eure-wedding-david-boies-prop-8-lawsuit_n_1030869.

"Soul Brothers Top 20." *Jet Magazine,* June 27, 1968.

Southern, Eileen. *The Music of Black Americans: A History.* 3rd ed. New York: Norton, 1997.

Stacey, Judith, and Elizabeth Davenport. "Queer Families Quack Back." In *Handbook of Lesbian and Gay Studies,* edited by Diane Richardson and Steven Seidman, 359–63. London: Sage Publications, 2004.

Supreme Court of the United States. *Obergefell et al. v. Hodges, Director, Ohio Department of Health, et al.* 576 U.S. ____ (2015). Decided June 26, 2015 https://www .supremecourt.gov/opinions/14pdf/14-556_3204.pdf.

Titon, Jeff Todd. "Reverend C. L. Franklin: Black American Preacher-Poet." *Folklife Annual* (1987): 86–105.

Tölölyan, Khachig. "Rethinking Diaspora(s): Stateless Power in the Transnational Moments." *Diaspora: A Journal of Transnational Studies* 5, no. 1 (1996): 3–36.

Vilensky, Mike. "Behind the Scenes of a Wedding Party." *Wall Street Journal*, October 25, 2011. http://www.wsj.com/articles/SB10001424052970204777904576651503458440 940.

Ward, Elijah G. "Homophobia, Hypermasculinity and the US Black Church." *Culture, Health & Sexuality* 7, no. 5 (2005): 493–504.

Watney, Simon. *Imagine Hope*. Reprint, London: Routledge, 2000.

White, Bill, with Bryan Eure. "One Couple Looks Back at a Year of Marriage." *Huffington Post*, October 23, 2012. http://www.huffingtonpost.com/bill-white/one-couple -looks-back-at-_b_2007050.html.

Wilson, Olly. "The Association of Movement and Music as a Manifestation of a Black Conceptual Approach to Music-Making." In *More Than Dancing: Essays on Afro-American Music and Musicians*, edited by Irene V. Jackson, 9–24. Westport: Greenwood Press, 1985.

Woletz, Bob. "Bill White and Bryan Eure." *New York Times*, October 23, 2011. http://www .nytimes.com/2011/10/23/fashion/weddings/bill-white-bryan-eure-weddings.html? _r=0.

EIGHT

—ɯ—

TRYING TO GET THE GIG

"Ethnic" Weddings from the Musician's Perspective

MICHAEL ALLEMANA

PLAYING DIFFERENT KINDS OF GIGS is something of a Chicago tradition. I remember one week when on Saturday I played a Jewish wedding; the following Monday, background music in a private hangar at Midway Airport for an Irish American billionaire; and on Wednesday, a concert performing Romanian folkloric music. Chicago drumming legend Red Saunders said that in the 1930s, musicians learned whatever musical style kept work coming in, and for many of us, this continues to be the case.[1] Since the mid-1990s, I have been a professional jazz guitarist in Chicago. For many years, my main gig was performing weekly on the South Side of Chicago with the late jazz saxophonist Von Freeman, who used to tell me stories of gigs he played to support his family, such as with polka bands and "walking the bar" in South Side clubs.[2] To make ends meet, I have found myself doing what local musicians endearingly call "jobbing," working with different wedding bands or playing background music at corporate events.[3]

Many of my colleagues take jobbing gigs performing for "ethnic" weddings—Jewish, Italian, Irish—and mixed weddings for couples of different ethnic and religious backgrounds. They accept these gigs more often than not for the paycheck but occasionally for the musical challenges and satisfaction they provide. As both a practicing musician and an ethnomusicologist-in-training, I think about what happens at these events. What knowledge does one need to work an ethnic wedding, navigating through known or unknown traditions? How is the repertoire chosen? How do musicians know what to do and when to do it? How and why do they cultivate their relationship with the wedding families? What strategies do performers use to connect with the wedded couple, their families, and invited guests? And how does music make an event meaningful for both the wedding couple and musicians?

In the following pages, I explore these questions in conversation with four Chicago musicians, analyzing their experiences by navigating between my perspectives as a longtime musician and neophyte scholar. Musicians play an important role in articulations of cultural identities and family histories through planning with their clients, preparing the repertoire, and providing music. Working to construct the soundtrack of a marriage ceremony and celebration requires a dialogue between the diasporic sentiments of the wedding families on one hand and the musician's skills, knowledge, and experience on the other. This dialogical musical space hopefully leads to a cohesive and memorable event. Underlying this dialogue are musicians' allegiances to particular aesthetics and to the practicalities of moneymaking—because for us, as performers, it is, first and foremost, the work that we do.

THE MUSICIAN, THE CLIENT, ETHNIC IDENTITY, AND DIASPORA

I use the terms *musician, client, ethnic,* and *diaspora* in particular ways to elucidate the work my colleagues do. The term *musician* describes a professional performer who, while trained in and passionate about a specific musical area, takes a variety of gigs to earn a living. As freelancers, these performers aim to play their best, fully engaged in every musical moment. Another type of player, a "jobber," performs only jobbing gigs and pursues no other musical interests. Usually jobbers are not exceptionally skilled, have a jaded attitude, and are not highly regarded by other musicians.[4] Though sometimes wedding bands consist of both types, the colleagues I interviewed are of the former category.

Musicians refer to the people who hire them, whether a bride, a groom, the couple, the parents, or anyone else, as *clients*. It is important to remember that though these musicians care about the musical product they provide, this a work-for-hire relationship. Like any other business, they are selling their services. One of the first interactions with clients is to have them sign a contract and pay a 50 percent deposit. The client expects the service they pay for to be performed well, which means they get the music they want, when they want it. To be successful, musicians must make themselves versatile to please the client, which often leads to more gigs.

I don't recall my colleagues using the words *diaspora* or *diasporic,* instead referring to ethnic weddings. I use *ethnic* to describe social and cultural boundaries clients draw to identify themselves and their groups in relation to others. Clients and musicians consider these boundaries in different ways in relation to music. The client asks for songs associated with one or more cultural traditions; musicians focus on repertoire, social interactions, and the sequence of wedding events.

The dialogue between client and musician is important because it enables them to engage in cultural and musical discourse. Close communication with a wedding couple and their families leads to what Homi K. Bhabha terms "signification through which statements *of* culture or *on* culture differentiate and authorize"—in this case musical expressions.[5] When musicians perform at a wedding, they engage in a sonic construction of an authorized musical difference with which the client explicitly identifies. Working with many clients, I have come to understand that "the concept of identity is strategic and positional. Identities are never unified," but fragmented and fractured.[6] Accordingly, music contributes to strategies that the wedding party and musician employ to voice complex fragmented identities that are part of everyday living.

Scholars of diaspora debate whether to define the term as a specific phenomenon or as a fluid social process.[7] Based on conversations with my fellow musicians and being aware that they don't use this term, I use *diaspora* here as a way to describe the dialogic relationship between a socially constructed homeland and the actual lived experience that immigrants have in a host country.[8] As Clifford explains, "Diaspora cultures mediate separation and entanglement: living here and remembering another place."[9] Music sonically mediates between *here* and *there*.[10] As evident from the experiences of my colleagues, a diasporic consciousness of here and there in music, entwined with generational history, plays an important role in determining what musicians perform. For instance, a wedded couple and younger attendees may demonstrate affinity with American popular music, whereas the parents of the bride or groom want to honor elder family members by requesting a few Yiddish folksongs.

"Ethnic" and "diaspora" are relative terms with meanings that are continually in negotiation. I do not intend to weigh into this scholarly discourse but attempt to understand how musicians deal with this in practice. By combining their musical knowledge with the ability to communicate the ethnicity their clients expect, musicians work to make music-for-hire not look transactional, showing in music their understanding of the client's diasporic sentiments.

GETTING A GIG

The following ethnographic example of one wedding I played illustrates how notions of ethnicity might emerge within the phases of negotiation, preparation, and performance.

April 2011. I receive an email from Tomoko, a Japanese immigrant and yoga instructor. She writes that one of her yoga students, a colleague of mine, recommended me to perform at her upcoming wedding. Her fiancé is James, a writer and a third-generation Italian American from Chicago. Tomoko explains that they are looking for a jazz group for their wedding reception. I let her know I am available and discuss pricing. She responds that most of the 250 guests are older Italian Americans who love to dance and "love all the Italian jazz singers," such as Frank Sinatra, Tony Bennett, and Dean Martin. She asks for bossa novas composed by Antonio Carlos Jobim. We negotiate the type of ensemble and agree on my working jazz trio of guitar, Hammond B-3 organ, and drums.

With the band, hours of performance, and pricing set, we discuss specific songs for the reception. She emails me an iTunes link for a CD, The Music of Antonio Carlos Jobim "Ipanema," by the Japanese Brazilian vocalist Lisa Ono, a well-known bossa nova singer. Tomoko asks us to perform tunes from this collection during cocktails, singling out "Aguas de Março" as her favorite. Her fiancé's requests include the jazz standard "How Deep Is the Ocean," arranged by Nelson Riddle for Frank Sinatra, and the Italian American favorites "Mambo Italiano," "Sway," and "Volare." For the couple's first dance, she asks for Cole Porter's "Night and Day." Since we rarely play Italian popular songs and "Aguas de Março" has a complicated form, I make lead sheets for the band (which adds to my collection, a benefit of doing these types of gigs).[11] The preparations go smoothly, and we arrive ready to perform.

The reception takes place during the afternoon in the main dining room of the Union League of Chicago, a storied social club in downtown Chicago. The venue is a large banquet hall with intricate large vases in the corners, chandeliers hanging from high wood-covered ceilings, a long table with flowers for the wedding party, and tables set up in front of the wedding party for the guests. The stage faces the wedding party table, the guest tables, and a space for dancing. We start playing at 1:00 p.m. as guests arrive. During the first set, we perform mostly jazz standards and bossa novas. At 2:30 p.m., the band takes a break, and I announce on a microphone some performances by friends of Tomoko and James. The first is a classical rendition of George Gershwin's "A Foggy Day," delivered by a female soloist who teaches classical singing and a male pianist. Next the duo expands to a trio, adding a female singer from Japan who performs "Hana" by the Japanese composer Rentaro Taki. Finally, I announce the last selection, the "Terzetto String Trio in C Major" by Antonin Dvorak, performed by a female Japanese immigrant violist and two violinists, a female Chinese immigrant and her American-born sister, all members of the Chicago Symphony. After these performances, we return to play the first dance for Tomoko and James. She dances with her new father-in-law while James does the same with Tomoko's mother, her only family member who was able to make the trip from Japan. As we play the Italian American tunes, the dance floor fills up with the older guests. Tomoko, James, and his parents thank us for our performance. It's another successful wedding gig, another fun time playing with my boys, another paycheck, and even a recommendation to perform at the groom's sister's upcoming wedding.

The music at this wedding overall was a medley reflecting multiple identities and tastes, ultimately providing a sense of diversity, with everyone included and entertained. At the same time, I fulfilled a business transaction, pleasing the client by performing what was expected. Playing for this wedding required from me, as the bandleader, a rather diverse set of musical experiences and repertoires and the ability to write lead sheets and organize sets. Music at the wedding articulated a wide variety of diasporic affiliations—Italian, Italian American, and Japanese—and particular musical tastes: bossa novas, jazz, and classical chamber works. The diverse wedding soundscape mediated and tied together significant moments of family history "for which melodies are the milestone."[12]

SCENE AND MOTIVATIONS

It is important to understand the environment in which musicians work. They are part of a scene (such as jazz, jobbing, concert, corporate event) that is composed of a spatial sphere (where they work) and a social sphere (the musicians with whom they perform). Though experienced musicians sometimes play in new spaces, they are already familiar with many clubs and banquet halls. For example, if the space is a local jazz club, they will know the staff, the owner, the size of the stage, and the quality of the acoustics. The colleagues they perform with at jazz clubs are probably musicians they value as highly skilled and with whom they share some aesthetic allegiance. If the venue is the banquet hall of a downtown hotel, a musician who often plays for weddings will know where to park, what door to enter (e.g., the loading dock), and the quality of the band's food on the break (such as the "bandwich").[13] They anticipate that the musical experience may not be artistically fulfilling and that guests will talk through the performance. The musicians engaged at these gigs may or may not seek aesthetic allegiance.

To what extent do musicians seek artistic satisfaction or work for cash? In my experience, three factors define musicians' attitudes toward such gigs: whether they enjoy performing the music, whether they like to play with the band, and whether they are compensated fairly. On one hand, I might take a gig that pays well and, smiling, play music that I don't enjoy with musicians I don't like because I need the money. On the other hand, I might accept a gig that pays poorly over one offering an impressive amount because the first engagement matches my artistic goals. Musicians who perform for ethnic weddings work both ends of this dichotomy. Weddings generally pay $300 to $400 per musician, as opposed to $50 or less in a small jazz club. The music requested by clients often includes popular numbers that musicians do not enjoy playing. However, for some of my colleagues, certain musical traditions may be attractive and challenging or may provide a way to musically interact with guests in a way that a musician finds meaningful and enriching.

THE CATS

The four musicians interviewed for this chapter participate in various local scenes, including Latin jazz, salsa, klezmer, wedding bands, jazz, and world music. They all perform regularly and have years of ethnic wedding experience. I have worked with three of these musicians in contexts ranging from weddings and jazz clubs to supermarkets. My access to these musicians was quite easy—one phone call or email to set up a time to meet.

Jeff Stitely is an accomplished jazz drummer, tabla player, and performer of Ghanaian drumming traditions. He founded Stitely Entertainment, a successful company that since 2000 has been supplying music for weddings and corporate events throughout Chicagoland. Most of his bands' repertoire is American popular music; however, they also perform standard Jewish repertoire (Stitely is a convert to Judaism and performed for five years in the Maxwell Street Klezmer Band) and some other ethnic traditional music. He and I have known each other since the early 1990s when, as a young musician trying to break into the jazz scene, I would go to hear his jazz organ group at the Bop Shop, a club in Chicago's Wicker Park neighborhood that closed in the mid-1990s. During my years in Von Freeman's quartet, Stitely would fill in periodically. I have also worked a few gigs for his company.

I park my car in front of a small office building in Evanston on a quiet tree-lined street. Buzzed into the building, I walk to Stitely's office; he greets me warmly. Musical instruments, including a bouzouki and a tabla, decorate the room where he works. Eager to discuss his experiences, Stitely hands me a list of ethnic weddings his company has performed. We reminisce about the importance of Von Freeman to the Chicago jazz scene, our experiences playing in African American jazz clubs on the South Side, and jazz groups Stitely led in the early to mid-1990s. Once we start talking about his company, he describes animatedly and in detail a variety of wedding performances. Throughout the conversation, Stitely shows that he cares about the individuals that hire him and appreciates the musical experiences he gains.

Alex Koffman, a violinist, was born and raised in Belarus, growing up ethnically Jewish. He immigrated to the United States in 1990, settling in Chicago. He joined the Maxwell Street Klezmer Band that year and has been its musical director ever since. The ensemble, known for its Klezmer repertoire, works

Figure 8.1. Alex Koffman, violinist and leader of the Maxwell Street Klezmer Band. *Photo courtesy David B. Sutton.*

concerts and weddings. Musicians on the Chicago scene highly respect his musical knowledge and technical skill, many having performed in his band. We have not worked together, but we have socialized frequently.

Before interviewing Koffman, I meet him in a Northwestern University classroom where he delivers a lecture about the history and performance practices of Klezmer music for a music appreciation course. (We are both visiting Inna Naroditskaya's World Music Culture class.) Explaining the roots of Klezmer music, Koffman tells how one should listen to Klezmer and performs a short piece. I am impressed how his entire body becomes involved, moving gracefully with each musical phrase in a slight back-and-forth motion. He closes his eyes, his face expressive. Finishing playing, he discusses the history and intricacies of Klezmer in its homeland in East Europe, tells about old performers, explains the American revival of Klezmer, points out characteristic elements, and demonstrates them by playing.

I interview Koffman after his lecture in Naroditskaya's class. His love for Klezmer, music-making, and his audiences radiates throughout the entire conversation, enhanced by his bodily gestures. He speaks about the importance of connecting with his clients and audiences, illustrating how he does this musically by singing phrases and repeating them on violin. He often pauses, looks right at me, as if checking if I got his point. Suddenly in a louder voice he exclaims, "There is nothing like it!" The rises and falls in his vocal register illustrate to me the deep meaning he finds in his musical endeavors.

Nicolae Feraru, a Romanian Gypsy, is a virtuoso cimbalom player from Bucharest. During his youth in the 1960s, he learned cimbalom from his father. In the 1970s and 1980s, he toured with the Romanian National Folkloric Orchestra, working with important Romanian musicians such as panflutist Radu Simion and vocalist Gica Petrescu. He received political asylum in the United States in 1988 and settled in Chicago in 1994, taking a job at a dental equipment factory where he worked until 2008. During this time, on weekends he performed at restaurants and played concerts. For six years (2006–12), we played in the same local ensemble, Gypsy Rhythm Project, which, led by violinist Steve Gibons, performed Romanian music and American jazz. In 2013, Nicolae was awarded a National Endowment of the Arts National Heritage Fellowship.[14]

When I arrive for the interview at Feraru's Northwest Side apartment, he greets me in his usual jovial way, cracking jokes in his heavily accented English and offering me pastries his wife just baked. His living room is full of cimbaloms, some without legs leaning against the wall, just as I remembered from years back when we rehearsed here. He repairs and builds cimbaloms for himself and his son and sometimes sells them on eBay. As I set up my video camera in his dining room, he tells me that he is upset with my university (University of Chicago) because he hasn't been paid yet for a gig he did there three months ago. When Feraru is passionate or upset about something, he looks you directly in the eye, raises his right hand, points his finger, and repeats his point several times. We sit down at his dining room table and converse freely about his life and performing experiences.

As we wind down the interview, he asks me to follow him into his living room so he can show me a video taken the previous month at his son's wedding. In the video Feraru is sitting at his cimbalom during the reception and playing an up-tempo piece, his grandson on his lap, his fingers flying over the cimbalom strings at a speed that still leaves me in disbelief. He holds the boy's hands to the cimbalom mallets while he plays. He tells me his father taught him the same way. While talking, he gets up from the computer and walking from one cimbalom to the next—his living room is a kingdom of cimbaloms—on each one he plays fragments of the songs we just watched on the video. Then he plays "Manea," a fast hora we used to perform together. Whenever Feraru is involved in music-making, he bounces his head quickly and smiles, drawing/forcing the listener into his irresistible musical world filled with virtuosity and passion.

Victor Garcia is an accomplished jazz trumpet player, percussionist, and salsa singer and dancer. He is in his midthirties. Born in Chicago of Mexican immigrant parents, in his youth he played guitar and sang in his father's wedding trio, with his brother on bass. He refers to this as an important period of his musical development because he transcribed all the songs for the group. Garcia performs in Latin American wedding bands, including salsa and mariachi, and is one of the top-call jazz trumpeters in the city. He is an average-sized man with a strong build and good looks; when he plays, he commands the attention of his audiences. We have performed together in a variety of situations, including small jazz groups and big band concerts.

When I call Garcia, he answers while playing his congas and drumming for me some rhythms he just learned. He says he is feeling inspired by the gig he had the night before with Edwin Torres, a percussionist who toured with the late Cuban bassist Cachao. We talk about our families and recent gig stories, making each other laugh. One of Garcia's endearing characteristics is that he loves to kid around, and we continue joking for around fifteen minutes before getting to our discussion. During the interview, he keeps the tone relaxed, calling me "bro" and "dude" and making a few subtle dirty jokes. He speaks about his early musical training and his knowledge of the Latin music scene in Chicago with authority and detail. He has remarkable knowledge of the diverse repertoire and an even more impressive awareness of the social and musical changes that have taken place over the past three decades in the Latin American communities of Chicago.

These four musicians provide intimate insight into the work of musicians performing ethnic weddings. Next I discuss how they interact with clients, how they conceptualize and understand the music the bride and groom ask them to perform, and how clients and musicians construct and experience weddings. By examining social interaction, musical preparations, cultural and business negotiations, and performance from the musician's perspective, I hope to show how music mediates diaspora consciousness.

INTERACTIONS, NEGOTIATIONS, AND PREPARATIONS

These four musicians, coming from diverse backgrounds, take different routes to wedding employment. Sometimes their opportunities come through reputation, such as Koffman's association with the Maxwell Street Klezmer Band; ethnic affiliation, as with Garcia or Feraru; Google search status, as with Stitely's company; or simply word of mouth. The way clients find these musicians colors their first interaction. For example, Stitely told me that a client drawn to him via a Google search for "Chicago wedding bands" generally relies on Stitely's advice for selecting songs appropriate for the ceremony and celebration. Feraru is respected as a master of Romanian folk song, so the parents of a bride or groom express confidence in his supply of the exact music needed at each moment. Koffman sees the first encounter as a personal relationship: "When there is somebody calling us, it's like dating. I carefully have this first date: let's talk and see who you are. Let's see if we are the right choice for you. They say 'we like you, we like you' and things like that, but half of the family is very religious and orthodox. I say, guys, forget about it, I do not do it . . . that is what this first date is about."[15]

During these first meetings with the client, important decisions are made about how music will be used and what songs selected. To land the gig, the musician guides the potential clients through musical possibilities, perhaps agreeing with their requests and maybe suggesting traditional and popular music selections, all the while negotiating how to meet the desires of family members and friends. It is a delicate dance between the wedding couple, the parents, and the musician. Stitely explains: "I'm a salesman as well. I'm trying to get the gig. And there's these complex relationships going on. If you only deal with the bride and don't address the parents, you lose it because the parents have their own ideas of what they think. Or vice-versa. I've lost more weddings because I've only talked with the parents and I don't get access to the kids and the kids make their own decisions and I've never got the chance to get a relationship going. It's all about relationships."[16] A client who likes what the musician presents will sign the contract; the musician continues developing strong relationships with the people planning the wedding. Or the clients already know the band, so the musicians don't have to try selling their services.

Preparation is essential for weddings to be pulled off successfully. The musician must have years of training and experience as well as mastery of multiple repertoires to perform whatever songs a client requests. According to Koffman, many people know that music is a necessary part of a wedding, so they come to him just as they choose a caterer or floral designer. Often, clients have not thought through what it would take to perform the songs they enjoy, so Koffman conducts his interviews with them by posing questions. His Klezmer group performs mostly at Jewish weddings, and instead of beginning the conversation by proposing a standard playlist, he seeks to understand specifically what they want. Agreeing to perform musical pieces that the band is unable to provide would harm its reputation. In his preliminary questions, Koffman tries to find out how clients identify themselves to see if he can fulfill the wedding's expectations:

The questions that I would start asking are: there is a big difference between American Jewish, regular secular, somebody who is not religious, just normal professionals or whatever, a business man calling for their children's wedding.

Those people are a little different because they will always be interested in making sure that all guests will be entertained with all kinds of today's popular music. To a certain degree I have to make sure we can cover it. But most of the time, I notice if they call me on my Klezmer line, they already know they shouldn't ask for rap or something that goes too far. Then I try as much as possible to find out what their roots are, where they came from, if it's long generations of Americans here or maybe it's a second generation, and they still have somebody and their family elders that know this music and remember it and would really appreciate it.[17]

Koffman gets a sense of clients to see if he can cover the musical traditions, genres, and styles needed to please the wedding families and guests. At the same time, his reputation as a master of Klezmer makes him an authority.

Each musician's specialized experience and repertoire define how the musician and client interact. Stitely tends to get clients who want American popular music. Garcia explains that since he performs a large pan-Latin repertoire, he must be ready for a variety of requests. His band has a reputation as a top salsa group, but when he is being hired for a "jobbing thing," he sometimes has to transcribe songs for the event. Garcia explains: "Juan Luis Guerra: I had to transcribe a whole album of his before because it was a family that had Dominican members. Or Marc Anthony, I've had to transcribe a ton of Marc Anthony, La India. Lately they like bachata a lot; I transcribed one bachata at the beginning of that craze."[18] Garcia says, however, that there is a limit to what can be transcribed for one event.

A wedding band is not going to profess to play any song because in reality, you have to work to make that happen, whether someone has to write out the chart, and you are going to have to ask a singer to learn it. The same thing with me; if they are asking for a particular song, that's fine, and I'll go to my singer and tell him I need you to learn these three to five songs and that's reasonable. He knows a lot of the other stuff that we are doing. But I can't have somebody learn a night's worth of music.[19]

These types of engagement with the client—asking questions and getting a feel for the desired musical environment—help musicians prepare. Yet a musician's reputation also enables a client to skip this process. Feraru comments that when people call him, it's because he is known as a performer of a variety of Gypsy music. Clients tend to ask him how many musicians he would like to bring for the performance rather than request specific songs: "I say it depends on how much you pay. I can have five, six, seven, ten . . . not less than three. Sometimes I know when they talk with me, I know from what region they are because they have the accent. Moldavia is different, Oltenia is totally different. In Bucharest, we pretend we speak the very clear language, because it is the capital. But others speak the dialect. . . . There is a big difference from one city to another in Romania. You have hora, serba in Romania, but if you go to Oltenia, they have a different rhythm."[20]

The negotiations between client and musician may become rather complicated. At times, the musician must mediate negotiations between the bride and groom, which can involve differences in taste and ethnicity, or between the wedding couple and the parents, which often reflect generational differences. All four musicians said that no matter how intense these negotiations might be, the bandleader must solve them so that musicians can provide a fun and memorable wedding celebration. Stitely admits that at times there are great discrepancies between groom and bride—one likes the song selections and the other "absolutely cannot stand them, ready to run out of the room." It comes down to finding "that common ground where you play music both really appreciate and then hitting those gray areas where it is really important to only one."[21]

It's not unusual for parents to request music from their homeland and for the young people to ask for American dance music performed by a DJ. Stitely and Koffman said that parents honoring their mothers and fathers may wish for a polka or an old Yiddish tune. Koffman explains that these tunes can have a profound effect on older guests: "There are some tunes I know that they know, and right away I'd place them in and we would play them and you can see the older people sitting, they are sort of half asleep, then the songs starts and you can see their mouths moving to the Yiddish lyrics. They get up, [Koffman stands up, imitating an elderly person] and she or he starts dancing. It's wonderful!"[22] When Garcia's group performs, it may play salsa for the parents on the first set, but for the main portion of the evening, the band plays American dance tunes, what Garcia jokingly calls "booty music." For this to happen successfully, Garcia must develop relationships with both the parents and the wedding couple.

The musician must also think about uniting the couple with all the guests. Koffman compares this to the culinary arts: "I say, guys, this is what you like, but if we are going to play only this music the other people will just get tired. Is this what you want? And hopefully they are not stubborn and listen to me; I have a lot of experience in this situation. It's like being a good chef. We'll mix it up, so that people have a lot to listen to."[23] Negotiations become more complex when a bride and groom have different ethnic backgrounds. At the wedding of an Italian groom and a Jewish bride, Koffman played a hora and tarantella in the same song since both are based on similar rhythms. Similarly, at the wedding reception of a Mexican bride and Puerto Rican groom, Garcia performed with a mariachi group during dinner and then with his Latin jazz group for the dancing. Stitely had an American bride who requested a didgeridoo performance for the wedding ceremony as a surprise for her groom from Australia. She wanted to honor his homeland at the ceremony—he had requested only a song by the

Australian pop group Men at Work. Another time, Stitely worked a wedding of a Hindu bride and Muslim groom. The bride's parents refused to attend the wedding. Stitely chose to play mostly American dance music, which somehow diminished the tension. In all these situations, musicians develop strategies to resolve familial and diasporic complexities.

UNDERSTANDINGS OF MUSIC

In all of the interviews, my fellow musicians discussed the use of musical instruments.[24] For musicians, the instrument is an extension and expression of their personal musical voice. As Feraru explained, his first wife is the cimbalom, his actual wife comes second, "because you keep your cimbalom with you all the time, your wife stays in the house." For him, instruments embody authentic Gypsyness—the cimbalom, the panpipe, the *cobza*, the *tambal* drums, and all other instruments he chooses to play Romanian, Serbian, or Bulgarian Gypsy weddings.

For the client, an instrument can also represent ethnic identity. At Irish weddings that Stitely performs, couples often request bagpipes for the ceremony or the Shannon Rovers, a local pipe and drum band, for receptions. With salsa bands, adding a vocalist makes a difference in how guests participate. According to Garcia, "even if we play danceable Latin jazz music, nobody really dances to it. It's a listening music. They'll sit in their chairs and groove, but when there is a singer involved, people all of a sudden get inspired to dance."[25] Instrumentation can sonically color different parts of diasporic identity. Koffman explains that with standard Klezmer instruments, his group can play recent pop hits, providing a sonic/visual mix of living *here* and remembering *there*. He plays the pop melodies "straight down" on his violin, noting, "It will come out a little bit different, but we try to stick to the original."[26]

Depending on the community they serve, my colleagues employ different approaches. Stitely says that at Irish weddings, clients tend to express strongly their "Irishness," even if their family has been in the United States for many generations. This means he must have "Danny Boy" and "Wild Irish Rose" ready at some point in the celebration. When he works Italian weddings, he always performs "Volare" and "That's Amore." For Jewish weddings, the prelude music tends to be selections of popular and classical music, and the recessional, "Siman Tov U'mazel Tov." As Stitely explained, his Jewish clients sometimes like to "go out Jewish style." Stitely specializes in American popular music, and his repertoire encompasses everything "from Sinatra to Bruno Mars." Most of his clients who request songs with strong ethnic associations ask for dance sets of popular music. He explains: "I've done Persian weddings; other than playing their iPod on the breaks for their parents and grandparents, they want American dance music. They want to be seen as Americans with their friends is my sense."[27]

Musicians also categorize repertoire by country of origin. Feraru elaborates: "We play Russian, Hungarian, Romania, Slovak, all kinds of music, not just one type." He believes that the most influential Gypsy music is from Romania, and many of the songs played by musicians in Serbia and Hungary come from Romania, including "Ciocarlia" and "Hora Staccato," famously performed by Jascha Heifetz and Grigoraş Dinicu. Feraru believes that each country of origin has a specific musical character expressed in musical elements. When he refers to the different tempos, Romanian music is very fast, Hungarian is very slow, Serbian music is somewhat faster without much variation in style, and Bulgarian is the most difficult to play because of complex varied meters. But there are great differences within each of these traditions: "If I go somewhere in Romania I don't know exactly what style it is because from one city to another it is totally different. We have many: serba, hora, geampara . . ."[28] He thinks of the diverse musical landscape of his native Romania as superior to other Eastern European musics. Garcia likewise thinks about repertoires and individual musicians by country of origin. With a client from the Dominican Republic, he knows to have merengue songs ready. With one of Cuban origin, Garcia prepares material from the film *Buena Vista Social Club*. For a Puerto Rican, he must rehearse songs by Papo Lucca, Tito Rodríguez, Gilberto Santa Rosa, and Héctor Lavoe.

For Koffman, versatility in multiple genres and ethnic traditions makes his group a true Klezmer ensemble. He explains, "I am proud to say we are today's Klezmer because we need to go and be able to fit any party's needs, even if we have to play rock." He told me that if a client requests opera or has an elderly family member that used to play jazz, he has "classical music" and may invite a guest to join in a traditional jazz piece. For Koffman, Klezmer means the ensemble's flexibility and depth of musicianship.

PERFORMANCE CONNECTIONS

The ways musicians deliver music for weddings demonstrate how they contextualize their performances. For example, when playing at a jazz club, musicians have total control over their repertoire, aesthetic approaches, and sets, but when it comes to ethnic weddings, the client has a lot of leverage over what a band performs; the ensemble must play what clients request. This restricted context structures the meaning of performance for musicians.

There are certain moments in a wedding sequence when clients feel especially proud to celebrate their diasporic origins and they connect through music. The emotional temperature rises during the dance. Stitely's band may not have the repertoire to cover some traditional styles, so he raises the energy level by playing dance music with no downtime between songs. Koffman carefully observes how the bride, groom, and wedding party walk, using the speed of their walking as his tempo marker, changing the tempo as their walking rhythms slow down or speed up. Importantly, his musicians know he is going to do this and follow. Koffman explains: "For example, when there are children that go before the bride, I might be playing the same melody, but I'll switch and go to the upper register and play pizzicato so it sounds very cute and when you play that you always are sort of welcoming people's emotions. So I'm playing around all the time with this stuff."[29] Musicians are aware of the movements and dynamics on the wedding floor.

Feraru spoke often about authenticity in music. For him, the music can only be "real" or "authentic" if performed by a "true" practitioner. The Gypsy is a pure musician, according to Feraru: "Between Romania and Gypsy, you believe me, I think it's two nations, like America. Who has the ear for music? It's the black people and the Gypsy. If you take any Gypsy from the street, when he sings, he sings very good."[30] He makes a distinction between Gypsy and Romanian clients. According to Feraru, a Gypsy wants the best musicians; a non-Gypsy Romanian hires four musicians to fulfill a service. A Gypsy client lets the musicians assemble their ensembles and never bothers the musicians on the stage except to request something, which leads to a large tip for the musicians. The non-Gypsy Romanian orders the musician around. He explains: "Romanians dance a lot, and the Gypsy not too much. They like to hear the song and they respect a lot the musician. Do they come to the musician and say, 'Stop, I want this'? No, because they respect. But the Romanians, they can say stop and say they want geampara, hora, I want this, and you must follow what they want. But the Gypsy, no, they not do this."[31]

He also makes a distinction between Gypsy and Romanian in the meanings of songs: "In the Gypsy music, they talk about family, you are poor, you don't have the money, you have the family in the hospital, somebody died, the Gypsy music, the most of them they cry. But in the Romanian music, the music is about flowers, about love, totally different."[32] Feraru feels he can provide authentic Gypsy music of any origin because he has traveled over Eastern Europe and performed with Gypsy musicians from different regions: "I can play Hungarian because I went there. If you want to learn Brazilian music, you must go over there. So it is not fake. I give you an example with milk. If you want the original milk, you must go to the farm and get the real milk. Milk is like music. You never can play the original way unless you go over there to stay and study. You must go over there, find the guy that does not read music, and find what is over there."[33]

Feraru is quite theatrical. Koffman, seeking to connect with the celebrating crowd, also sees the wedding space as theatrical: "When you play in today's weddings, . . . think about it as a big theater going right now. . . . And the people who are around you and the musicians we are all characters of the theater. It's a theater! This is something that is very unique. It's life. And it should have that that human touch."[34] To give a "human touch" to his performance, Koffman strategically uses the dinner set to play "something refined from the good concert repertoire so that people will at least know that these are musicians of stature."[35] The "human touch" for him involves connecting the wedding couple with their parents and older Jewish guests. Making the point that he is not a deeply religious person, Koffman finds profound meaning in identifying with his audience musically.

Musicians have observed loss and change in their wedding work as well. Garcia explained that at the Latin American weddings he now performs, many children speak little or no Spanish. Often the bride and groom ask the band to play salsa for the first set so that they can appease their parents. The rest of the evening ends up being a DJ playing songs one would hear in a dance club. He comments: "The music is not really being passed forward as it once was. It is a finite community. . . . It's a Latino wedding but we have just a little piece of it and then the rest of the night is a DJ."[36] Another change Garcia has seen is that salsa bands are paid so little for weddings that he only plays a few weddings per year; standard American weddings and his jazz work pay significantly more.

For these musicians, the replacement of live musicians with DJs signifies musical change, a lower quality of music, and the changing tastes (for the worse) of the younger generation. Koffman discusses how DJs have altered the employment landscape. Having grown up with DJs, the young generations view digital musical media as more socially relevant than Klezmer. He's had to make adjustments to keep his ensemble working. Unable to compete with techno modern dance music (what he calls "studio tricks and effects"), Koffman now provides a DJ for band breaks and the main dancing set. Feraru sees DJs as a symbol of young people's tastes. The parents usually hire him since they are paying for everything; they hire a DJ for dancing to satisfy the bride, groom, and younger guests. He sees this change further reflected in the venues families use for weddings, which have moved from churches to hotel banquet halls.

CONCLUSION: GETTING MORE GIGS

Musicians performing ethnic weddings deal with multiple tasks. They bring their skill, experience, and ways of conceptualizing music into dialogue with the diasporic sentiments of their clients, connecting emotionally with the wedding couple, relations, and guests and creating a celebratory environment for all. Two stories, one told by Koffman and the other by Stitely, describe moments of excitement and emotional elation at events they worked. Koffman tells about how he once used music from *Fiddler on the Roof* to lead the bride into the wedding ceremony:

> There is one scene in *Fiddler on the Roof* . . . where the bride is escorted by the violinist and musicians. So it came to me that the bride was really open to all kinds of experiences. It was very important for her music. It is a little theater when people are walking down the aisle, . . . a special occasion. So she [one bride] was asking for some suggestions and something just came to me and I borrowed this from *Fiddler on the Roof*. I said, "What if I just lead you in?" She did not understand, so I am describing to her what I want to do. . . . I've never done this before but I kind of feel that this is right. She goes, "Oh my God, it feels so good. Let's do it." And when I was playing it, I put myself on the spot through such an intense range of emotions, that I was almost choking myself. I was fully involved, something was channeling through me. I was leading her and she was crying and I still feel goosebumps because it was so right. It was such a true connection, such true feelings, and people who were there no matter how busy they were with their cell phones or whatever they came from, at this moment they were all together for something. If you don't have it for real, if you don't have that emotional exchange for real, people will continue to do this. [Koffman pretends to look at a cell phone.] If it's for real, they will stop doing what they are doing. Everyone wants to feel, to be part of that incredible feeling. And I felt that. And from the ceremony we grabbed them so tight that anything we would play, they would go, "Oh my God!" I know it wasn't something super different. . . . We connected so deeply.[37]

Stitely shared the story of a mixed marriage where the groom was American and the bride from Lithuania. To resolve the division between American and Lithuanian guests, his band alternated sets with a Lithuanian band. Stitely recalls:

> We had a contract the American way: you sign a contract and it's for a certain amount of money, you play the gig, they pay you that money, they may or may not tip you. Then that band showed up, four people—accordion, keyboard, drums, and a singer. They played twice as loud as we did. I'm not kidding. As people danced, the singer would get out on the dance floor and sing to people. I don't speak the language so I don't know what was going on, but it was almost like a salsa band where a cat is blowing, improvising lyrics, it felt like that. Because he was going up to people and singing to them for long periods of time, it was almost like he was telling a story. And they were throwing money at him, tens, twenties, fifties, and after the end of their set a broom came out and swept up all the money and put it in a bucket. I know they made twice what we made. It was an insane amount of money that this band made.[38]

Stitely provides more insight into the way he thinks of music as a soundtrack for the events in people's lives:

> Two people are growing up listening to certain music in their home[s]; there is a soundtrack for high school dates and high school friends; there's a soundtrack to college, to the bars they partied at, to the fraternity or sorority, to the sports group, wherever they hung out in college, there was a soundtrack to that. Music is powerful! Music evokes memories. And so, what I try to do is to find the pieces of music that have a powerful emotional connection to them with certain periods of their life.... Whether it's ethnic or not, that's what I'm trying to do.[39]

The common thread in these musicians' stories is how music brings families, guests, and musicians together for a memorable and meaningful celebration of marriage. At the same time, they are for hire and must have the skill to perform something transactional and yet meaningful, personal. For a wedding couple and their families it is a one-time event. Musicians make their living by playing as many events as they can. Their task is to seek more and better-paid wedding gigs while making each into the single most important, emotionally fulfilling event in the life of the family. In their day-to-day experiences, working musicians attest to the power of music to evoke memories of *there* and provoke emotional connection to *here*, central to the diasporic experience.[40]

MICHAEL ALLEMANA is a PhD candidate in Ethnomusicology at the University of Chicago and a professional jazz guitarist.

NOTES

1. Saunders, *Red Saunders Oral History Interview*, tape 1, side 1.
2. A saxophonist walking on top of the bar at a club to impress the audience—a common African American practice in the 1940s. See Cottrell, *Saxophone*, 294.
3. Chicago musicians use the word *jobbing* to mean a type of gig that feels more like a job as opposed to gigs that are artistically fulfilling. On the East Coast, musicians use the term *club date*. See MacLeod, *Club Date Musicians*.
4. Also called *weekend warriors*, a derogatory term for not very accomplished musicians who play only on the weekends (i.e., they have day jobs).
5. Bhabha, *Location of Culture*, 34, emphasis in original.
6. Hall, "Introduction: Who Needs 'Identity'?" 3.
7. On defining diaspora, see Safran, "Diasporas in Modern Societies," 83–99; Tölölyan, "Rethinking Diaspora(s)," 3–36; Cohen, *Global Diasporas: An Introduction*. For those that theorize fluid processes, see Clifford, "Diasporas," 302–38; Gilroy, "Diaspora," 207–12; Hall, "Cultural Identity and Diaspora."
8. Braziel and Mannur, *Theorizing Diaspora: A Reader*, 5.

9. Clifford, "Diasporas," 311.

10. Ramnarine, "Musical Performance in the Diaspora: Introduction," 2.

11. Jazz musicians and bandleaders of wedding bands collect lead sheets, the notated melody and harmony of a song, to bring to gigs in case other musicians aren't familiar with a particular tune.

12. Slobin, "Music in Diaspora," 244.

13. A poor-quality sandwich served to the band on their set break while guests enjoy a full gourmet meal.

14. Feraru, "NEA National Heritage Fellowships: Nicolae Feraru."

15. Alex Koffman, interview with the author, November 4, 2015.

16. Jeff Stitely interview with the author, November 2, 2015.

17. Koffman interview.

18. Victor Garcia, nterview with the author, May 13, 2016.

19. Ibid.

20. Nicolae Feraru, interview with the author, May 4, 2016.

21. Stitely interview.

22. Ibid.

23. Koffman, interview..

24. See Kartomi, *On Concepts and Classifications of Musical Instruments.*

25. Garcia, interview.

26. Koffman, interview.

27. Stitely, interview.

28. Feraru, interview.

29. Koffman, interview.

30. Feraru, interview.

31. Ibid.

32. Ibid.

33. Ibid.

34. Koffman, interview.

35. Musicians perform as the guests dine.

36. Garcia, interview.

37. Koffman, interview.

38. Stitely, interview.

39. Ibid.

40. Slobin, "Music in Diaspora," 244.

BIBLIOGRAPHY

Bhabha, Homi K. *The Location of Culture.* London; New York: Routledge, 1994.

Braziel, Jana Evans, and Anita Mannur. *Theorizing Diaspora: A Reader.* Malden, MA: Blackwell Publishing, 2003.

Clifford, James. "Diasporas." *Cultural Anthropology* 9, no. 3 (1994): 302–38.

Cohen, Robin. *Global Diasporas: An Introduction.* Seattle: University of Washington Press, 1997.

Cottrell, Stephen. *The Saxophone*. New Haven: Yale University Press, 2013.

Feraru, Nicolae. "NEA National Heritage Fellowships: Nicolae Feraru." *National Endowment for the Arts*. Accessed October 24, 2016. https://www.arts.gov/honors /heritage/fellows/nicolae-feraru.

Gilroy, Paul. "Diaspora." *Paragraph* 17, no. 3 (1994): 207–12.

Goldschmitt, Kariann. "Doing the Bossa Nova." *Luso-Brazilian Review* 48, no. 1 (June 2011): 61–78.

Hall, Stuart. "Cultural Identity and Diaspora." *Framework* 36, no. 1 (1994): 161–74.

———. "Introduction: Who Needs 'Identity'?" In *Questions of Cultural Identity*, edited by Stuart Hall and Paul Du Gay, 1–17. London: Sage, 1996.

Kartomi, Margaret J. *On Concepts and Classifications of Musical Instruments*. Chicago: University of Chicago Press, 1990.

MacLeod, Bruce A. *Club Date Musicians: Playing the New York Party Circuit*. Urbana: University of Illinois Press, 1993.

Ramnarine, Tina K. "Musical Performance in the Diaspora: Introduction." *Ethnomusicology Forum* 16, no. 1 (2007): 1–17.

Safran, William. "Diasporas in Modern Societies: Myths of Homeland and Return." *Diaspora: A Journal of Transnational Studies* 1, no. 1 (1991): 83–99.

Saunders, Red. *Red Saunders Oral History Interview: Jazz Oral History Project of the National Endowment of the Arts*. Institute of Jazz Studies. Rutgers University, 1978.

Slobin, Mark. "Music in Diaspora: The View from Euro-America." *Diaspora: A Journal of Transnational Studies* 3, no. 3 (1994): 243–51.

Tölölyan, Khachig. "Rethinking Diaspora(s): Stateless Power in the Transnational Moment." *Diaspora: A Journal of Transnational Studies* 5, no. 1 (1996): 3–36.

NINE

—◆◆◆—

JEWISH WEDDING MUSIC IN
THE NEO-KLEZMER ERA

HANKUS NETSKY

MY VIEW OF THE JEWISH wedding has never been all that typical. My mother's family included five of Philadelphia's most experienced and sought-after Jewish wedding musicians. Marvin Katz, my mother's younger brother, played trumpet with a variety of "outside" groups,[1] and Harold Katz, my mother's older brother played piano with many bands, including Meyer Davis, the city's top society band. In that case, he performed as Harold Karr or Harold Rogers, since having an overtly Jewish name meant you might be denied admission at certain exclusive resorts. My grandfather Kol Katz was a bandleader who played the drums professionally for forty years. Sam Katz, his brother, played the trumpet, and Jerry Adler, another great uncle, played the clarinet. By the time I was a teenager, Uncle Jerry was widely considered the last of the old-time Jewish wedding musicians on the local scene.

As a child, attendance at a wedding or bar mitzvah naturally meant keeping track of which relatives were playing or, if none were, whose band was playing and who was playing each instrument in the band. I also made a mental note of the musical choices the bandleader made, knowing that, given the vocational trajectory of my mother's family, it was not unlikely that in a few years, I might very well evolve into one of those well-dressed gentlemen on the bandstand (albeit hopefully with no need for the seemingly obligatory hairpiece) and, with a little luck, I'd be the one up front calling the tunes.

Jewish weddings also had a more personal impact on my extended family, decidedly not in the direction of marital bliss. On several occasions, weddings held on Thanksgiving caused my uncle Marvin to show up late for Thanksgiving dinner at his own house. His lack of availability on weekends because of weddings and Bar Mitzvahs led to an early divorce and a reluctant end to his musical career in order for him to preserve his second marriage. On what seemed like a happier note (for me, anyway), my grandfather regularly farmed my grandmother out to our family for the entire weekend. I later realized that this arrangement probably wasn't my grandmother's first choice; she simply didn't want to be abandoned for two entire days and nights every week.

THE LAST GASP

Growing up in the 1950s and early 1960s, I was largely unaware that the weddings I attended in my early years were, more or less, contemporaneous with the last gasp of Philadelphia's flourishing ethnic Jewish music scene, a scene that had survived relatively unchallenged and unchanged since the late 1930s and that I assumed would survive forever. Had the older Jewish wedding musicians recruited me as an apprentice at an early age, something that would have delighted me to no end, I might have learned a unique and highly structured musical routine that demanded great versatility and also provided a congenial (if extremely quirky) social network.

As I have chronicled elsewhere in great detail,[2] Philadelphia's Jewish weddings evolved in fascinating ways along with other aspects of the American Jewish immigrant story. That story began in the late nineteenth century with Eastern European Jewish immigration to the United States, in the case of Philadelphia mostly from Ukraine, but also from Belarus, Moldova, Romania, Lithuania, and Polish Galicia. Early Jewish immigrant weddings were religious and chaotic, replete with musical repertoires still intact from particular ancestral towns and home-cooked food served by relatives to guests seated at long tables.[3] By the 1920s, Jewish caterers and florists had become well established, and a diverse musical repertoire had been cobbled into a unique and specific playlist that all of Philadelphia's Jewish wedding musicians and many non-Jewish ones who played with the Jewish musicians needed to know by heart. This story repeated itself all over the world in the various urban centers to which Jews migrated during the tumultuous late nineteenth and first half of the twentieth century.

Mostly because of the tension between second-generation Jewish brides and their immigrant parents, 1940s and 1950s American Jewish weddings tended to be a blend of American sophistication and old-country ethnicity, but by the 1960s, musicians had added a hint of ersatz Israeli identity to the mix. By then, traces of Eastern European Jewish ethnicity were quickly going out of style. Unlike the healthier path toward acculturation followed by Greek, Armenian, Italian, Irish, and Polish immigrants, the mainstream Jewish community received special assistance from Jewish educators who worked diligently to pass on the anti-ethnic and anti-Yiddish bias of the finally victorious Zionist movement.

Along with establishing a much-needed safe haven for oppressed Jews from around the world, Zionism, ironically enough, also strongly encouraged Jews everywhere to drop their "ghetto" customs, language, and music, especially after the Holocaust had taken its own brutal toll on them. The *bulgar* (a Romanian staple of immigrant weddings) became repackaged as the Israeli "hora," and other dances were soon characterized as corny and archaic reminders of roots that, by then, assimilated American Jews mostly laughed about; somehow, our real cultural roots were to be found (or, more accurately, constructed) somewhere in a far-off desert. Meanwhile, beginning as early as the late 1890s, Reform and Conservative Jewish religious leaders started championing the concept of Jewish identity as something bound up exclusively with the expression of religious ideas.[4] Their efforts in this regard only accelerated after World War II.

Jewish wedding musicians were, at best, caught in the middle of these bold experiments in cultural engineering. A wedding was, after all a "liminal" occasion, a time when, like on the Jewish High Holidays, the spirits of the ancestors came back to mingle with their offspring. But what if they hardly recognized those offspring? The musical career of Philadelphia Jewish bandleader Cal Shaw (born Carl Schwartz, active as a musician between the mid-1960s through the early 1990s and still active as a florist) represents a defiant and valiant effort to strike a balance between old and new at a time when the old was decidedly passé. It also serves well to stand in for what I might have encountered, had the Jewish wedding trade become my calling at an earlier age. Here Shaw describes his initiation into the "business": "I started out in 1966 or 1967 working for a bandleader [Dave Cantor, a musician from the Ukraine] who played for "New Americans," most of whom were Holocaust survivors. He was in the music business and in the flower business. He had a friend who was in the photography business who was also a "New American" ... at that time, a lot of the new immigrants [settled] in Vineland [New Jersey] and [when they had a wedding or party], they would sign up for flowers, music, and photography at the same time."[5]

His patrons were a generation behind many other Americans, and they were much prouder of their European roots: "The people I played for lived in Oxford Circle and South Philly [Philadelphia's most ethnically concentrated working-class Jewish communities]. Their families came over directly from Europe. They didn't have a lot of money. Some of them put their small row houses up for second mortgages just to make the daughter a wedding. My mother was in the flower business with me and she would always throw in extras because she felt sorry for the mother."[6] In the "New Americans" community, Jewish mothers still ruled the roost, even in the 1960s: "The mother picked the flowers, the mother picked the décor, the mother picked the caterer, the mother picked everything. All the bride and groom had to do was show up."[7]

The music at these weddings was also an echo of European days, and immigrant bandleaders trained their young protégés to follow their lead, even though their tastes hardly reflected contemporary American style trends: "I [came up] in the remnant of the typical Jewish wedding where you played a lot of *freylekhs* [lively circle dances]. In those days, very few people read music on the job. You'd call the tune, call the key, kick off the tempo and that was it. I have phrase for it: It was the end of the *geshmak* [flavorful] wedding, when you felt so at home, when the bartender would tell you his troubles. As for the food, it was either roast beef or chicken . . . it was easy."[8]

Shaw, who had started his career as a child entertainer on Steele Pier in Atlantic City, also made sure that the parties where he led the band were memorable. Inspired by the older musicians who taught him the trade, he went the extra mile to conjure up attractive images of the "Old Country":

> They would remember me for the rest of their lives because I didn't just play music. I would do a kazatsky [a Cossack dance from Ukraine that involved getting on the floor and kicking out your legs] in the middle of the dance floor. When I played a Bar Mitzvah, I had the Bar Mitzvah boy sit on my lap and kick out his legs. Then I'd have the father get on my lap and kick out his legs. I got everyone in the room into the circle when we did a freylekhs. If there were people trying to hide in the back of the room, I would go back there with the microphone and get them up to join the circle.[9]

Shaw managed to stay active playing his brand of Jewish music through the early 1990s. By then, total assimilation was in full bloom for third-generation Jewish families from more affluent neighborhoods, and a large number of bandleaders (including thirty-five from one agency alone) were available to provide what that crowd wanted: "If you lived in Lower Merion, if you lived in Gladwynne, if you lived in Center City in a high-rise, then you would hire a Bobby Roberts, Mark Davis, Jay Jerome, these bandleaders really set themselves apart. They provided continuous 'society' music and only a minimum of Jewish flavor."[10]

The country club–style party or the party with a DJ and eight dancers didn't impress Shaw in any way. He still longs for the days when the bandleader knew everyone in the room and everything about their families: "There are some [business] people, like the owner of the small grocery store on the corner, that are no longer in business. The small bandleader is no longer in business. What had been over two-hundred dates a year [became] seventy-five dates a year. You had to do a lot more rock 'n' roll by the 1990s. These days, the drummer barely even plays. A lot of the time, the band plays with a [prerecorded] track."[11]

MEANWHILE, OVER IN THE SOVIET UNION

Given my family's roots in Bessarabia (present-day Republic of Moldova, an area annexed to the Soviet Union in 1940 that has always played by its own rules) and southwestern Ukraine, it might also be worth taking a look at the Jewish weddings I might have played, had my family never immigrated to America—and had miraculously survived. Like many Jewish Americans, I grew up believing what I was taught in Hebrew School, that Jewish life in various parts of Central and Eastern Europe (including the Soviet Union) simply stopped after the Holocaust. To some extent, this was true, but we tended to hear only the official reports, not about what was actually going on underground or in more remote areas well outside the largest cities. Many years later, after meeting Jewish wedding musicians from Moldova after the breakup of the Soviet Union in 1990, I learned a very different story.

I met accordionist Edward Kagansky backstage after one of my concerts in Toronto. He and his family had left Kishenev for Cuba in the late 1980s, later settling in Burlington, Ontario, where he found work as a laborer and wedding musician. "I know all of the music you played tonight and a lot more," he told me after that concert. As it turns out, before leaving the Soviet Union, he had performed at Jewish weddings in Moldova since the late 1960s, having learned the Jewish repertoire from Yefim "Naches," an octogenarian *badkhn* (folk poet) and charismatic entertainer whose career dated back to prerevolutionary days.

Clarinetist German Goldenshteyn came from Molov, a nearby town. He learned to play clarinet in an orphanage during World War II and learned to play Jewish weddings from surviving Gypsies who retained the old Jewish repertoire. He relocated to Brooklyn in 1979, bringing with him a hand-notated volume containing over six hundred Jewish wedding tunes. By the early 1990s, he was teaching his repertoire to any of us who were interested at such festivals as KlezKanada and Klezkamp.[12]

For these men, a 1970s Jewish wedding celebration bore a profound similarity to weddings of much earlier times, performed on unamplified instruments to a rhythmic accompaniment provided on a *poyk*, a small marching tenor drum with an attached cymbal. Yes, the Jewish religious ceremony took place in a darkened apartment behind pulled shades, and for the first hour or so and at the celebration that followed, the musicians made sure that the repertoire was officially approved Soviet fare: songs the musicians knew from playing lots of non-Jewish weddings. But after the Communist Party officials left (and they knew that they shouldn't stay very long), the celebration could go on for many days, at least for as long as the guests still had tips for the musicians, the vodka flowed, and the spirit of Jewish irony was alive and well. "When you were hired for a wedding, the family didn't pay the band; the band gave the family a deposit for the opportunity the wedding created to earn money, lots of money. . . . No small weddings like here—three, four, five hundred people was a wedding."[13]

It would be impossible to even imagine twentieth-century American Jewish families allowing weddings like the ones German and Edward described: "When we played in some towns we'd arrive at two in the morning. We'd have a list of the wedding guests and their addresses and we'd go to their houses and play a lively tune under each of their windows. Eventually the head of the family would come down, usually in his underwear, since it was the middle of the night, and give us a tip—and then we'd move on to the next house. Since the *balabos* [head of the household] would usually be very sleepy, we often got very large tips this way."[14]

These very large wedding celebrations took place in large tents, and as each family came in, the musicians would play a different march for each family—and each family would tip the musicians. This routine continued throughout the party: "While people were getting seated, we'd play dance tunes, requests, and they'd pay us for each of these . . . and the tables were long. They'd stretch from Boston to Washington. We'd walk around and play a short piece for each group of guests. This is how we earned our sustenance. It would all go into one cashbox. Sometimes we'd use the bass case, and we'd fill it so much that we wouldn't be able to close it."[15]

As for the dancing, the guests would turn their suit coats inside out, making them look like Hassidic garb, and they would dance like Hassidim, only wilder. The musicians would play all of the "banned" music, along with plenty of older tunes from the days before World War I, and as klezmorim had always done, they'd mix them with local non-Jewish dances, including bulgars and Romanian horas, dances that American musicians still erroneously think of as Jewish. And like the American musicians I've chronicled elsewhere, Bessarabian klezmorim had their own special brand of pranks. Smaller pranks were called *Donkyebar* and larger ones were called *Tolstoybar*:

> When someone bothered you, made requests without paying, repeatedly requested the same song, we'd call that person a Dostoyevsky because, as you know, Dostoyevsky was the author of *Crime and Punishment*. People like this could ruin the whole wedding, so we had special ways of getting rid of them. We would prepare a special drink; we'd fill a glass half full with vodka and then cap it off with wine. The next time the fellow made a request, I'd ask his mother's name and, if he said "Rukhl," I'd say, "Let's drink to Rukhl."
>
> He'd drink from his glass, and within ten minutes he'd be asleep. I would drink from a normal glass of vodka and, in those days, I could drink many of those.

A similar technique could also be used for animal control. One time I was playing a wedding for about eight hundred people. As soon as we started with the mournful music, a dog started howling. I took some bread, soaked it in the vodka/wine mix and threw it to the dog. No one heard from him for the rest of the wedding.[16]

In 1970s small-town Bessarabia, very little had changed since the nineteenth century. Music at a party had to be acoustic and portable. If the wedding took place at the top of a steep mountain, Edward Kagansky recalls leaving his accordion at the foot of the peak and switching instead to a smaller brass instrument that he hardly played; as long as he could make some noise with it and keep the rhythm, everything was fine. One time, he decided to bring a boom box along to a wedding so that there might be continuous music when the band took a break, since that's what he'd heard bands in the United States were doing. To his chagrin, as soon as he turned it on, the father of the bride came over with a baseball bat and smashed it to pieces—so much for any pretensions of modernity in that part of the world.

AN ALTERNATIVE ROUTE

While Cal Shaw was keeping the Jewish ethnic flame burning in northeast Philly, and Edward Kagansky was climbing mountains and preparing special cocktails in Bessarabia, I was growing up in a very different musical scene in Philadelphia's West Mount Airy, still one of the most diverse and stable urban neighborhoods in the United States. My musical training took more of an "artistic" route: I took classical piano and oboe lessons and had a strong interest in jazz starting in seventh grade, when I was initiated into a quartet by three top-notch black musicians who were a year ahead of me in junior high and already sounding like professionals at age fourteen.

By the time I was sixteen, I was directing Central High's marching and jazz bands (gleefully taking up the slack for staff and budget cuts in Philly's school department), playing in three different jazz and blues bands, and preparing to enter a conservatory with a college music teaching career as my goal. I also performed regularly with big bands, gospel groups, folk groups, and ensembles that played traditional Greek and Caribbean repertoire. When the occasional bar mitzvah or wedding came along, I would take the gig and plow through it like the pro I soon hoped to be, but my family regularly warned me that the career and musical repertoire that went along with it simply didn't have a future.

Of course, there still was an ethnic Jewish music scene at the time, but it was entirely based on nostalgia. The brochures for the 1977 Jewish Welfare Board (the major New York–based Jewish music presenter) roster and the early 1970s roster of New York's Charles and Howard Rapp agency, New York's top Jewish booking agents, read like a Jewish "Who's Who" of the 1940s, a list that included the Barry Sisters, the Zim (Zemel) Brothers, Mimi Sloan, comedian Emil Cohen, and Italian Catholic Yiddish opera star Jeannetta LaBianca.

These acts didn't appeal to me, and since I was already playing Greek ethnic music, I believed there had to be something else out there. I was nineteen when my uncle Sam introduced me to the recordings of Naftule Brandwein and Dave Tarras, two virtuosic klezmorim. Somehow, these guys sounded nothing like the Jewish music on the radio or in commercial circulation at the time, and they totally caught my imagination. Here was a seemingly forgotten Jewish dance repertoire (very different from the 1960s Jewish wedding repertoire) performed with the kind of virtuosity and artistry that, given my reference point of local wedding bands, I couldn't even have imagined.

I joined the faculty at New England Conservatory in 1978, the second faculty member hired to teach in a relatively new multiethnic improvisation department. I was delighted that I had found a Jewish ethnic music repertoire that seemed worthy of passing on to my students, Jewish or not, and they were glad to take on its multiple challenges. My Klezmer Conservatory Band, a Jewish concert ensemble specializing in Jewish dance and Yiddish theater music, gave its premiere performance in February 1980, and the reception to our concert tours, radio broadcasts, folk and jazz festival performances, and recordings was way beyond anything I could have anticipated.

WHERE ETHNICITY MEETS POST-ETHNIC (AND POST-JEWISH!) ETHNICITY

In retrospect, I came to see that this completely unplanned resurgence of older ethnic Jewish music was, perhaps, in some ways part of a much larger trend in the Jewish community that was starting to bubble up beginning in the late 1960s. In his book *American Post-Judaism: Identity and Renewal in a Post-Ethnic Society*, Shaul Magid observes that postwar secularity brought Jewish ethnicity back to the forefront. According to Magid, in the 1970s, my generation reclaimed the ethnicity that had been hidden by the assimilation of our parents, but given our generation's tendency to be selective about choosing only the aspects of ethnicity that we felt like using and our other tendency to create new contexts for it (reclaiming Jewish wedding music as concert music, for example), a kind of postmodern "postethnicity" emerged. As Magid puts it, "Contemporary cosmopolitanism and postethnicity acknowledge that ethnicity plays a role in individual and communal identity, but identity and community are generally founded on voluntary and socially constructed affiliations."[17]

Magid saw the neo-klezmer movement as one of the newer Jewish constructs that took its place beside movements including Havurah Judaism and Jewish renewal. As he pointed out, Reform Judaism officially severed its tie to any trace of Jewish ethnicity as early as 1885, and he cited as further evidence the growing popularity and influence of the more recent Jewish renewal movement spearheaded by Rabbi Zalmen Schachter-Shlomi, a renegade Chabad Lubavitch emissary who also articulated the idea of creating the "non-ethnic Jew.

So, how does all of this apply to contemporary Jewish klezmer weddings? Sometimes it applies perfectly and, sometimes, not at all. Even back in the 1960s, when families might have been completely suppressing their ethnicity in their day-to-day lives, as soon as Aunt Zelda and her clan arrived at the party, all bets were off. And, these days, with so many couples choosing to bring traditional music and dance into their wedding parties, we might be reaching a new phase that deserves another look. It wasn't so easy to sever the Jewish religion from foods our grandparents loved and music our great-grandparents danced to after all, especially when a younger generation longed to connect to a history and culture that was deliberately exorcised from their education. In my experience, overt expressions of traditional Jewish ethnicity have actually been making a profound comeback in recent years, propelling such trends as artisanal gefilte fish, a proliferation of seltzer machines, and, in Boston, green bagels on St. Patrick's Day.

Anyhow, whatever it was we symbolized or represented in the 1980s, it didn't take long before the inevitable calls came in: "We're getting married next June. . . . Can you guys play at our wedding?" "Ah, weddings—I know about those!" I thought to myself. "Why not?"

We played our first "klezmer" wedding in the summer of 1981, and soon enough, I realized that we were responding to some sort of perceived need both within the Jewish community and outside it, where "Jewish" is still very much one of the most familiar forms of American ethnicity. The overwhelming acceptance of klezmer as "authentic" Jewish ethnic expression in non-Jewish circles (including huge crowds at European festivals in Germany and Poland and, when we perform with Itzhak Perlman, at quintessential American venues including Carnegie Hall, Radio City Music Hall, Tanglewood, Ravinia, and the Hollywood Bowl) is, after all, what really put the klezmer revival on the map. My band brought Yiddish songs of all sorts (fully intact—no medleys!) and virtuosic klezmer dance tunes to folk and jazz festivals, internationally broadcast radio shows such as *A Prairie Home Companion* (a show we performed on twelve times), multiple film scores, and (after joining forces with Perlman) three international PBS Great Performances specials. The cache that came from universal marketability as well as heightened publicity in the world of artistic expression inevitably gave klezmer revival bands a potentially huge advantage when we threw ourselves into the mix with other kinds of Jewish wedding bands.

Also, by the time we came along, very few conventional wedding bands were capable of making the shift to playing classic klezmer. Playing virtuosic music of any sort shows a serious commitment to technical and musical details that, for most commercial musicians, would have required too much time, especially in a business that was primarily focused on other musical styles. The most the society bands could do would be to hire one klezmer to give them a little bit of Jewish flavor, as they did with guitarists in the 1960s when rock 'n' roll came in.

Looking back at the clientele that sought my band out for their weddings over the years, various types emerged—couples who wanted to honor the culture of their grandparents (or, in one case, seventy family members who were killed in the Holocaust), couples who had seen us play in local jazz clubs and concert halls, couples who knew someone in the band, academics who saw us play at local Hillel fundraisers, and, the most reliable source of clients, couples who heard us play at other weddings. Film director Michal Goldman was inspired to make the classic klezmer revival documentary *A Jumpin' Night in the Garden of Eden* after hearing the band play at her sister's wedding and, in the movie, made sure to capture the band's performance at the wedding of her ninety-year-old uncle. I was recently in touch with the Yagers, a family who hired my band four times, to play at both of their daughters' bas mitzvahs as well as at both of their weddings. I was not surprised to learn that their faith in us was sealed when they first heard us play on a broadcast of *A Prairie Home Companion*:

> Our introduction to klezmer music on the radio by the Klezmer Conservatory Band not long before Alison's bat mitzvah in 1986 was really a reintroduction, as some of the melodies could be dredged up from our memories. Many of them were very familiar to our parents, all of whom had had exposure to Yiddish culture. The music resonated with our sense of our heritage and felt so much more authentic for a Jewish ceremony than contemporary secular music. Also, we were completely smitten by the exuberant, joyful, and danceable quality of the music. At all four events, our family and friends, many of whom were not familiar with klezmer music, were unanimously enthusiastic about the beautifully rendered melodies.[18]

I have no reason to be fishing for testimonies at this late stage in my career, but without casting any aspersions, it is safe to say that we were different than the groups that were out there playing weddings in our early years. By the 1980s, there were really two kinds of American Jewish wedding bands, the kind that played for the Orthodox crowd and the kind that played for pretty much every other kind of Jewish wedding. The Jewish component in the first kind of wedding consisted of a highly specialized repertoire, including Israeli dances, *bedeken* music (for a ceremony that takes place just before the *khupe* [wedding canopy] ceremony itself, when the groom lifts the bride's veil in order to verify her identity, as the biblical Jacob failed to do when he was tricked into marrying his first wife, Leah), contemporary Hebrew processionals, Hassidic rock hits, Yeshivah line dance tunes for the women, any of hundreds of possible specific (to each Hassidic dynasty) *Hashem* tunes (lively dance tunes with biblical- or prayer-based texts), a *ketsed m'rakdim* ("parade before the bride," where the attendees act out various pantomimes about what the bride can expect in the coming years), and music to follow the *sheva brukhes*, the seven blessings that follow the *birchas ha-mazon* (grace after meals). Since Philadelphia's Orthodox community was small, insular, and self-sufficient, it was the kind of wedding no musician in my family would have been familiar with at all, but as someone who left for Boston in his late teens and was affiliated for several years with the Orthodox community there, I was fairly familiar with it.

The Jewish component in the second type of wedding consisted exclusively of a hora set, generally including "Siman Tov U'mazel Tov" (A Good Sign and Good Luck), "Hava Nagilah" (Let Us Rejoice), and "Haveynu Sholom Aleykhem" (Let There Be Peace). Horas were followed by popular modern Israeli tunes and well-known Hassidic songs by Isachar Miron and Shlomo Carlebach such as "Rad Halaila" (A Circle Tonight), "V'haer Eyneyu" (Our Joyous Observance), and "Sisu Et Yerushalayim" (Come to Jerusalem). If the crowd was completely assimilated or if the bride or groom were marrying outside the faith, then Israeli pop and Hassidic repertoire was replaced with a jig, tarantella, polka, and, in Philadelphia, the obligatory Mummers' strut. At some point during the hora medley, it would be de rigueur to lift the bride, groom, and various members of their extended family up on chairs, a custom taken directly from the Orthodox ritual. If the band played any Yiddish repertoire at all, it would most likely be cobbled into a nostalgic medley consisting of "Belz, Mayn Shteytele Belz" (My Little Town of Belz), "Sheyn Vi Di Levone," (Beautiful as the Moon), and "Bay Mir Bistu Sheyn" (To Me, You're a Beauty).

Most people who wanted us to play at their wedding had something entirely different in mind, at the very least a "klezmer" dance set consisting of meticulously ornamented virtuosic dance tunes that they knew from our concerts, broadcasts, and recordings. Generally, they'd want at least two sets of that type of repertoire. As for the rest of the party, it could go in pretty much any direction and, indeed, did. I fondly recall Rastafarian/Jewish weddings at a Jewish hippie commune in Brighton, Massachusetts (replete with smoking marijuana as part of the ceremony), a Hindu/Jewish wedding with Ram Das (Richard Alpert) himself officiating, and lively parties under the spirited supervision of the Bostoner Rebbe, Rabbi Levi Horowitz, Shlita. We've shared the bandstand with Boston's top swing bands, Afro pop bands, and Afro-Cuban ensembles. At David Mamet's wedding, we switched off sets with premier Scottish fiddle virtuoso Johnny Cunningham (hired to honor the ethnicity of his bride, actress Rebecca Pigeon), and at Caroline Kennedy's wedding, we strolled to ready the crowd for the primary entertainment, a thirteen-piece ensemble fronted by singer/songwriter Carly Simon. At the wedding of Itzhak Perlman's daughter, Arielle, her dad joined forces with us in playing the main dance set, as many of the world's top virtuosi looked on.[19]

Many patrons seeking out neo-klezmorim to play at their parties are interested in the cultural cache and even "hipness" of the Jewish ethnic roots movement, a movement that defies ownership by any ideology. In its recontextualized form, klezmer provides a safe backdrop for intermarried couples who want their weddings to include elements of Jewish cultural identity outside of a religious context. In the LGBT community, klezmer and Yiddish has become a "queer" form of expression of Judaism itself. Neo-klezmorim have also had great success playing non-Jewish weddings. I recall playing one such wedding for patrons who had chanced upon us and our music on the street in Harvard Square and simply thought it would be more fun to hire us than to engage a slick commercially packaged ensemble that played "ordinary wedding music."

The revival of Jewish dance has gone hand in hand with the revival of klezmer music, and on many occasions, "dance motivators" have joined forces with us to show the modern crowd how to dance like their ancestors would have wanted them to. I am always delighted when patrons want to take the time to learn a *patsh tants* or Russian *sher* since it's the dancing that really takes the party to the next level. I know that, when a wedding party really gets going, it's a feeling that, for me, is unequaled in any other musical experience.

There have, of course, been plenty of occasions when my band has been hired to perform as just another Jewish wedding band. I remember feeling that way when we played our first wedding in Philadelphia. There, presiding over the party was Harry Davis, a legendary caterer from one of Philadelphia's oldest music and catering families. It seemed to me that he had been in the business seemingly since even before my grandfather's time. Luckily the couple wanted mostly Jewish music, and Harry seemed pleasantly surprised that someone from the Katz family could still run a credible Jewish affair.

FALLING SHORT IN STAMFORD

At other time we were, honestly, completely out of our league. At the request of their daughter, the Hornick family transported my entire band to Stamford, Connecticut, to play at a lavish six-hour Jewish wedding party in the Grand

Ballroom of the Marriott. The bride and groom were big fans who would have danced with their friends all night to Israeli dances, freylekhs, and bulgars, but that was not what their parents had in mind at all. In the course of the affair, I struggled to summon the spirit of every one of my relatives who had ever played a party, somehow coming up with a bossa nova set, a waltz set, several big-band swing sets, a polka set, a Broadway set, a Latin set, a Motown set, a Beatles set, and a bit of funk for after hours. Somehow we were still alive at the end, and Mr. Hornick did pay us, but I was painfully aware that my ragged klezmer crew would not have given Glen Miller, Lester Lanin, or Tito Puente a run for their money.

After that experience, we seriously went to work crafting a formula that would credibly fill the needs of many kinds of clients. Noticing that we were often sharing the stage with other bands that were brought in to provide swing, Latin, reggae, or soul, our manager and bassist, Jim Guttmann, decided to augment our typical wedding ensemble, adding one of Boston's top swing tenor saxophonists, Cambridge's most respected soul singer, and an excellent reggae, rock, and R & B guitarist. To this day, playing parties with this ensemble is one of my favorite endeavors.

CLUELESS IN BROOKLYN

Another memorable party produced a very different result. A female friend from a prominent secular Yiddish-speaking family asked me to put together a band consisting of specific Jewish musicians she knew from "klezmer revival" circles to play her Hassidic wedding at the Kamenetz Yeshivah in Borough Park, Brooklyn, in the heart of the Bobover community. It would include myself, Yiddish singer Michael Alpert, clarinetist Andy Statman, and whoever I thought might be appropriate to round out a six-piece group. I chose to bring in trumpeter Frank London and my band's bassist and drummer.

My band had already played quite a few Hassidic parties in the Boston area. Those were fairly easy, since we didn't have much competition and the Bostoner Rebbe and his sons were supportive, helpful, and actually fond of the klezmer repertoire. As in many places, Boston hadn't actually had a local Hassidic band since the death of the city's last European-born klezmer in the late 1970s, so the only alternative would be bringing a group in from hundreds of miles away.

I knew a lot of the typical repertoire because of attending Hassidic religious services, purchasing *Hassidic Israeli Club Date* (a wonderful anthology published by Tara Music, precisely for the purpose of getting non-Orthodox musicians through Orthodox Jewish weddings) and because I had learned the music recorded on *Hassidic Israeli-Survival Kit*, a homemade cassette that

New York musician Pete Sokolow shared with his colleagues, mostly so that they wouldn't embarrass him on the bandstand.

It's worth mentioning that, more than any other single musician, Pete Sokolow provided a valuable link between the world of the wedding musician and the klezmer revival crew. A precocious jazz saxophonist and stride pianist whom had mastered bebop at an early age, Sokolow entered the New York Jewish wedding scene in the 1950s, an era when the Epstein brothers and Dave Tarras were still quite active. By the time of the 1980s klezmer resurgence, he was a fixture in the Hassidic music trade that, in Brooklyn, had replaced the older scene built on freylekhs and bulgars. He approached the new "highbrow" klezmer world with the healthy skepticism of a true New York pro, but Klezmer Plus, the group he started with Henry Sapoznik, founder of the revival band Kapelye, partnered with various wonderful older local clarinetists to compete with the more mainstream commercial bands. Pete would have been the perfect choice for a gig at the Kamenetz Yeshivah. But he wasn't there, and between the six of us, I was pretty sure the only one who had even attended a Hassidic wedding was me. I suddenly remembered that the brother of the groom (also the caterer) had sent me a cassette with contemporary Hassidic songs I didn't know that sounded like *Saturday Night Fever* on steroids. What if that was the music they expected us to play?

Actually, things went pretty well at first. Hassidic weddings begin with two separate parties, and in this case, the band was assigned to the bride's side, the side that came from a strong secular Yiddish background. Our repertoire of Yiddish folk and theater songs and occasional Israeli dances was well received, and when the groom's party came to get us for the bedeken, it was clear that they wanted the usual repertoire. We were also well prepared for the processional, in this case a traditional Bobover wedding march, although when it came time to play it, my erstwhile colleagues on the clarinet and trumpet decided it might be fun to turn it into something more akin to a New Orleans funeral march. Luckily, somehow, no one else seemed to notice this. After the ceremony we gave the crowd a rousing "Od Yeshoma" (There Will be Rejoicing) for a recessional and a lively first dance set.

I must admit that we were a little taken aback when we were seated. It was the Hebrew month of Adar, and there is a lovely tradition that goes back hundreds of years in the Hassidic community of making that rather frigid time of the year a special month of *tzedakah*, doing kind acts and giving special support to those in need. In Borough Park, this meant that the community's beggars were invited to every wedding held during that month and were, of course, seated at a table with the other representatives of the lowest strata of Jewish society, the klezmorim. When the waiter came over with the large trough with the scraps from the other tables, we had no choice but to dig in, lest our even hungrier compatriots gobble everything up.

Soon enough, the adventure continued, and we were back on the bandstand in the midst of the most challenging and surreal situation I think I ever encountered in my career as a bandleader. A group of around twenty tall Hassidic men in furry white rabbit costumes suddenly entered the room and the brother of the groom started yelling at us: "Play the song for the rabbits! Play the song for the rabbits!" The leader of the Dancing Rabbits, a fixture for many years at Adar weddings in Borough Park and, as it turned out, a group that raised lots of money for the benefit of the poor in the community, handed me his business card and smiled. I, of course, reciprocated with a completely blank stare, but we had to do something. Conjuring up my best bandleader instincts, I called the most intense Hassidic song I knew, and somehow the ersatz rabbits put on their show despite our ignorance.

WEDDINGS ARE FOREVER

I never returned to the Kamenetz Yeshivah, but it wouldn't surprise me at all if Frank London and Andy Statman have been back there many times. For both of them, playing at Brooklyn's Hassidic weddings soon became a staple of their income, for Frank as a commercial musician always hungry for new repertoire and extra income and, for Andy, as a member of the local Hassidic community.

It's actually hard to find anyone in the neo-klezmer movement who doesn't include weddings as a basic staple of their work. In addition to her concert work, former Klezmatics member Alicia Svigals now runs a function business that employs over fifty musicians on any given weekend, and our manager and bassist Jim Guttmann sends our wedding bands all over the world. The simple fact is that rewarding as a concert music career may be, it is the wedding that created the need for couples to rejoice and dance, and without it, the klezmer tradition probably wouldn't exist.

When it's well played, traditional Jewish music provides something irreplaceable at Jewish weddings and the weddings themselves can be an incomparable source of inspiration for Jewish musicians. For Jewish families, it provides that ancestral connection that shows them who they truly are and where they come from. For anyone, it can provide a link to a proud ethnic tradition filled with party music designed to express ironic joy even in times of great hardship. For now, that tradition is here to stay and, with a little *mazel* (good luck), perhaps it always will be.

HANKUS NETSKY, a multi-instrumentalist, composer, and scholar is co-chair of Contemporary Improvisation at New England Conservatory. He is author of *Klezmer: Music and Community in Twentieth-Century Jewish Philadelphia.*

NOTES

1. Musicians in Philadelphia use the term *outside* to refer to work "outside" a regular musical contract, contrasting such work with an extended engagement for a theatrical pit orchestra or ballet company or similar. In other cities, various other terms are used for such work, including *casuals* (Los Angeles), *club date* (New York), and *general business* (Boston).

2. See Netsky, "Klezmer in Jewish Philadelphia, 1915–1970," 52–72; Netsky, "Klezmer: Music and Community in 20th Century Jewish Philadelphia"; Netsky, "Evolution of Philadelphia's Russian Sher Medley," 288–314; and Netsky, *Klezmer: Music and Community in Jewish Philadelphia.*

3. See Patten, "Amusements and Social Life: Philadelphia," 233–48.

4. For more on these ideological shifts, see essays by Theodore Herzl, David Phillipson, and Solomon Schechter in Reinharz and Mendes-Flohr, *Jew in the Modern World,* 533–38, 490–93.

5. Cal Shaw. Interview with the author, July 23, 2016.

6. Ibid.

7. Ibid.

8. Ibid.

9. Ibid.

10. Ibid.

11. Ibid.

12. KlezKanada and Klezkamp were the two best-known North American Yiddish music and dance festivals. Klezkamp was founded by author and musician Henry Sapoznik and ran from 1985 until 2014. KlezKanada, founded by Yiddish activists in Montreal, has run every summer since 1996.

13. German Goldenshteyn. Interview with the author, July 1999.

14. Ibid.

15. Ibid.

16. Edward Kagansky. Interview with the author, July 1999.

17. Magid, *American Post-Judaism,* 19.

18. Henry Yager, email communication with author, August 10, 2016.

19. As of the date of this publication, you can still watch this set on YouTube: "Perlman Wedding Klezmer Hora," https://www.youtube.com/watch?v=CMIEr4COomE.

BIBLIOGRAPHY

Netsky, Hankus. "The Evolution of Philadelphia's Russian Sher Medley." In *The Art of Being Jewish in Modern Times,* edited by Barbara Kirshenblatt Gimblett and Jonathan Karp, 288–314. Philadelphia: University of Pennsylvania Press, 2008.

———. "Klezmer in Jewish Philadelphia, 1915–1970." In *American Klezmer: Its Roots and Offshoots*, edited by Mark Slobin, 52–72. Berkeley: University of California Press, 2002.

———. *Klezmer: Music and Community in Jewish Philadelphia*. Philadelphia: Temple University Press, 2015.

———. "Klezmer: Music and Community in 20th Century Jewish Philadelphia." PhD diss., Wesleyan University, 2004.

Magid, Shaul. *American Post-Judaism: Identity and Renewal in a Postethnic Society*. Bloomington: Indiana University Press, 2013.

Patten, Charlotte Kimball. "Amusements and Social Life: Philadelphia." In *The Russian Jew in the United States*, edited by Charles S. Bernheimer, 233–48. Philadelphia: John Winston, 1905.

Reinharz, Jehuda, and Paul Mendes-Flohr. *The Jew in the Modern World*. London: Oxford University Press, 2010.

TEN

—ෲ—

SOUND UNIONS

The Work of Music Specialists in Chicago's
South Asian Wedding Scene

KALEY MASON AND AMEERA NIMJEE

We promote cultural awareness and exchange through entertainment and education.... Mandala Ensemble would love to bring South Asian performing arts to
you. Showcase Indian dance, music or Bollywood at your corporate event, private
function or home.... You know you want Mandala at your wedding!

—www.mandalaarts.org

WEDDING PERFORMERS ARE UNIQUELY EQUIPPED to acknowledge, manage, and bridge social variation in celebrations of affinal union. Hence most
weddings and commitment ceremonies involve professional and/or semiprofessional music specialists, a category of waged or gifted affective labor that may
include singers, instrumentalists, dancers, and DJs. In this chapter, we examine
wedding work from the point of view of each one of these music specialists in
Chicago's South Asian communities. Borrowing the concept of affective labor
from feminist sociology of work,[1] and following the spirit of Studs Terkel's anthology of oral histories of everyday workers in the United States,[2] we present a
series of portraits exploring the creative and socioeconomic conditions within
which ordinary artists supplement their living with ritual and entertainment
work at South Asian wedding events. In addition to taking a fresh look at the
culturally specific enskillment, entrepreneurship, and experience required to
be a successful performer at South Asian weddings, we consider how diasporic
contexts present a distinct set of challenges for music specialists charged with
the task of performing sound unions—what we understand to mean an embodied musical framework for braiding together homes with homelands, betrothed
individuals, their families, and wider ethnic and religious communities.

Chicago and its suburbs are home to one of the most diverse South Asian populations in North America. Several blocks along Devon Avenue boast the second-largest concentration of South Asian businesses and immigration services in the United States. Since the first Indian-owned business was established on Devon in 1973 (the Indian Sari Palace), South Asian presence has grown exponentially in the wake of changes in US immigration policy implemented in 1965.[3] With the lifting of restrictions on quotas based on national origins, families were able to immigrate to the United States as a unit, and highly educated workers were given priority if their skills and knowledge met the demands of the US labor economy.[4] Today, many of the early immigrant families have moved on to Chicago's suburbs, including Glenview, Rosemont, Schaumburg, Naperville, Lisle, Downers Grove, Lombard, Skokie, and Oak Brook, which remain hubs for continuing South Asian immigration. Consequently, these suburbs have become burgeoning centers for South Asian restaurants, grocery stores, clothing shops, and banquet halls. Many of these institutions provide or advertise services that specialize in weddings—from events planners, banquet hall managers, and caterers to photographers, florists, fashion sales representatives, jewelers, mehndi/henna artists, and music specialists.

The market for wedding services in Chicago's South Asian communities has expanded dramatically over the past decade, as evidenced by the establishment of the Asian Wedding and Lifestyle Expo held at a convention center in the suburb of Rosemont from 2007 to 2011. In addition to advertising live performances, the 2011 expo promised to be a one-stop event for essential wedding services including DJs; live bands; and *dhol*, *tabla*, and *sitar* players; as well as dancers and dance companies. These wedding expos continue to take place throughout the year, hosted by banquet halls, hotels, and other venues that are common spaces for hosting South Asian weddings.

WEDDING MUSIC AS AFFECTIVE LABOR

Music and dance studies answered the 2008 global recession with a "labor turn," a shift toward theorizing the performing arts as embodied practice engaged in the production of value as well as social life itself.[5] Representing growing concern for creative economies and livelihoods in the face of precarity, this line of inquiry grew out of renewed interest in the political economy of music in the early 2000s.[6] Meanwhile, over the same period questions of embodiment, emotion, intimacy, touch, and sentimentality figured prominently in the humanities and social sciences. It was a short conceptual leap to begin thinking about affect and labor in productive tension with one another as "affective labor." In 1999,

Michael Hardt described affective labor as the work of constituting communities and collective subjectivities.[7] For Hardt, this form of labor had become both
a lucrative commodity under late capitalism and a platform for subversion and
resistance to the exploitation of human life.[8] Before his call to take affective labor seriously, however, feminist sociologists of work were already writing about
the deeply unequal gendered dynamics of feminized labor—creative activity
described variously as "women's work" or kin and caring labor. Writing about
the labor of airline stewardesses in the early 1980s, Arlie Hochschild coined the
term emotional labor to refer to "the management of feeling to create a publicly
observable facial and bodily display."[9] In her view, as soon as emotional labor
could be sold for a wage, it acquired exchange value as distinct from the use
value that this same kind of emotion management had in other domains of
life, for example in childrearing and homemaking. Despite the possibilities
for braiding material and affective dimensions of musical experience together,
music scholars have only begun to explore how the idea of emotion work might
be heuristically applied to performing art worlds.[10] By bringing the experiences
of South Asian music specialists into conversation with discourses of "affective
labor," we aim to illuminate some aspects of the political economy of wedding
music and affect.

For instance, music specialists give tangible form to the diffuse circulation of affective energy at life cycle events. In this way they help reproduce
the social relations that sustain life. Performers at weddings and commitment
ceremonies play a vital role in ritualizing the transmission of feelings and emotions that foster the bonds required for reproduction. They help create wedding
affect-cultures, to borrow a term from Rosemary Hennessy's recent work on labor
activism in the industrial borderlands of northern Mexico. According to her, an
affect-culture "is the transmission of sensation and cognitive emotion through
cultural practices"[11] and include birthing, caregiving, teaching, and healing. To
this list of feminized, mostly unwaged labor, we add *wedding*, the act of joining
two individuals in union. Performers are invariably key contributors to the production of wedding affect-culture as conduits for making vague feelings material in the form of physiological intensities and social interactions. According to
Hennessy, "As intangible as a rainbow and as indispensable as a bridge from here
to there, affective capacities are essential to the making of a truly living time."[12]
Since music and dance intensify the embodied experience of these affective
capacities, there can be no sound wedding union, no "truly living time," without
the work of music specialists. We believe this is as true for diasporic Indian wedding scenes as it is for each wedding affect-culture featured in this volume. It is
to this musical work of nourishing and sustaining South Asian affect-cultures
of weddings that we now turn. Drawing on collaborative ethnography, media

sources, conversations with music specialists, Ameera Nimjee's background as a professional dancer, and our experience learning from each other in a graduate seminar that Kaley Mason led on affective labor at the University of Chicago, we examine the understated role of musical labor in the economic, aesthetic, ritual, and social life of weddings.

THE KARNATIC SINGER: BRANCHING
OUT IN SOUTH INDIA

Minu Pasupathi has been actively performing and teaching Karnatik classical music since she moved to the Midwest in 1998 from Chennai, South India. A graduate of the prestigious Madras Music Academy, she began teaching classical music lessons to South Asian heritage children shortly after settling in the suburb of Schaumburg where she founded her own music school. With over seventy students, Akshaya Music Academy has become one of the most successful South Indian classical music studios in the metropolitan area. Despite her dense teaching schedule, Minu continues to cultivate her art as a performer, singing regularly at local temples, including the Hindu Temple of Greater Chicago and the Sri Venkateswara Swami (Balaji) Temple in Aurora, as well as at public concerts throughout the Midwest. Versatile in her musical outlook and craft, she enjoys performing South Indian classical repertoire as well as devotional hymns, film songs, and fusion music.

Although we have known Minu since 2011, it was not until Kaley initiated a conversation about wedding work that we realized the extent to which she honed her skills as a singer while performing at marriage receptions in South India. And yet, as she immediately clarified in our interview, she has rarely performed for weddings in Chicago since those formative years in India. She explained: "In Chicago I've been to South Asian weddings, but I haven't performed. . . . They usually have instrumental; they don't have vocal performances, . . . because people of all languages can enjoy it much better . . . because it has no language when you don't have the words. . . . And also it would be like nice background music for the enjoyment. . . . But in India, it's like the total opposite. I've performed classical and I've performed light music for wedding receptions in India."[13]

Our conversation thus turned to her experience back home. After her formal training, Minu began accepting invitations to sing as a professional artist at local weddings. Her reputation grew through word of mouth. If her family knew the bride's family, they would treat the payment more like a gift (pay whatever you like), but when the family was unknown, they would negotiate for a fee proportionate to the degree of social distance from her family. There were no formal

Figure 10.1. Minu Pasupathi performs alongside a vocalist, mridangist, and violinist at a wedding in Rameswaram, 1995. *Courtesy of Minu Pasupathi.*

contracts and no wedding planners then. As a young unmarried woman, she would go to these gigs accompanied by her father and male melodic and rhythmic accompanists, usually a violinist and *mridangist*. The photograph, taken by her father in 1995 at a marriage hall in Rameswaram, shows a younger Minu singing into a microphone, confidently poised while seated wearing a vibrant pink sari with gold trim, her accompanists on either side of her on a raised platform.

Minu described how a typical wedding gig might unfold. Unlike the ensemble of double-reed *nagaswaram* and *tavil* players—the *mangala vadyam*—whose auspicious sound is considered obligatory throughout Hindu weddings,[14] singers would typically perform for three hours at pre- or postwedding receptions. Like most Indian musical events, concerts always begin with a devotional invocation (*sloka*) to Lord Ganesha and often end with an upbeat performance. The singer might give a light music concert with an emphasis on film songs or a full Karnatik classical music recital. Whatever the repertoire, there is often more flexibility when compared with other performance settings. She explained:

> MINU: We kind of prepare only a few songs. Our preparation lasts for only one hour. The other two hours plus are always requests from the audience, because they want this, and that [chuckles], so we should be well prepared for that. So it's always more of an impromptu session.

KALEY: So you have some pieces you planned to perform, but you leave a lot of space or opportunity to respond to the requests from the wedding guests.

Whereas in conventional public concerts, soloists perform a set program with some variation depending on the mood and spirit of the moment, at a wedding reception, guests and the families shape the direction and content at the concert and earlier in the days leading up to the reception. She spoke about the planning involved:

MINU: The first thing I would ask them is what kind of songs are they looking for particularly, because sometimes the bride and the groom might have some favorites. Or they might have some family favorites, so we ask for that. . . . If they are very particular about a few songs, we only go with their favorites. We don't even have our own. We just go with whatever they request.

KALEY: What kinds of songs do they request?

MINU: Usually they request a lot of songs that are very popular in the film industry, or in the Karnatik style, like by very famous artists like M. S. Subbulakshmi Amma. . . . They want that, just to attract the audience and keep the moment live [chuckles].

KALEY: Did you ever get any surprise requests?

MINU: Oh yeah, a lot. [Laughs]. Some people [laughter] . . . some people are really good music *rasikas* [knowledge listener, connoisseur], and they ask you for really nice songs, which motivates and inspires you to learn more, but some of them are like . . . no offence, but they ask us to like kind of combine a cinema song with Karnatik in the same *raga* [formulaic design of modal melodic improvisation in South Asian music]. . . . It has no connection with this. We'll be like: "Ah, okay, maybe next time, because these don't match at all. They're totally different, but thanks for asking."

KALEY: But when you do have knowledgeable rasikas, do they make requests for specific ragas?

MINU: Sometimes they ask for ragas, but mostly they ask for kritis [devotional art songs], the compositions. . . . Or they might ask for the composer. They might ask: "Do you know any Meera Bhai *bhajans* [hymns]? Do you know any Purandara Dasa kriti." . . . A lot of Kannada-speaking people would want Purandara Dasa. . . . And a lot of Hindi-speaking people would like Tukaram, or Kabirda's bhajans, or Meera Bhai's bhajans. Or Tamilians would ask for Papanasam Sivan kritis.

The ability to satisfy requests at wedding concerts is one way performers try to build their reputation for making connections with audiences while also facilitating bonds and bridges between guests who relate through music. Another way is to learn how to anticipate the tastes and emotional responses of mixed audiences in the absence of requests or knowledge of the wedding crowd. One of the most insightful exchanges in our conversation took place when Minu recalled learning how to engage listeners by attending receptions for the purpose of studying how guests responded to the creative choices of experienced singers: "There's a term in Tamil called *jana ranjagam*, which means appealing to all kinds of audiences. So that's my priority. I generally list out the songs. I used to go to concerts at different weddings. Not my performances but other people performing, and I kind of made notes, like which are the songs when the audience would tend to listen. Which of them would they tend to ignore. I kind of made two different tables, likes and dislikes. Most of my list consists of the likes, so that I'm always appealing to the audience."

Knowing which songs tend to be widely popular at weddings was only one strategy Minu developed as a young singer-entrepreneur. There were other ways she would make her performances jana ranjagam.

> It's good to perform some unique songs, and I love making up my own songs, for example with the names of the bride and groom. If I know the family close, then I try and take some important likes and dislikes about that family and incorporate that in the words to the famous tune, so that people are like "Wow, that's really amazing," and they really come and interact with you. . . . It's like more of a conversational concert I would say. I would tell the people: "Guess what, I'm going to sing a song now. Listen to it carefully because I'm going to ask you two questions." Whoever answers will win a CD of mine. So it's like they are attentive and they answer. Even little kids, they're very curious to get the gifts so they sit and listen to it and answer the questions. So if it's more interactive, people really love it.

In this discussion, she also emphasized the performer's role as host, going beyond providing background music to entertaining guests with games and playful banter at the couple's expense. At the same time, she revealed how singers can exploit their position on the dais to promote their musical service and art more broadly through the circulation of recordings. This enterprising practice can be traced to the decentralization of consumer-grade recording and playback technology in the 1980s,[15] first in analogue form as cassette culture and later in the 1990s through the proliferation of small studios with digital work stations. The potential to diversify ways of supplementing livelihoods, however, is contingent on creating the right mood for the performance, which can only be done if the listening audience is actively engaged in *musicking*, to borrow Christopher Small's gerund for capturing the spectrum of musical experience that animates performance events.[16] When asked what makes a successful wedding performance, Minu reached for the Tamil term *kalai kattudhal*, which she understood to mean the experience of being well-received after branching out in full swing, to hold the attention of not only audiences but also musicians. Skilled soloists, she explained, create programs that use a variety of different *talas* (rhythmic cycles) and ragas to make the performance more engaging for accompanists. As part of the wider creation of affect-culture at a wedding reception, the classical singer's goal of reaching out to be well received by attentive listeners, then, is a discursive way of saying that music materializes emotions and connections; it fuses social relationships while serving as an auspicious agent for sound marriage beginnings and ultimately the reproduction of human life.

Our conversation closed with a discussion of some of the changes in wedding musical practices Minu has noticed over the years on trips back to India. The same digital revolution that made producing and distributing music easier for live musicians has also replaced them, as more affordable karaoke retro shows increasingly supplant light music orchestras and classical ensembles in South India. Singing, though, is still considered indispensable, although professional singers are now faced with the challenge of using prerecorded tracks, which, Minu lamented, seriously limits the scope for innovation. In Chicago's South Asian wedding scene, however, singers are largely absent in part due to language barriers. Instrumental performers, dancers, and DJs, on the other hand, have become preferred affect-cultural builders of "multi-local belonging" at home in the diaspora.[17]

THE VEENA ARTIST: KEEPING THE
ENERGY OF THE UNION TOGETHER

Saraswathi Ranganathan is one of the finest Indian musicians to make a home in Chicago's South Asian diaspora. Like many Indian musicians who migrate to North America, she has cultivated a sense of multilocal belonging since arriving in the United States in 1999 from Mysore, South India. Although she is the bearer of a classical tradition of *veena* artistry inherited from her mother and grandmother, she also embraced a cosmopolitan musical outlook early in her musical career. Her latest double album captures her musical experience of multilocality well. Depicting a bucolic image of a swan by a river on the cover (the swan and river are symbols associated with the Hindu goddess Saraswathi), *The Magic of Veena* pays homage to the Karnatik classical music canon. The second album, *Refreshing Raga Blues*, consists of original compositions in an experimental vein, an aesthetic visually reinforced with a photograph on the cover featuring Saraswathi holding her veena in front of the Chicago skyline. A recording artist, concert performer, and teacher, Saraswathi also performs regularly at Hindu, Muslim, and Christian weddings for Chicago's South Asian communities.

Figure 10.2. Saraswathi Ranganathan performs at a Muslim wedding at the DoubleTree by Hilton Chicago, Oak Brook, May 2016. *Photo by Subramanyam Ranganathan.*

For Hindus, the long-necked plucked veena is considered not only a sacred instrument, but it is also deeply auspicious when played at key moments in the marriage ceremony. For Muslims, the veena is often an acceptable compromise if the wedding organizers are unable to find a North Indian Hindustani sitar player. For both communities, the instrument is soothing to the ears as a discrete form of Indian background music for receptions. In a conversation with Kaley, Saraswathi expressed mixed feelings about the wedding industry in the diaspora. When asked how she would describe the differences between playing for weddings in India and Chicago, she paused, then offered the following reflection:

SARASWATHI: In India . . . The way you receive someone is very important. How you receive them with a warm welcome. A musician, in a wedding, they're usually received . . . "Oh, please come in. Here is where you sit." They take your instrument from you and place it near the stage. Then they ask someone to get you some coffee. They'll get you water, something to eat. And then once you're done with the sound and everything, they'll say please come and have some snacks. They offer you some samosas. So it's almost like even if they do not know you, they treat a musician with great love. I mean, there are lots of people who don't really care. But by and large, on average . . . from my experience, they do all this and then during the concert, they ask you to play these types of songs. . . . There is always a crowd and everyone gets food no matter how late it is. Sometimes when you're done [with] a wedding it's almost midnight. But then after it's done, then again they take the musicians over to a place to eat. Sometimes they even get it from there and give you the plate to eat. They make you sit down and make you feel comfortable, "Please eat." They help you pack and when you're done they come to the car and say thank you. It's their extended family kind of treatment you get. It's beautiful. . . . Whereas here, it's completely impersonal. Not one wedding I've ever been to has ever asked me if I wanted any food. They won't even ask you if you want water. You just come in and set up. If there is no place to sit down, you just put your own comforter, arrange your own mics and amplifiers, and then, when you're done, you get paid, and you leave.[18]

KALEY: Would they pay you in cash?

SARASWATHI: Some of the Indians pay you in cash. When you go formally through an event planner, they pay you after the fact. They mail you a check.

KALEY: Like an institution.

SARASWATHI: Yeah, like that. Well, it's always good to receive payment the day of, because I have to pay the others.

Saraswathi's discussion of the stark contrast between welcoming wedding performers as honored guests and treating them like wage laborers resonates well with the increasing commercialization of intimate life, a global trend that feminist sociologists have been tracking for decades. The rise of the professional wedding planner as a key figure in a booming industry is emblematic of the new scale of excess and spectacle that has characterized the gradual shift toward viewing weddings as a consumer lifestyle choice among privileged classes, and even for families who are considerably less privileged. In an earlier part of the conversation, Saraswathi commented on the irony that the professional South Asian class is willing to invest unprecedented resources into wedding plans yet is unwilling to pay much at all for freelance musicians who nonetheless continue to be viewed as spiritually, culturally, and socially essential.

Despite some of the challenges and frustrations associated with wedding gigs in Chicago, Saraswathi also spoke about the careful steps she takes to ensure that she meets expectations, and more importantly, that her musical labor holds the energy of the wedding union together. Versatility is key, and so is trying to tell both sides of the story. Drawing on the example of interfaith weddings, she elaborates:

SARASWATHI: In interfaith weddings what I do . . . for example in a Hindu-Christian wedding I learn what's that . . . Canon in D . . . and other songs that they play.

KALEY: Sure, the standard Western wedding repertoire.

SARASWATHI: Yeah, I learn those, so I kind of try to present both sides of the story through my music, which is kind of cool. In the Muslim weddings I play a lot of Bollywood mix songs. So if you have to play at weddings, my observation is that you have to be very versatile, because it's all about the bride and groom and their day. You just try and understand, so I try to ask them beforehand about what they want, like some of their parents' songs. So that's how I plan the music I play at weddings.

In order to tell both sides of the story effectively, Saraswathi always tries to learn as much about the families and their communities as possible. This can be a challenge in the metropolitan big business of wedding planning. When families hire event planners, the task of finding the necessary services and professionals is often delegated to members of a larger team, which means performers often never meet the families or even learn their names ahead of the wedding event. At the very least, Saraswathi hopes someone can tell her the names and the religious communities involved, but planners are in some cases not legally permitted to reveal names, and they often don't know the religious identities. Sometimes, she manages to learn details from people who usher her into the hall or from name board displays, which help her decide if she needs repertoire for Telegu, Kannada, Muslim, or Christian guests.

When asked about the kind of requests that come her way, without hesitating she exclaimed, "Bollywood takes the cake every time!" But then she turned to a thoughtful reflection on music that should not be played at weddings.

SARASWATHI: For instance, somebody will come and ask you for "Narayana Ninna Namada Smaraneya." It's a beautiful song in Kannada. But it's about calling out to God when you're in great difficulty . . . like someone is really not happy. . . . You have to make sure that all your ragas that you play, all the songs that you play, they're all happy songs.

KALEY: So which ragas would you play and which ragas would you not play?

SARASWATHI: Something like Subha Pantuvarali I would not play in a wedding. It's more of a sad raga. Or something like Kalyani. I would play Kalyani. I would play Hamsadwani. I would play Mohanam. . . . Those ragas I would play. . . . Madhyamavati is supposed to be a *mangala karam*. *Mangala karam* means causing auspiciousness. So I would play Madhyamavati.

Despite the fact that many people are unaware of the emotional significance attached to specific musical gestures like ragas or song tunes, Saraswathi explained that she refuses to honor requests for music associated with sadness or separation. As an artist, she feels it is her responsibility to politely steer guests to other more spirited and joyful selections. For her, keeping the energy of the union together is the traditional duty of musicians. In her words, the music should serve "a higher positive spiritual vibration within the space and also for the couple."

THE DANCERS: CHOREOGRAPHING
AFFECT AT A WEDDING

For Ameera, attending South Asian weddings in the diaspora has always meant watching, participating in, and even "gifting" dance. Friends and family members prepare choreographed dances, and later participate in spontaneous folk and popular dancing at the several events that make up a wedding. Pranita Jain is a *bharatanatyam* dancer and Artistic Director of Chicago-based Mandala Arts—the institution to which we refer in the opening epigraph of this chapter. Ameera has worked with Pranita for five years, collaborating to produce staged shows and other performances, including those at South Asian weddings. Pranita stated in an interview with Ameera that the presence of dance at diasporic weddings is the result of both tradition and evolution.[19] She elaborated:

> PRANITA: Dance and music have been part of the Hindu wedding rituals since the beginning. It's not just Hindu tradition; music has always been part of a [South Asian] wedding. But to give music a more visual form, dance comes in.... Growing up in India, and I come from a Rajasthani background, at that time the women would take out the *dholki* (drum) and play, and back then they would dance the traditional folk dance. Just the family members would get up and do it. I grew up in a conservative Rajasthani family, where women would dance and men would not participate, in this middle-class mentality. Only men danced in the *baaraat*. Now everyone dances in the baaraat and *sangeet*.[20] And then the tradition transformed from the courtyard where everyone would get together and dance to setting up a stage. So now it's a show, where the family members perform, and now the bride and groom dance too. And now it's about the performance of the bride and groom, and family members get less of a chance, especially if they don't or can't dance. So if they don't, they call professionals [to dance].
> AMEERA: So it's not necessarily about the family but that you have to have dance at the wedding, and we don't care how it happens.
> PRANITA: Yes. And it goes from hiring the local dance company to hiring internationally touring artists to perform. I toured the Rajasthani Manganiyars from India, and I got lots of calls to ask if they would perform at this and that wedding.

Pranita emphasized later that though wedding performances are now staged, there is a difference between wedding work and stage production within the framework of how a dance company organizes its performance output.

PRANITA: Whether we do private client events such as weddings, it is the earned revenue stream that helps the rest of the not-for-profit activities [of Mandala] breathe. They're lucrative. They're no stress. Instead of stage production, you simply go and do it. The stress is dealing with the client before the wedding. It's a very emotional moment for the family. And we want to be mindful that we uphold their joy in the celebration. A stage production is about the [dance] company. The family gigs such as a wedding is about the emotions of the family and their emotional state. A lot of our job is to keep it participatory, to make them feel that it's their choice of music and how they want the dancers to appear. So we are there to enhance their personal experience.

AMEERA: So is this an understanding in accepting a contract?

PRANITA: We do have a very clear agreement that we sign. We've had issues where they did not want to pay after the wedding. So now I'm very clear with the dancers [to] make sure the check is with you before you start performing.

Pranita described that Mandala dancers have been required to perform choreographed pieces and, later in the evening, encourage others to participate in more informal dancing. She stated that this happens across South Asian subcultures and religious backgrounds. In her experience, Hindu weddings have always featured dance. In the diasporic case, Muslim and Christian weddings also feature dance, as a cultural marker for their South Asian-ness. From Pranita's perspective, while family members and friends can do some of this affective work through dance, Muslim and Christian families hire dancers to perform, teach, and choreograph, ensuring that dance is present at a wedding.

Shereen Ladha is a Toronto-based choreographer, dancer, and YouTube personality, whose channel "dancewithSL" is followed by over seventy thousand subscribers. She discussed the economy of wedding work in an interview via Skype, in which she explained:

SHEREEN: I didn't think of weddings initially as a source of income. I don't think you do all that training [as a dancer] to dance at weddings. But it's become so popular because people want to showcase their culture and have entertainment, and that's where the money is. We were doing shows, and then we did this wedding and that wedding and that wedding. I'll do one film per year—one unionized project per year, or I can do fifty weddings. The money is really in the weddings.

AMEERA: So what goes into accepting a wedding contract?

SHEREEN: So the process is that someone will email on my website or will have seen us at another wedding or performing anywhere. They're required to fill out a form indicating the date, venue, the time we'd have to be there. And then there would be a rate card, going by number of dancers and performances. One dancer, one performance is $200. If it's two performances, there's kind of an economy of scale on their side, since they're not paying twice, so more dancers becomes more and more "worth it." If there are customized things, it can get very expensive. These customized things are like if they want a specific song that isn't in these preset mixes we do. Oftentimes the bride and groom want to dance in the performance, something like a Bollywood movie, so that's custom as well. And that requires lessons at an hourly rate.[21]

Shereen went on to describe the contexts in which she provides dancers to perform. These include "opening a dance floor," similar to the affective work that Pranita described of Mandala dancers. Others are in the form of a "surprise performance," in which the hired performers appear in the middle of an "already hype party." Shereen's yearly approach to her wedding dance business is to choreograph a few standard mixes of four songs in advance of "wedding season" in Toronto, from April to August. These mixes feature some of the newest songs released in Bollywood film soundtracks. In addition she creates packages of songs, including classical, *bhangra*, and *garba* mixes that are thematically associated with special requests, especially in the cases of Punjabi or Gujarati weddings.[22] She rehearses these choreographies with her dancers, who perform them almost each weekend during wedding season, as is the case in the photograph below. The period of preparation ensures that wedding season features the work of performing, with limited attention to customization and rehearsal. This allows Shereen to capitalize on the work available through requests and contracts.

Shereen's business model also takes into account her work as a YouTube personality, since she charges more for performing particular choreographies that she premieres on her channel. Upon further inquiring about the impact of her online work, she described:

SHEREEN: I get people all the time, tagging on social media and in emails, saying, "We learned your choreography and performed it here." A lot of people use that choreography for performing at weddings, which I think is awesome because lessons are expensive, and if you want to learn from a choreographer that is geographically far away, it used to be impossible.

AMEERA: So if you were to speculate on the future of hired dancers at weddings, given the ability to learn choreographies for free, would you say there will be less and less of an economy for hired dancers at weddings?

SHEREEN: I don't think it's eliminated Bollywood dancers—hired entertainment at weddings. There will always be a distinction between "we can do this ourselves" versus "we now have to hire." Just like it is with hairdressers and makeup artists [and tutorials online]. People aren't cheaping out on weddings anytime soon.

Figure 10.3. Two dancers choreographed by Shereen Ladha perform at the wedding of Aleem and Shelize Jadavji in Toronto, October 2015. *Photo by Ikonica.*

It seems that Shereen makes a distinction between hired dancers for teaching and choreographing family performances, the affective work of encouraging others to participate, and dance as showpiece entertainment. All three feature heavily in a diasporic South Asian wedding.

Preeti Veerlapati is a Chicago-based *kuchipudi* dancer and former artistic director of Kalapriya Center for Indian Performing Arts. On dance as entertainment, Preeti explained:

> I don't really do wedding gigs. When it's not your own family, I don't feel the connection as much. And I'm not an entertainer. I am a performer, and I think dancers who dance at weddings are entertainers. They're there for entertainment. Yes, they can be performers as well but . . . even if you ask my mom, when she found out I did my first wedding [as a dancer], she said, "You're a wedding dancer now?" There's a stigma against it, too, in society where you're a wedding dancer versus a legit[imate] dancer on stage and in performance. At the end of the day the dancers are there because they're there to entertain, and bring up the festivities and keep the party going.

Preeti's anxieties on being perceived as an entertainer relate to historical practices of entertainment in Indian aesthetic history. Courtesans were musician-dancers who enjoyed varied social statuses as masters of music, dance, etiquette, and poetry during the nineteenth century in particular. They had some proximity to sex work, and as such were complex figures in the history of entertainment.[23] Today, women who continue these liminal forms of entertainment are known colloquially as *mujra* and *kothi* dancers.[24] Pranita and Shereen expressed their apprehension about being associated with mujra culture when hired to entertain at weddings. Shereen elaborated:

> We've been asked to dance, and I've never done these, at all-male functions before the wedding. And it makes me feel uncomfortable. It always feels that way at Muslim weddings, but never at Punjabi weddings. You feel like you're performing at a real show at Punjabi weddings. There's no seating chart, twelve hundred people that show up, there's always a baaraat, and there's an open bar. Bollywood dance is glitzy and glamorous, so it feels fitting at such a big spectacle at a Punjabi wedding. There's also a culture of tipping at these weddings. It's great to get tipped, but on the other hand it looks bad. When people throw money at you in a bhangra dance when you're fully covered and it's mostly men, it's fine. But on the other hand, it's not totally comfortable when you're doing a Bollywood dance in a little top—it doesn't feel right for people to throw money at you. There's a definite difference among Indian subcultures regarding what it feels like to be dancing at these weddings.

Dancers confront the living issues of the history of entertainment, theological and cultural belief systems, and gender in performing at weddings. Preeti, Pranita, and Shereen point to the lucrative nature of these gigs and have organized systems and economies to respond to the demand for dancers in South Asian diasporic weddings. As music specialists, dancers perform affective labor by constructing and participating in the circulation of feelings and emotions at weddings, turning them into choreographies and opening up dance floors for the dance-based expression of these emotions. We now turn to the figure of the DJ, who provides another perspective on this affective economy.

THE DJ: "MIXING" A MARRIAGE

Of each music specialist we interviewed during the research for this chapter, the DJ's role is the most paradigmatically different. Ameera discussed the kinds of affective work at play with Chicago-based DJ Aumir Ahmad at a cafe in the city's West Town neighborhood. Having frequented many South Asian weddings, birthdays, ritual celebrations, and even clubs and parties, Ameera thought she knew the role of the DJ at a wedding—to sustain a dance floor. Aumir indicated that this is one of the most important elements of the gig, but also illustrated the months of work and relationship-building with a wedding couple that take place prior to a wedding event.

Aumir began his business of DJ-ing at weddings, parties, and other private-client events several years ago. He has become a "preferred vendor" at several wedding venues, including banquet halls and hotels in Chicago's suburbs. He also appears and is advertised at wedding expos, hosted by the same venues. In this way, Aumir participates as a music specialist in a larger network of wedding laborers, allowing for them to draw on systems of collaboration and referrals when contracting new work. Upon accepting a contract, Aumir explained:

> Usually I give an inquiring couple a free consultation. Typically the first question I get is "How much do you charge?" And that's such a difficult question because there's no stencil, it's such a customized thing. I'll listen to exactly what they're trying to do or create. And then I give them my advice, and to give them more value, I'll help them through a basic idea of their itinerary as they shop around for vendors. For example, if they have a wedding at which they have over five hundred guests, and if you have buffet stations, up-lighting, and customized gobos, and then a DJ, it's going to require a lot of power. You want to do your best to avoid technical difficulties. And one of my big things is safety on power. So I ask them, "What are you doing to make sure you're backed up?" So I tell them, "Talk to your venue, talk to your other vendors." Then we go through the itinerary, and for example, they say that they want to have a skit that requires five microphones. I say you gotta think about that, because a typical DJ has two mic inputs, and then pricing comes in. Another example—lighting. If you do down-lighting in your room, like if you have a really nice purple. Talk to your photographer and videographer, because the room might look really nice, but then you get your photos back, and everyone is purple. And you're not necessarily thinking about this.[25]

While Aumir works as a music specialist, he illustrates that the DJ is part of a wider network involved in wedding design more broadly. Aumir negotiates with sound and lighting companies, photographers and videographers, wedding planners, and of course the couple and their families to construct an event that reflects the desires of the couple with the resources available. Aumir explained that typically, he accepts a contract six to seven months in advance of the wedding event, and spends time building a relationship with and getting to know the couple. He does this to learn the kind of environment, feel, and mood they seek to create during their wedding, and to whom the wedding is catered, whether family, friends, or themselves. Working in this way, Aumir has amassed equipment that allows him to increase the capacity of his supply in this economy, including speakers, subwoofers, dance floor lighting, mic setups, mixers, mixing boards, and other DJ equipment. His other "supplies" include preferred relationships with companies that provide these resources, allowing wedding couples the ability to enter this already negotiated network to access lower prices and systems of communication that have worked at past events.

In addition to the preparatory work that begins after accepting a contract, Aumir explained in detail the processes that accompany "loading into" a wedding. Having worked with the wedding couple to curate lists of songs that correspond to a wedding's various ceremonies, Aumir creates and sustains the moods associated with these elements. His choice of music for a Punjabi baaraat, usually played to underscore a live dhol player, is totally different than the *nasheed* (genre of Islamic vocal music) that softly accompany a Muslim *nikkah* (ceremony of Muslim marriage contract). These are different than the songs for cake cutting, bridal party entrances, and transition music between speeches, which the bride and groom sometimes choose for sentimental and/or mood-setting purposes.

Aumir does the affective work of establishing and continuing the moods, emotions, and feelings sought by the wedding couple to facilitate the participation of families and friends in their celebration. In selecting what to play, he consults the "top 40" lists of the many countries of prominent family members to see what would emphasize and heighten the affects in circulation. While in the moment of play, some songs are set, and he works them in according to the ceremony they are meant to accompany. In other situations, such as "opening the dance floor," he relies on his experience as a DJ to improvise in the moment, drawing from a larger band of repertoire, mixing one song into another.

> A lot of DJs tell me, "Why don't you just leave a playlist going [during dinner]"? And I don't like that because what I like to do is tease the crowd with music and see what they're responding to, to see what's going to work on the dance floor. And then I would open the dance floor. This is one of the most important things in my opinion. The first twenty minutes of how you open the dance floor can set the tone for the rest of the night. I start slowly, and in that first twenty minutes have an awesome buildup and then hit other genres. If I've gone through different music that everyone seems to like, they'll think, "This DJ can appeal to everyone," and they're a lot more inclined to stay. This is crucial.

Aumir's perspectives demonstrate that in addition to a DJ's job being so intricately tied to encouraging dancing at a wedding, it is also one of constant negotiation. Aumir prepares repertoire selection for months prior to a wedding event. He consults online song lists and blogs and revisits the larger design of the wedding to curate a "mood" through music. On the day of an event, he negotiates with wedding guests, reading their participation and responding accordingly, the affective labor of "keeping them happy and dancing."

This constant negotiation occurs even in less "visible" circumstances. Aumir recounted some of his experiences DJ-ing at Muslim weddings, during which women who wore hijabs (headscarves) took them off in the company of other women to dance and celebrate a marriage: "At Muslim mendhis [a ceremony in which a natural dye is applied to the hands and feet of a bride, as part of South Asian wedding ceremonies] I usually offer to put a draping or curtain in front of the DJ booth. There will usually be one girl—perhaps a family relative—who comes back and forth to say, 'This [song] is working; this isn't,' and I continue to do that until the women are finished dancing and have put their hijabs back on. And then I move the curtain back. I would show you pictures, but I don't have them, of course [laughs]."

Aumir's work underscores why the framework of music specialists must also include DJs, who, like dancers and instrumentalists, help materialize emotion and feeling through the embodied experience of everyone present. The DJ, however, is also an integral professional service in a network of designers who collaborate over several months in dialogue with the couple to construct and curate the wedding they envision with their families. The DJ negotiates with the couple, their families, and the guests to create, inflect, sustain, and "mix" a spectrum of appropriate emotions for wedding occasions.

CLOSING THOUGHTS: "BOLLYWOOD TAKES THE CAKE"

Indian filmmakers often punctuate and develop their narratives with diegetic performances to the extent that to "talk of Bollywood is inevitably to talk of the song and dance sequence."[26]

Mehfil ta sajjdi	The party rocks
Ke mehfil ta sajjdi	The party rocks
je nacche jeeja-bhaabi	when Uncle-Aunty dance
Ke mahfil ta sajjdi	The party rocks
je nacche jeeja-bhaabi	when Uncle-Aunty dance
Ke mahfil ta sajjdi...	The party rocks...
Turn the table	Hurry up DJ, turn the table
bass bana chal jaldi move it DJ	and blast the bass
Ke mehfil ta sajjdi	The party rocks
hip hop da chaska leejay	when we do hip hop
Ke mehfil ta sajjdi	The party rocks
jab naach nachave DJ	when the DJ makes you dance
Ke mahfil ta sajjdi...	The party rocks...[27]

These lyrics are from the film song "Baari Barsi," the opening "item number" in the Hindi romantic comedy, *Band Baaja Baaraat* (2010), a story of two young entrepreneurs, Bittoo and Shruti, who establish a wedding planning business together and eventually fall in love. In this scene at a community wedding, the father of the bride (the patron-client) asks Shruti to get the dancing started. Switching from her role as wedding planner to performer, Shruti begins singing "Baari Barsi," a Punjabi-language *boli* song that usually features in Punjabi weddings, to "rock the party" and get everyone dancing. As her song and dance routine intensifies, more and more attendees join in laughing, clapping, swirling, and smiling. The song's picturization dramatizes the way in which music specialists create scintillating sound unions—malleable musical frameworks that harness the incipient affective energy of lifecycle events to create the kind of intimate recognition required to reproduce social life itself.

The film also foregrounds the commodification of affective labor as a lifestyle choice in a rapidly expanding middle-class market for wedding planning and design services. Working with florists, caterers, music specialists, and other subcontracted services, the protagonists commercialize the affect-culture of weddings. Instead of families cultivating relationships directly with the service-providers they need to create the appropriate moods, emotions, and sensibilities for weddings, today India's privileged classes are hiring planners whose business models reduce emotional life to a consumer choice. As demonstrated in the film and in our interviews, music specialists remain central in this increasingly commercialized intimate domain, although the conditions in which they work have changed dramatically in some cases. This point was poignantly captured by veena artist Saraswathi's fond memories of being treated with the warmth and respect reserved for members of an extended family at weddings in South India. For her, working for wedding planners has the advantage of supplementing her income for a limited time commitment, but it also has the drawback of alienating her from the families, thereby making her affective labor more difficult in the absence of personal connections and knowledge of her patrons' sensibilities.

Moreover, Bollywood films themselves depict lifestyles people seek to emulate. Jigna Desai argues: "Most [NRI] viewers are seen to consume [Bollywood] films as prefabricated transnational commodities providing comforting and familiar emblems of normative social values neatly wrapped in packages of glossy celluloid. The film is designed to make NRIs tearful, but is also designed to encourage the consumption and conflation of family and capitalism in India for the cosmopolitan bourgeoisie."[28] While acknowledging the heterogeneous viewership of Bollywood films abroad, Desai notes that India's Hindi-language film industry circulates nostalgia to encourage commoditized engagement among diasporic South Asians in particular. Bollywood films offer models for diasporic South Asians to live by, thereby encouraging the consumption of values for approaching social relationships in the act of consuming films.

If the wedding planning business depicted in *Band Baaja Baaraat* demonstrates the commercialization of lifecycle events such as weddings, it also encourages a new way of relating to the musical work of weddings. Many of the music specialists we interviewed highlighted the connection between diasporic weddings and Bollywood, whether through requests to play film songs or to perform and teach film choreographies. Dancer Shereen Ladha went so far as to claim that Bollywood films determine the kinds of themes, color schemes, clothing, food, music and dance to have at weddings "here." The influence of Bollywood cinema in South Asian weddings is clearly ubiquitous. Wedding couples and their families increasingly look to Bollywood to re-create larger-than-life scenes and fantasies in banquet halls and hotel venues, playing out narratives and song themes in real life. Diasporic wedding planners and clients, like the characters in our Bollywood scene, are as a result moving the celebration of conjugal union into the realm of spectacle, the success of which remains contingent on the energy and participation music specialists bring.

Our collaborative research has offered a glimpse of the shifting work worlds of music specialists, including how they mobilize a range of trade skills and knowledge to create, materialize, and manage emotions in marriage arenas. The wedding affect-cultures they play a vital role in shaping a gamut of feelings, from affection, flirtation, excitement, and even seduction to nostalgia, longing, and of course, belonging. Singers, instrumentalists, dancers, and DJs thus go beyond punctuating rituals and ceremonies with vivid soundtracks and backdrops. Rather they channel and make tangible the affective energy communities need at lifecycle occasions to reproduce who they were while also charting who they aspire to be.

KALEY MASON is Assistant Professor of
Music at Lewis & Clark College.

AMEERA NIMJEE is a PhD candidate in
Ethnomusicology at the University of Chicago.

NOTES

1. Hochschild, *Managed Heart.*
2. Terkel, *Working.*
3. The Immigration and Nationality Act of 1965, also known as the Hart-Celler Act.
4. Rangaswamy, "Asian Indians in Chicago."
5. See Srinivasan, *Sweating Saris*; Peterson, "Sound Work," 791–824; Tatro, "Hard Work of Screaming," 431–53; Baade, Fast, and Grenier, "Musicians as Workers," 1–9; Morcom "Terrains of Bollywood Dance," 288–314.
6. See Qureshi, *Music and Marx*; and Webber, *Musician as Entrepreneur.*

7. Hardt, "Affective Labor," 89–100.

8. See also Hardt and Negri, *Multitude.*

9. Hochschild, *Managed Heart*, 7.

10. Thompson and Biddle, "Somewhere between Signifying and the Sublime."

11. Hennessy, *Fires on the Border*, 50.

12. Ibid., xxi.

13. Minu Pasupathi, interview with the authors, November 21, 2016.

14. See Terada, "Performing Auspiciousness,"103–38.

15. Manuel, *Cassette Culture.*

16. Small, *Musicking*, 9.

17. Ramnarine, *Beautiful Cosmos*, 9.

18. Saraswathi Ranganathan, interview with the authors, November 6, 2016.

19. Pranita Jain, interview with the authors, October 31, 2016.

20. Baaraat and sangeet refer to two traditions that figure prominently into many weddings. The baaraat indicates the procession of a groom and his family toward the bride. This procession is usually accompanied by musicians who play portable drums. The groom and his family dance as they move along with the procession. A sangeet, meaning "music," in many South Asian languages, is an evening dedicated to singing, playing, and dancing in advance of the marriage ceremony.

21. Shereen Ladha, interview with the authors, November 2, 2016.

22. Bhangra and garba are two forms of dance that are associated with the regions of Punjab and Gujarat, respectively. Bhangra has become a highly athletic form that features dance teams performing in world competitions. Garba is a Gujarati folk dance in which its participants dance in concentric circles.

23. See Chakravorty, *Bells of Change*; Qureshi, "Female Agency and Patrilineal Constraints," 312–31; Soneji, *Unfinished Gestures.*

24. Morcom, *Illicit Worlds of Indian Dance.*

25. Aumir Ahmad, interview with the authors, November 6, 2016.

26. Gopal and Moorti, "Introduction: Travels of Hindi Song and Dance," 1.

27. "Baari Barsi," a wedding song used in the film *Band Baaja Baaraat*, Yash Raj Films. Director Maneesh Sharma, 2010

28. Jigna Desai, "Bollywood Abroad," i, 132.

BIBLIOGRAPHY

Baade, Christina, Susan Fast, and Line Grenier. "Musicians as Workers: Sites of Struggle and Resistance." *MUSICultures* 41, no. 2 (2014): 1–9.

Chakravorty, Pallabi. *Bells of Change: Kathak Dance, Women and Modernity in India.* London: New York: Seagull, 2008.

Desai, Jigna. "Bollywood Abroad: South Asian Diasporic Cosmopolitanism and Indian Cinema." In *New Cosmopolitanisms: South Asians in the US*, edited by Gita Rajan and Shailja Sharma, 115–37. Stanford: Stanford University Press, 2006.

Gopal, Sangita, and Sujata Moorti, eds. "Introduction: Travels of Hindi Song and Dance." In *Global Bollywood: Travels of Hindi Song and Dance*, edited by Sangita Gopal and Sujata Moorti, 1–60. Minneapolis: University of Minnesota Press, 2008.

Hardt, Michael. "Affective Labor." *boundary 2* 26, no. 2 (1999): 89–100.

Hardt, Michael, and Antonio Negri. *Multitude: War and Democracy in the Age of Empire.* New York: Penguin Books, 2014.

Hennessy, Rosemary. *Fires on the Border: The Passionate Politics of Labor Organizing on the Mexican Frontera.* Minneapolis: University of Minnesota Press, 2013.

Hochschild, Arlie Russell. *The Managed Heart: Commercialization of Human Feeling.* Berkeley: University of California Press, 1983.

Manuel, Peter. *Cassette Culture: Popular Music and Technology in North India.* Chicago: University of Chicago Press, 1993.

Morcom, Anna. *Illicit Worlds of Indian Dance: Cultures of Exclusion.* Oxford: Oxford University Press, 2013.

———. "Terrains of Bollywood Dance: (Neoliberal) Capitalism and the Transformation of Cultural Economies." *Ethnomusicology* 59, no. 2 (2015): 288–314.

Qureshi, Regula Burckhardt, ed. "Female Agency and Patrilineal Constraints: Situating Courtesans in Twentieth-Century India." In *The Courtesan's Arts: Cross-Cultural Perspectives,* edited by Bonnie Gordon and Martha Feldman, 312–31. New York: Oxford University Press, 2006.

———. *Music and Marx: Ideas, Practice, Politics.* New York: Routledge, 2002.

Peterson, Marina. "Sound Work: Music as Labor and the 1940s Recording Bans of the American Federation of Musicians." *Anthropology Quarterly* 86, no. 3 (2013): 791–824.

Ramnarine, Tina K. *Beautiful Cosmos: Performance and Belonging in the Caribbean Diaspora.* London: Pluto Press, 2007.

Rangaswamy, Padma. "Asian Indians in Chicago: Growth and Change in a Model Minority." In *Ethnic Chicago: A Multicultural Portrait,* edited by Melvin G. Holli and Peter d'A. Jones, 438–62. Grand Rapids, MI: Eerdmans, 1995.

Sharma, Maneesh. *Band Baaja Baaraat.* Directed by Maneesh Sharma. Yash Raj Films, 2010.

Small, Christopher. *Musicking: The Meanings of Performing and Listening.* Middleton, CT: Wesleyan University Press, 1998.

Soneji, Davesh. *Unfinished Gestures: Devadasis, Memory, and Modernity in South India.* Chicago: University of Chicago Press, 2012.

Srinivasan, Priya. *Sweating Saris: Indian Dance as Transnational Labor.* Philadelphia: Temple University Press, 2011.

Tatro, Kelley. "The Hard Work of Screaming: Physical Exertion and Affective Labor among Mexico City's Punk Vocalists." *Ethnomusicology* 58, no. 3 (2014): 431–53.

Terada, Yoshitaka. "Performing Auspiciousness: Periya Mēlam Music in South Indian Marriage Ceremony." *Wacana Seni Journal of Arts Discourse* 4 (2005): 103–38.

Terkel, Studs. *Working.* New York: The New Press, 1972.

Thompson, Marie, and Ian Biddle. "Somewhere between Signifying and the Sublime." In *Sound, Music, Affect: Theorizing Sonic Experience,* edited by Marie Thompson and Ian Biddle, 1–24. New York: Bloomsbury, 2013.

Webber, William, ed. *The Musician as Entrepreneur, 1700–1914.* Bloomington: Indiana University Press, 2004.

MOUNTAIN WEDDINGS
IN CHICAGO

TIMOTHY J. COOLEY

FEBRUARY 2010, ZAKOPANE, POLAND. MY WIFE, *Ruth, and I stay in the spectacular log home of Halina and Tomasz Lassak. Snow is falling; we have views over a narrow valley up into the majestic alpine Tatra Mountains. We are here for the funeral of Władysław Styrczula-Maśniak, a prominent violinist in the regional* Górale *(Highlander, Mountaineer) style. Born here in the Polish Tatras, he lived most of his adult life in Chicago.*

I met Halina and Tomasz through Władysław in 1991, when all three were playing together in a traditional Górale string band for a wedding in Chicago. Knowing I was interested in music from the Tatra Mountain region (*góralska muzyka*), Górale musicians started inviting me to traditional weddings. Two years later, in September 1993, I attended and documented Halina and Tomasz's wedding, also in Chicago. Now nearly two decades after first meeting and encountering each other on occasion in Chicago and in Poland, we speak warmly and freely as old friends.

This afternoon, nearly a decade after first meeting them, I sit with Halina and Tomasz in their new house financed by years of labor in Chicago. Halina is explaining some of the challenges of weddings in diasporic Górale communities. She kindly corrects some of my interpretations of Górale weddings and funerals published a few years earlier,[1] and offers me new insights about the challenges for the Górale diasporic community in Chicago during Poland's post-communist, pre–European Union years. Though travel to and from Poland was especially difficult and expensive at that time, many in the Chicago Górale community still managed to maintain very close connections with Poland. Through extraordinary effort, they cultivated core aspects of their mountain village traditions in the urban flatlands of Chicago. For example, special foods and clothing were brought in from the Tatra Mountains or painstakingly made

Figure 11.1. *From left to right:* Musicians Andrew Tokarz, Maciej Lasniak, Władysław Styrczula-Maśniak, Halina Maciata, and Tomasz Lassak, playing for the wedding party of Krystyna Knapczyk and Władysław Kania, Chicago, 1991. *Photo by Tim Cooley.*

locally. The effect may have seemed incongruous to others, but as every immigrant knows cultural practices and products transcend place and may even gain meaning and power with every mile traveled. Perhaps most importantly, family and friends would journey from Poland for a wedding no matter the cost and inconvenience. When in Chicago, they would be accommodated and treated with respect—in the Górale manner. This means, among other things, providing seemingly endless quantities of food and drink, local transportation, and live music played by specialist musicians steeped in the Górale style and repertoire. Of course as with all human organizational efforts, compromises had to be made, but on the day of the wedding, there would be no mistaking a Górale wedding, whether in the Tatras or in Chicago.

As we finish our discussion of weddings among the Górale diaspora, Halina offers us tea and coffee, which we enjoy. Ruth and I then strap on our boots and take a short walk in the fresh snow falling in the shadows of the Tatras. We stop by a secondary structure next to the Lassak's home. The lower level is a stable where a fine horse is housed. Tomasz is an excellent singer as well as a violinist, and he now has his own horse, making him available for the honor of serving as a pytaca for others' weddings.

—ᴍ—

In the introduction to this book, Inna Naroditskaya notes that weddings are a metaphor for diaspora, which "engages simultaneously in preservation and compromise." My experiences documenting Polish Górale weddings in Chicago as well as in Poland confirm this. In this chapter I show some of the ways that compromise is itself a means for preserving beliefs, lifeways, performative traditions, and more, both in diasporic communities and in the motherland. Compromise, after all, is the essence of marriage, fueled ideally by love, passion, and even the occasional abandonment of reason, all contained by conventions and traditions that seem to mushroom at weddings. And the passion and dreams of all marrying couples must be tempered by the demands of work, financial limitations, children, families residing in several countries, and more. While weddings may in fact be the performance of compromise, they are also a ritual of preservation and its sibling, sustainability, while families, communities, and institutions all work to preserve and sustain their bloodlines, belief systems, forms of governance and social control, and cultural practices for another generation. Herein lies the tension that drives my interest in weddings among those who identify as Polish Górale in the Chicago area diaspora, and in their Polish motherland. What motivates young people in the urban flatlands of Chicago, Illinois, to have a traditional Górale wedding, defined in so many ways by the rural alpine Tatra Mountains of Poland's southern borderlands? And what is at stake? What qualities of Górale tradition call for preservation in diasporic communities? And what impact does this have back in the Polish motherland?

In this chapter I interpret weddings of couples who identify as Polish Górale in or near Chicago, Illinois, and who choose to have what they themselves call a "traditional" wedding.[2] I show that what is considered traditional is an actively negotiated category that references and reenacts past weddings in sometimes inventive ways. Concepts of tradition with this diasporic community are rooted in the material reality and the imagination of their mountainous motherland, particularly the Tatra Mountain area with its distinct regional folkways. My interlocutors in Górale communities in Chicago and Poland emphasize rootedness in place and practices held to be from the Tatras, so I too will ground notions of tradition there.

PLACE, LIFEWAYS, LEAVINGS, AND DIASPORA

Górale are a cultural group, arguably an ethnic group, in or from the Tatra Mountain region of the southern tip of Poland, bordering Slovakia.[3] The root word of the moniker is *góra*, which means mountain. Thus Górale are mountaineers or highlanders (as Górale themselves often translate the term). Using a convention established by ethnomusicologist Louise Wrazen,[4] I use the plural

Polish word *Górale* as both noun and adjective, singular and plural, when writing in English. The picturesque Tatras Mountains are geologically young alpine formations, the tallest peaks of the long arch of the Carpathian Mountains that run from the Czech Republic, through the border between Poland and Slovakia, the southeast corner of Ukraine, a bit of Hungary, and much of Romania. While the steep alpine quality of the Tatras would become a draw for tourists beginning in the last quarter of the nineteenth century, the rough terrain, minimal arable land, and short growing season contributed to the area being one of the last settled in Central Europe, especially on the cold northern side in Poland, a subregion known as Skalny Podhale (rocky piedmont), or simply Podhale.

Lifeways and cultural practices are historically related to seasonal migratory shepherding found throughout the Carpathians, as well as to a Robin Hood–like social hero from the Slovak side of the Tatras named Juraj Jánošík (1688–1713), who led a band of *zbójniki* (highland robbers). Both lifeways are celebrated today in songs, musical genres, and dances and remain key symbolic markers of primarily male Górale identity revolving around ideas of pastoral self-sufficiency in harsh mountain conditions and righteous protest against political and economic oppression.[5] I bring these up here because I interpret the migratory patterns set up by transhumance grazing cycles and living on the lam in the Tatras as foundational to the long history of seasonal and long-term migratory work patterns embodied by Górale then and now. Romanticized preindustrial migrations, I suggest, provide a narrative for contextualizing industrial-era and present-day migratory patterns that draw Górale out of their beloved mountains to metropolitan centers for employment at first in Kraków, Budapest, and Vienna but increasingly in the twentieth and twenty-first centuries farther afield to, for example, London and North America, including most notably Chicago. For practical and political reasons, as Górale traveled to increasingly distant locations for employment, the migration season became longer, often lasting years, thus forming what became diasporic Górale communities. I interpret the Chicago Górale diasporic community, which coalesced in the first half of the twentieth century, as an extension of this history and the tradition of migrations of necessity.

Perhaps these departures intensify the longings many Górale migrants have for Podhale and the Tatra Mountains. Among my Górale acquaintances who have been living in Chicago for years—owning a house and raising children there—a surprising number intend to return to the Tatras. Several have built or are building homes in Podhale with money earned in the United States. Górale's identification with the Tatra Mountinas, even when living abroad for years, is actively encouraged by individuals and organizations both within and from beyond the community. This in turn encourages the continuous engagement with traditional music and dance practices among Górale in both North America and Poland.

Fueling the dynamic between preservation and compromise, the distance and duration of migration increased in direct correlation to the decreasing viability of traditional lifeways in Podhale. While still a feature of the Polish Tatra's economy, seasonal migratory pastoral lifeways were attenuated during the twentieth century and largely replaced by seasonal tourism that required an expanded service industry. The in-migration of seasonal tourists to the Tatras differs from earlier migrations to and from the Tatras, resulting in a politics of difference that contributed to a codification of cultural practices, including musical practices, considered traditional and/or regional.[6] Of significance for this study of diasporic weddings, the codification of cultural practices defined as Górale occurred in tandem with the recognition of the critical mass of Górale immigrants in North America during the interwar period when Poland enjoyed its reemergence as an independent state. The center of this diasporic blossoming was in Chicago, and the solidification of the Górale diaspora there was facilitated by musicking, reminding us that identities are created in their performance. I will dwell on this moment for a paragraph since it sets up many of the conditions for Górale diasporic weddings in Chicago still today.

During Poland's brief independence at the end of the First World War, a heady time of reconstruction and national reinvention, The Polish Tatra Society (Polskie Towarzystwo Tatrzańska) and the Highlander Alliance (Związek Podhalan)[7] engaged a graduate student of geography and forestry named Stefan Jarosz to travel to North America with the goal of encouraging return tourism to the Polish Tatras.[8] Arriving in 1927, Jarosz published an announcement in Chicago's Polish-language newspapers of a slide show of photographs of the Tatra Mountains. The advertisements include a photograph of Jarosz wearing a traditional Górale outfit. Contemporary accounts claim that Poles with roots in Podhale flocked to the events, where in addition to projecting images of the Tatras, Jarosz also hired a local band of Górale musicians and sang a few Górale songs (including one about Jánošík, the legendary highlands robber).[9] In Chicago, Jarosz met lead violinist Karol Stoch from the village of Ząb in Podhale, an excellent musician in the Górale style. Together they made the first commercial recordings of Polish Górale music.[10] Jarosz helped form the first Highlander Alliance of North America (Związek Podhalan w Północnej Ameryce), which remains the center of Górale activities in North America today, while also facilitating substantial cooperation with Związek Podhalan circles in Poland.

These early international exchanges reveal some of the paradoxes of diaspora. I have uncovered photographs of Stoch between 1927 in Chicago and 1934 during one of his return visits to Podhale. In the photographs of Stoch visiting Poland, he wears a cosmopolitan three-piece suit, while in Chicago he sports elaborately embroidered felt trousers, linen shirts, and a felt jacket or cape that form an unmistakable sartorial image of Górale identity.[11] Thus in his dress, he shows his otherness both in Chicago and when he returns to his place of birth— a double sense of removal experienced by some who have joined dynamic diasporas. Alternatively this might be interpreted as cosmopolitan achievement where the global reach of one's community is celebrated.

WEDDINGS AND THE PERFORMANCE OF IDENTITY

My personal experiences with Górale and their distinctive weddings began exactly sixty years after Karol Stoch made his first recordings of Górale music in Chicago in 1927, yet the clothing that marked Stoch as Górale as well as the tune-families he recorded were still recognizable among Górale in 1987, and they still are today. This observation is not to suggest that these musical and sartorial symbols of Góraleness are static. The performing style continues to change as does the *strój* (regional costume), though sometimes subtly. The three-piece suits Stoch wore when visiting Podhale in the 1930s may look similar to suits in fashion today, but they are also quite different. Similarly while Górale musicians today will recognize the tune families that Stoch recorded in the 1920s, his strident vibrato-free style is no longer in fashion, though his quick bowing and clear articulation is still appreciated. These subtle changes are of great importance, but in my estimation, the primary significance at a wedding is whether or not one chooses to wear Górale strój and hire a Górale string band in the first place. To do so is a clear, unmistakable statement of Góraleness and, in the context of Chicago, a statement of distinctiveness. Why might the draw to this distinction be especially powerful when a couple contemplates their wedding? Why do the performative trappings of Góraleness seem to have increased in prevalence in the ninety years since Stoch made his impact on the Chicago community?

Elsewhere I have documented and interpreted the tendency of some who identify as Górale in Poland to cultivate traditional lifeways, especially musicking, as statements of and the creation of identity.[12] I have also tried to address a related question about the impulse and the effort required to perform one's Górale identity in Chicago.[13] The urge among some young couples to have a Górale wedding, whether in Podhale or Chicago, is very similar—to ritually perform or "restore" past rituals[14]—while the contexts within which one creates such a wedding in the motherland versus in the Chicago diaspora are radically different. This contextual difference generates the tension of preservation and compromise at the center of this book, and it also generates, for me, much of the fascination and beauty of diasporic wedding celebrations.

This tension is manifest at Górale weddings in Chicago during many weekends starting in spring after Easter (weddings during the pre-Easter Lent season are rare among predominantly Catholic Górale), through summer, fall, and into early winter. As Halina Maciata reminded me when I misinterpreted the iconography on her wedding invitation, a multinational wedding takes planning, and things do not always go according to plan. Yet as a highly significant life cycle ritual in which a couple makes unambiguous statements about who they are and with whom they associate, they tend toward consensus. The bride and groom are individuals, but their wedding connects that individuality to families, villages, and often global religion-based diasporic communities. Weddings are opportunities for individuals and groups of varying sizes to perform ideas about what is most meaningful to them, and sometimes to enact contestations of those ideas. However, contestations are rare, usually subtle, drawing from extended association groups (such as a sense of American identity among some in the Górale diaspora), and therefore noteworthy. Here I consider weddings where the joining couple and their families have chosen to perform their identity as Górale by referencing specifically the Tatras and conceptions about what a traditional wedding was and could be.

Since the late nineteenth century Podhale became a popular destination for Polish seeking an adventurous excursion or vacation. This nascent tourism was encouraged by visitors writing about the regional folkways, including musicking, and these writings are our earliest ethnographic records of Górale. The ethnographic, scholarly, and popular attention in Podhale was intensified during the interwar period, only to be redoubled after the reconstruction and reorganization of Poland following World War II. This leaves us with some records of a few Górale weddings. I don't want to overemphasize the ethnographic record, though many Górale who choose to perform traditional music and dance are well aware of this published record. More significant are the recreations of the idea of a Górale wedding at weddings themselves but also on community stages and halls where the performance of a wedding is a staple of folkloric shows. Thus the idea of what a Górale wedding should be is informed by past weddings, song and dance troupes' rehearsals and performances of staged weddings, and ethnographic documentation. As I will show, individuals who engaged in the many song and dance troupes available for young people in Chicago and in Poland are much more likely to choose to perform their Góraleness at their own wedding.

Based on my own ethnographic observations of weddings in Chicago and in Podhale[15] together with published descriptions by Alexander Szurmiak-Bogucka,

Jan Gutt-Mostowy, and Urszula Lehr,[16] a wedding considered traditional would contain the following distinct (and thus transferable) ritual moments:

Before the wedding

1. *Inviting guests:* Bride and groom go throughout the village/community with two pytace) inviting people in person to the wedding. Ideally the bride and groom travel in a two-horse sleigh or carriage with the pytace leading the way on horseback.

Wedding day

2. *Groom's house and first blessing:* Pytace with the groomsmen and bridesmaids congregate at the groom's house where the groom's parents offer him a blessing. Sometimes a string band (three violins and a *basy*, which is a three-stringed cello-sized instrument) is hired to play regional music (*muzyka Podhala*). Afterward, all process to the bride's house.

3. *Bride's house and second blessing:* The procession to the bride's house. The groom is dressed in a new white shirt given to him by the bride (often provided by the groom's mother and ceremonially given to the bride). The groom's cape-like coat is tied with a white ribbon (rather than the typical red). The bride is dressed in white decorated with sprigs of myrtle by the wedding hostesses (generally including the bride's godmother). When dressed in their wedding outfits, they kneel for a solemn address by the wedding host, followed by their parents' blessing.

4. *Procession to a church:* The bride and groom, led by the pytace singing as they ride on horseback and followed by the wedding party in horse-drawn carriages or sleighs, proceed to the church. The musicians also travel in a horse-drawn carriage or wagon and play music while they travel. Others walk or ride in cars.

5. *Wedding Mass (ślub) at the church:* Music often provided by the church organist and chanter with the Górale string band providing music in some cases.

6. *Procession to wesele (wedding party):* Procession back to the bride's house (now often substituted by a restaurant or other public space), led by the singing pytace on horseback. The bride and groom ride with close family members in a carriage ideally pulled by a pair of white horses especially adorned for the occasion. The string band again is carried in a wagon or carriage and they play while they ride. The procession is halted by one or more fancifully decorated barriers set up by local youths demanding a ransom. In a playful interaction, the "beggars" are paid a bribe, often of alcohol,[17] before the gate is removed and the procession is able to continue.

7. *Wesele:* At the entrance to the bride's house (or other space) the bride and groom are presented with bread and salt. The string band greets guests with music as they enter the house. This leads to a celebration that often goes well past midnight and includes a feast, special homemade spirits, music, and dancing.

8. *Cepowiny:* The capping ritual wherein the bride has her bridal garland covered or removed and replaced with a scarf (symbols of maidenhood and of a married woman, respectively). The groom's feather (symbol of freedom and, according to some, a phallus) is removed from his hat. The entire cepowiny is accompanied by the string band and a specific set of *krakowiak*-type tunes. It is a long ritual ceremony with many significant moments requiring substantial cultural knowledge of all participants, which ideally includes many, if not all, present.

LONG AGO, FAR AWAY, HERE AND NOW IN CHICAGO

Some young Górale in Chicago look back in time as they imagine and thus begin the process of creating their hoped-for future with their partners. By restoring and reperforming visions of the longed-for imagined past,[18] a young couple pledges themselves to each other for an unknowable future. Whiteness, horses, bread, salt, green myrtle, music, tears, challenges, priests, food, different generations, more white, dancing, drink, and more food make for the performance of the past and future in the present that is a wedding.

I return again to Stoch, the violinist from Ząb who immigrated to Chicago in 1926, made the first commercial recordings of Gorale music in 1927, and was instrumental in the founding of the first Podhale Alliance of North America in 1929. Stoch met his wife in Chicago, and they were married there. His wife was also from Podhale, from the village of Czerwienne, not far from Ząb. In the 1930 memoirs of the first meeting of the Podhale Alliance of North America in Chicago, Stoch is described as a "typical highlander folk musician" who had played for more than seven hundred weddings in several states: so many weddings, so many questions. What we do know from the still highly regarded audio recordings made by Stoch in the 1920s to the 1950s, is that he was indeed a fine violinist in the Górale tradition and that he had an excellent band in Chicago. I extrapolate from this that many of those seven hundred weddings hired Stoch to perform Góraleness and to aid in a young couple's ritual enactment of Górale identity at their wedding. The real question for this study is why the same tune-families played by Stoch ninety years ago, as well as the strój he wore, are still recognizable markers of Góraleness both in Podhale and in Chicago today.

Chicago, October 2016. Not having lived in Chicago for about three decades now, I get lost because so many streets and landmarks have changed. Yet when I arrive at my destination, Chicago feels much like it used to. Tonight, driven by my host, Maria Krzeptowska, I am meeting with the leadership of the Highlander Alliance of North America. He greets me at the impressive headquarters of the Highlander Alliance at 4808 Archer Avenue, also known as the Dom

Podhalanski or Highlander House, which boasts more than a few rehearsal spaces for song and dance troupes, a banquet hall, bar, restaurant, offices, and a library into which we are invited tonight. A long table is set with kielbasa, cheese, tea, and so forth. Gathered is the current president of the Highlander Alliance of North America, Józef Cikowski, past presidents Stanisław Zagata and Marian Bryja, vice presidents Zdzisław Dorula and Zofia Bobak, the secretary Helena Studenska, and others. I give them a copy of my book, *Making Music in the Polish Tatras*, make a brief presentation, and explain my present interest in diasporic weddings. A Górale string band plays some tunes, Marian Bryja calls a dance *po góralsku* (in the Górale manner), and dances with my host, Maria Krzeptowska. I have known Marian and Maria, as well as several other dignitaries in the room, for decades. The music and the distinctive costumes worn by many in the room are re-performances of similar events that have taken place in this Chicago neighborhood for nearly a century.

As the official meeting winds down, I have the opportunity to interview two young couples about their visions for their future weddings. The young men, Dawid Walus and Piotr Waliczek, were in the string band that played for the gathering moments ago. Their girlfriends, Monika Kois and Zuzanna Soltys, danced and they two are in strój. A good number of the Highlander Alliance dignitaries remain for at least some of the interview, in particular Maria Krzeptowska and former Alliance president Stanisław Zagata both make significant interjections during the interview. The location, occasion, and those listening on certainly shaped the direction of the interview.

Monika Kois was born in Chicago in 1995 to parents from Chochołow, a village in Podhale renowned for its well-preserved nineteenth-century log homes. She shows a photograph of her grandparent's 1948 wedding in Chochołow, and then a strikingly similar photo of her parents' 1984 wedding in the same village. Both parents and grandparents had a Górale wedding, and the photos show many of the guests in Górale strój. In the earlier photo, Monika's grandmother Maria appears to wear a white Górale wedding dress and headdress, while her grandfather Władysław Kois wears a cosmopolitan suit and a white necktie. A Górale string band of three violins and a basy is featured prominently in the foreground. In the photo of Monika's parents' wedding, pytace flank the right and left sides of the wedding party and are easily identified by their distinctive long, dark coats adorned with sashes draped diagonally across their torsos. The mustachioed pytace on the left is Władysław Styrczula-Maśniak, the violinist I met in Chicago a few years after this photo was taken and whose funeral I attended in 2010 in Podhale. Monika's parents, like Władysław, migrated to Chicago, where they raised families. Looking at the photo, I wonder how many of the people I see immigrated to Chicago.

Figure 11.2. Wedding of Maria and Władysław Kois (seated center behind musicians, Władysław turning his head to look at Maria), Chochołow, 1948. *Courtesy of Monika Kois.*

Reflecting on these photos, Monika states: "I see how much my parents love each other, and my grandparents love each other too, so I kind of strive for the same thing as them. So I feel that is why I would want a traditional Polish wedding."[19] In an email exchange following up on this interview, Monika clarified: "For me, personally, I would get married traditionally 100 percent po goralsku (strój, blessings in the homes, pytace, etc.) if I were to get married in Poland."[20] She went on to explain that since her whole family has moved from Poland to Chicago, she is more likely to have her wedding here in Chicago. That being the case, she imagines a "white dress"[21] wedding that reflects who she is here in the United States: "a mixed individual with a taste of two different worlds (American and Polish), and that is how I would like to have my wedding. . . . Of course I would intertwine my goralskie traditions within my wedding day! I do want pytace, musicians, carriages, blessing from my parents (the MOST important tradition), and goralskie dance later on."

During our interview, Zuzanna Soltys and Monika would often finish each other's sentences. They are best friends, sing and dance in the same zespół, and go to the same church. Each comfortably assumes that the other will be a bridesmaid at her wedding. Zuzanna succeeded Monika as the Highlander Alliance *Królowa* (princess), an honorary position wherein the Królawa performs

Figure 11.3. Wedding of Jozef and Anna Kois, Chochołow. 1984. *Courtesy of Monika Kois.*

a representative role at public functions and is charged with raising significant funds for charity. While closer than sisters and often speaking as if with one voice, they nevertheless respond to situations differently. Following up our interview via email, Zuzanna emphasizes that "Goralskie weddings to me are the most creative, colorful, and passionate weddings. Everything is done with so much detail. Cepowiny for example, every guest can be a part of it and it truly feels like everyone is giving their blessings. Not only are you becoming one with your partner, you're being a part of something bigger with everyone's love and support. I have been involved with goralski all my life, if given the chance I would love to have a goralskie wedding. Goralski is truly a part of me."[22] Thus while Zuzanna imagines a Górale wedding, Monika qualifies her desires, noting that if married in Chicago, she imagines a wedding that, at least sartorially, would draw on American traditions. I note that she has a model of this already in her grandparents' wedding where her grandfather wore a suit rather than a strój. What self-identities did he wish to celebrate at his village wedding in Podhale?

Their boyfriends, Dawid and Piotr, bring perspectives from their experiences in Górale string bands at many weddings (though maybe not as many as Stoch). Playing a traditional Górale wedding, according to Piotr, involves arriving at the bride's or groom's house early in the morning and becoming an essential part of the wedding party. But they also play for other sorts of weddings: culturally mixed weddings, weddings for lowlander Polish couples, and so forth. For those weddings, they have learned additional repertoire but also play Górale music. They perform their Góraleness even for other Polish Americans who do not identify as Górale. Yet prizing Górale weddings, Dawid notes that "they are the most presentable weddings. . . . Nobody's going to look at a limo driving by. . . . When you see horses, a carriage full of musicians, two guys, pytace, in the front—[it's] something distinguishable." Piotr adds, "It's an all-day event for us. We go in the morning to a Polish wedding. We get there bright and early. We're part of the wedding party. We get there 8, 9, 10 a.m." Zuzanna interjects: "They are there too early and come home way too late." A Górale wedding takes commitment.

Reflecting on our interview, I recall that the two young couples were wearing Górale strój, as were a few others in the room. In a photograph from the evening, I am the odd one out. The images are evocative of place, people, and ways of living that Zuzanna finds very attractive, comfortable, reassuring, and desirable. On the walls behind are two images: on the left is a painting looking up a valley to Giewont Mountain, a distinctive granite peak that rises prominently above the town of Zakopane, arguably the cultural center of Podhale; to the right is a reproduction of the iconic medieval image of the Black Madonna (Czarna Maddona, also known as Queen of the Górale). One could read the image as nostalgically archaic, recalling religious icons from another era. Yet the strój worn by the Górale in the photograph is similarly preindustrial, requiring intensive skilled handwork rarely found today. The men's trousers, for example, reflect eighteenth-century Central European conventions and technologies—felting sheep's wool, tailoring, and extensive embroidery. Their manufacture is so labor-intensive that a pair cost around $400; of course, a single pair could last one a lifetime. Every type of clothing worn by my interlocutors—trousers, tooled leather shoes and belts, drawn thread–decorated linen shirts, pleated skirts, embroidered shearling vests, felt hats—is being manufactured by Górale in Chicago, and there is a lively trade of goods made in Podhale as well. There are places in Chicago where Górale in strój would be out of place, of another place, placeless, but not here, not in the chambers of the Highlander House situated in the heart of Chicago's historic Polish neighborhood.

A CHICAGO GÓRALE WEDDING IN POLAND?

My recent conversations with Górale in the Chicago community revealed a consistent concern that beyond the first generation of Górale Americans, couples might not choose a traditional Górale wedding. As we saw with Monika, even

Figure 11.4. *From left to right*: Dawid Walus, Piotr Waliczek, Marian Bryja, Monika Kois, Tim Cooley, Zuzanna Soltys, Adrian Chrobak, and Andrzej Bryja. October 20, 2016, Highlander Alliance, Chicago. *Photo by Anna Zalinska.*

individuals who are deeply invested in their Gorale identity nonetheless value their American identity and feel that this too should be expressed in their weddings. Is that a compromise or an innovation?

What if a Chicago Górale couple has the ambition and wherewithal to celebrate their wedding in Podhale, Poland? Andrzej Krzeptowski, born in Podhale and brought by his mother, Maria, to Chicago when he was two or three, was raised as a Górale. His father and Maria's husband, Andrzej Sr., joined the family in Chicago a few years later. Active leaders in the Chicago Górale community, Andrzej's parents have been key music and dance teachers at the Highlanders Alliance. Andrzej grew up playing violin and dancing in the Górale style. His wife, Maggie (Majerczyk) Krzeptowska, was born in Chicago shortly after her parents moved here from Podhale. The parents of Andrzej and Maggie were best friends. Taught Górale ways when growing up, Maggie recalls going to countless Górale weddings and other functions. And, as she explained, she started spending summers in Podhale with her family there when she was eight year old. "So I had both worlds. When I go back there, it still feels like home."

Andrzej and Maggie were married in June 2015 in Podhale. Their spectacular wedding demonstrated great attention given to Górale traditions. This included pytace traveling with the couple to invite guests before the wedding; on the day of the wedding, blessing ceremonies at the groom's home as well as the bride's home; pytace leading a long train of horse-drawn carriages between homes, church, and venue for the extended wesele with an elaborate capping cepowiny (ritual) around midnight. They had an additional celebration (poprawiny) the following day. Even by local standards in Podhale, this was a spectacular wedding, employing dozens of florists, chefs, tailors, horse carriage drivers, and so forth. It was a boost for the economy in Podhale, and also for the Górale cottage industries in Chicago where some of the traditional-style clothing was made. The groomsmen and bridesmaids, as well as many of their other friends and family members, live in the United States and had to travel to Podhale for the wedding. The bridesmaids and groomsmen all dressed in strój and took part in the cepowiny, even though not all were Górale or even Polish. They effectively performed Góraleness for their Górale friends' wedding.

About two months after the wedding in Podhale, Andrzej and Maggie had a reception and ceremony in Chicago, where they repeated their vows in the company of their friends who were unable to attend the wedding in Poland. While these dual ceremonies did accommodate their binational communities, it also allowed Andrzej and Maggie to express both their American and Górale identities. As Maggie explained when I interviewed her and Andrzej, "I just wanted the traditional Polish Highlander góralski wedding there, but also here I wanted to have the white dress and veil. So I got to have both."[23]

Having both required effort on several levels. Andrzej expressed that here in the United States, Górale parents have to deliberately teach their children about Górale lifeways—otherwise lost. He noted that children learn American culture, including English language, at school. Sustaining cultural practices from a different place requires consistent effort. When I ask why it was important for them to have a traditional Górale wedding in Podhale, Maggie responds: "We wanted to go back to our roots, and then we also wanted to carry on the traditions from our grandparents, our great grandparents, and the history that we have in our family. That's why we chose to go back to where they were born, the land that they were raised on, and in the church that holds so much history. So it made sense for us, being from the same culture, that we would go back to where it began."[24]

Both Maggie and Andrzej emphasize the spiritual significance of this mid-nineteenth century wooden church in Zakopane, the hometown of the Krzeptowskis. When I asked them to identify the most important part of a traditional Górale wedding, Andrzej opined, "First and foremost would be the church that we had an opportunity to get married at. . . . That is the biggest part because that is what marriage is. Everything else is just a celebration of what you just did [in the church]." Maggie agreed with Andrzej, and went on to expand the religious power of the wedding to their family homes: "Secondly I would say, the blessing in our home. . . . I mean, just knowing what they're telling us and what we have to carry in our lives together and hold together. And, you know, now we are one . . . just hearing it from your parents."

In this way, a diasporic wedding for the Polish Górale community in Chicago might involve a pilgrimage of sorts back to the motherland—a twenty-first century religious pilgrimage across political borders to ask God to aid in keeping Podhale and Chicago spiritually linked.[25] Podhale itself becomes a pilgrimage site, with its Tatra Mountains, Mount Geiwont with a fifteen-meter steel cross erected on its peak in 1901 visible from Zakopane on a clear day, old churches, cemeteries, shrines at crossroads, and family homes blessed each year by Catholic priests. There in Podhale, the wedding party can engage meaningfully on the relatively quiet streets in pilgrimage-like processions between sites of significance for series of blessings: from the groom's family home, to the bride's family home, to the church, and finally to the wesele replete with pre- or extra-Christian pagan rituals.

For Maggie and Andrzej, the wedding in Podhale began with a lot of work in Chicago, of course. Plenty of devilish details were dealt with in multicultural, multireligious, secular Chicago before anyone boarded a plane for Poland. It is only fitting that the wedding ritual is reperformed back in Chicago, back in the diasporic community, where their dual identities as hyphenated Górale Americans are asserted—horses not needed, though they are available even here.

TRADITION, INTERPRETATION, AND RESTORATION AS NEW

The problem with writing and publishing is the tendency of print to suggest stasis, fixity, and, in the worst cases, totalities. This tendency may be especially strong when one writes about this thing called "tradition" which must be new, renewed, restored,[26] reinvented, and reperformed in order to continue to remain viable and meaningful. A "traditional" wedding is, to the extent possible, a restoration of previous weddings, and it is in these restorations that a palpable sense of tradition is created and maintained. A couple cannot get married at their parents' or grandparents' wedding; they must have their own new wedding. At least this is how I see it; this is my interpretation and it may not mesh with the understandings of those people who allowed me to document their weddings and those who have taken time to share their thoughts about weddings with me. The problem is that my experiences of Górale weddings in Chicago are not representative. My experience and interpretation of these weddings reveals at least as much about me as those I presume to represent.

Brought up in a devout Protestant Christian teetotaling home, the Catholicism and appreciation of vodka among some of the Górale I first met was almost as new to me as was their music, dance, regional architecture, strój, alluring Polish dialect, borderland history, and so forth. Yet it was their musicking and dancing that caught my interest. Their typically three-violin and basy ensembles captivated me aurally. The virtuosic lead violin playing compared well with my already developed interest in American bluegrass and old-time fiddling traditions. The rhythmic and harmonic force of one or two accompanying violins plus a basy provided a full sound that excited my senses. The first Górale musicians and dancers I met immediately began to steer me toward the cultural contexts of this captivating sound by inviting me to rehearsals and performance events at the Highlander House on Archer Avenue. They also told me that the place to experience Górale musical practices in action was a wedding, and it is they who began inviting me to weddings, not the couples being married: "It's OK. I'm with the band." I soon learned that excuses for showing up at strangers' weddings with a camera and audio-recorder were not necessary. These were community affairs and my interest in Górale music seemed to make me an adoptive member of the community.

But not the whole community; just those devoted to performing their Górale identities with music and dance. The fact is that most individuals in Chicago with Górale heritage don't have traditional Górale weddings, though their weddings are still held to be traditional in meaningful ways, thus challenging any confined notions of what "traditional" and "Górale" mean. Take for example Monika Sobański-Krzysiak and Mark Krzysiak, married in September 2016 in Chicago. Both she and her husband identify as Górale: Mark was born in Podhale while Monika was born in Chicago. Her parents were born in Podhale, immigrated here independently, and met at the Highlander House on Archer Avenue, where Monika's mother was working. During a phone interview,[27] I asked Monika if she and Mark chose to have a Górale wedding. She responded, "We had a traditional wedding . . . because we didn't dress in the góralski outfits." Monika wore a white (or ivory) dress, and Mark wore a suit, thus a "traditional American wedding," as she described it. The use of the term *traditional* to describe both a Górale and an American wedding was used by different consultants in my interviews and conversations. I had to interpret "traditional" in the context, or ask for clarification. Mark and Monika drew from several traditions to construct, enact, and perform their wedding and thus represent to their family and friends a curated statement of their identity. This identity included symbols and acts that they associate with North America and symbols and acts that mark them as Polish and Górale. For example, they hired a Górale string band to play at their house for their blessing before the wedding and at the reception. In other situations, they dress in strój, but at their wedding, what they hold as American traditions were foregrounded, with elements of Góraleness having perhaps less prominent roles but present nonetheless. This wedding is probably more representative of Górale weddings in Chicago and resonates with what the younger Monika Kois imagines, should she be married in Chicago—a white dress wedding with some sartorial and performative symbols of Górale identity blended in. But my empirical and ethnographic knowledge of diasporic weddings of Górale weddings in Chicago is skewed toward those that reference the there and then: Podhale in the time of one's ancestors.

The time of one's ancestors is a movable feast—at least as fluid as our perceptions and understandings of the present. No wonder that what constitutes a traditional wedding is a malleable phenomenon, though one can identify stabilizing forces. Most prominent is the Catholic Church—these are Catholic weddings. That is the elephant in this chapter that I have done little to recognize. The sacred elements of Górale weddings seemed to be taken for granted or even deemphasized in the late 1980s and 1990s. Then again, I was with the band at weddings, and bands may or may not take part in the wedding Mass. My interlocutors back then in the final years of the twentieth century drew my attention to what happened before and after the wedding Mass—or maybe I gave less attention to the Mass for my own reasons. Whatever the case, during my more recent exchanges with individuals in the Chicago Górale community references to God, the church, and personal belief were prominent. Górale are very religious people, I was told on several occasions, and Monika Kois and Zuzanna Solty said they thought belief in God was, if not required by those who identify as Górale, necessary for experiencing the full effect of Górale traditions. Zakopane had a spiritual draw for Andrzej and Maggie Krzeptowski because it was in the Tatra Mountains but also because of the old wooden church that resonated with them spiritually. While some spoke of the cepowiny as having central importance in the later twentieth century, in 2016 the wedding Mass and the prayerful blessing of the couple at the bride's home before the Mass were brought up as the essential elements of a wedding.

In the three decades that I have taken notice of Górale weddings in Chicago, I have seen a significant increase in more thoroughly traditional Górale weddings (again, meaning the ability to reference Podhale of the past). The infrastructure in Chicago has developed to facilitate cultural practices and to produce objects associated with Polish Górale. Skilled craftspeople have set up shop, producing all items common in a Górale costume. When I began interacting with Chicago

Górale in the late 1980s, some were already moving beyond the city limits in search of more space. A handful of Górale are now grazing sheep and making the distinctive smoked cheese called *oscypek*, a delicacy that no wedding feast should be without. I was told in the 1980s and 1990s that this handmade, unpasteurized cheese was smuggled into the United States from Podhale for weddings. Having the cheese produced locally is significant.

Another dramatic infrastructural change is the availability of horse teams and carriages. Moving just a few miles beyond the city allows some Górale to raise and train horses to pull carriages or to be ridden by pytace during wedding processions. For example, Jan Słodyczka has three horses and several carriages and sleighs on his suburban Palos Hills property. Słodyczka believes that the first Górale wedding with horses in Chicago was in 1993. Twenty years later, NPR reporter Linda Paul wrote about a Chicago Górale wedding that featured five carriages and twelve horses, including two ridden by the pytace.[28] While many in the Górale community still live in the historically Polish neighborhoods of the near south side along or near Archer Avenue, many others are dispersed outside the city, even up into Wisconsin. This decentralization of the diasporic community may indicate integration into American society—and I am sure it does in some cases—but it also affords an interesting reinvestment in Górale cultural practices as some maintain horse teams and carriages, and others tend sheep and make their distinctive smoked cheese. Thus, the Chicago-area Górale community has collectively gone back in time and space to bring into the twenty-first century and to Chicago cultural practices and material culture from Podhale. This is motivated by no small degree by the desire of many to have a Górale wedding.

—⁓—

September 2016, Chicago, Illinois.

Well past midnight, Maria Krzeptowska and I sit in her living room and watch DVDs of her son's wedding. I met Maria and her husband thirty years ago at a Chicago Górale wedding—it might have been Halina and Tomasz Lassak's. I distinctly recall an after party with the band where Maria asked me to turn her out for a dance—to bring her to the dance area using particular turning steps. Embarrassed, I protested that I did not know the simple steps. Undeterred, Maria taught me on the spot and has been teaching me about things Górale ever since. More to the point, Maria and her husband have taught literally hundreds of children in Chicago to sing, dance, and play in the various Górale styles. They also teach them the distinct Górale dialect, history, and traditions. Over the years, we have crossed paths in Chicago and in Podhale. When I have needed a

Górale band in the Chicago area to illustrate a talk, or provide a demonstration, the Krzeptowskis have offered their talents, always showing up in strój and good spirits. I met her son, Andrzej, when he was a boy at one of these demonstrations. We go way back, and here we are again to look back some fifteen months at her son's wedding in Podhale. As always Maria is teaching, teaching me the detailed minutia of the symbolic meanings of objects and actions that flash by on the screen.

As we watch and talk, first Halina and then Tomasz Lassak appear on the video screen, and then their now-grown-up daughter. I remind Maria of Halina and Tomasz's wedding here in Chicago. Does she remember if that is where we first met? She doesn't. The Lassaks and Krzeptowskis were good friends here in Chicago back in the day. Of course they are honored guests at their son's wedding in Podhale—old friends from Chicago dancing together again in Poland. Mountains and oceans are crossed in an instant. Here and there, then and now, merge in memory and presence.

TIMOTHY J. COOLEY is Professor of Ethnomusicology at the University of California, Santa Barbara. He is editor with Gregory F. Barz of *Shadows in the Field: New Perspectives for Fieldwork in Ethnomusicology*, and author of *Making Music in the Polish Tatras: Tourists, Ethnographers, and Mountain Musicians* and *Surfing about Music*.

NOTES

1. Cooley, *Making Music in the Polish Tatras.*
2. My comparative base is ethnographic work in Chicago from the late 1980s to mid-1990s with periodic follow-up visits in the 2000s, most recently in the fall of 2016, and intensive ethnographic research in Poland in the mid-1990s, again with period follow-up visits and research trips. These experiences are illuminated with renewed conversations and correspondences with my research-collaborators in Poland and the Chicago area as I prepared this chapter. Thus my personal experiences with Górale weddings in Chicago and Poland were primarily in the 1990s and might be considered historical. The information I present on weddings in the first decades of the twenty-first century are secondhand and curated by the interpretive intelligence of my interlocutors and those who shot and edited the photos and videos I studied.
3. For an explanation of Górale as an ethnic category, see Cooley, *Making Music in the Polish Tatras,* 67–72.
4. Wrazen, "Traditional Music Performance among *Górale* in Canada," 175.
5. Cooley, *Making Music in the Polish Tatras,* 30–31, 147–49.
6. Cooley, *Making Music in the Polish Tatras,* 30–31, 72–82; Gromada, *Tatra Highlander Folk Culture in Poland and America,* 19–21.

7. The Związek Podhalan is a fraternal organization started in 1904 in Zakopane, the largest town in the Polish Tatras. The Związek Podhalan formed in response to the increasing influence in the region by outsiders, encouraged in part by the Polish Tatra Society, arguably the oldest tourist society in Europe.

8. Gromada, *Tatra Highlander Folk Culture*, 149.

9. Some Górale migrated to the United States in the 1870s and '80s. Mass migrations began in the 1890s and increased especially in the early twentieth century until World War I.

10. Cooley and Spottswood, *Fire in the Mountains*.

11. Similarly, Carlos Gardel, a tango singer from Argentina, appeared in gaucho attire when traveling abroad and in a three-piece suit when performing in Buenos Aires.

12. Cooley, "Folk Festival as Modern Ritual in the Polish Tatra Mountains," 31–55; Cooley, *Making Music in the Polish Tatras*.

13. Cooley, "Music of the Polish Górale Community in Chicago," 72–76; Cooley, "How 19th-Century Musical Folklore Created Poland's Górale Diaspora in 20th-Century Chicago."

14. Schechner, "Collective Reflexivity: Restoration of Behavior," 39–81.

15. Cooley, *Making Music in the Polish Tatras*, 225–26.

16. Szurmiak-Bogucka, *Wesele góralskie*; Jan Gutt-Mostowy, *Podhale: A Companion Guide*, 77–81; Lehr, "Obrzędowość Rodzinna" [Life Cycle Rituals], 319–20.

17. Gutt-Mostowy, *Podhale*, 79.

18. Here I reference Boym's sense of nostalgia as a mythical return. See Boym, *Future of Nostalgia*, 8.

19. Monika Kois, Zuzanna Soltys, Dawid Walus, and Piotr Waliczek, recorded interview with the author, Chicago, October 20, 2016.

20. Monica, email correspondence with the author, November 3, 2016.

21. A bride in a white dress was often used by Górale in our conversations as a marker of an American wedding.

22. Zuzanna, email correspondence with the author, November 4, 2016.

23. Andrzej and Maggie Krzeptowski, interview with the author, Chicago, October 21, 2016.

24. Maggie, personal communication, Chicago, October 21, 2016.

25. Bohlman, *Revival and Reconciliation*.

26. Schechner, "Collective Reflexivity."

27. Monica, phone interview, October 21, 2016.

28. Paul, "Traditional Wedding Brings the Polish Highlands to Chicago."

BIBLIOGRAPHY

Bohlman, Philip V. *Revival and Reconciliation: Sacred Music in the Making of European Modernity*. Lanham, MD: Scarecrow Press, 2013.

Boym, Svetlana. *The Future of Nostalgia*. New York: Basic Books, 2001.

Cooley, Timothy J. "Folk Festival as Modern Ritual in the Polish Tatra Mountains." *World of Music* 41, no. 3 (1999): 31–55.

————. "How 19th-Century Musical Folklore Created Poland's Górale Diaspora in 20th-Century Chicago." In *Music's Intellectual History: Founders, Followers & Fads; Proceedings of the First Conference of the Répertoire International de Littérature Musicale*, edited by Zdravko Blazekovic and Barbara Dobbs Mackenzie. New York: Répertoire International de Littérature Musicale, 2009.

————. *Making Music in the Polish Tatras: Tourists, Ethnographers, and Mountain Musicians*. Bloomington: Indiana University Press, 2005.

————. "Music of the Polish Górale Community in Chicago." In *American Musical Traditions*, edited by Jeff Todd Titon and Bob Carlin, vol. 4, *European American Music*, 72–76. New York: Schirmer Reference, 2002.

Cooley, Timothy J., and Dick Spottswood. *Fire in the Mountains: Polish Mountain Fiddle Music*. Vol. 1: *The Karol Stoch Band*. Compact disc recording with notes. Newton, NJ: Yazoo, a division of Shanachie Entertainment Corp., 1997.

Gromada, Thaddeus V. *Tatra Highlander Folk Culture in Poland and America: Collected Essays from "The Tatra Eagle."* Hasbrouck Heights, NJ: Tatra Eagle Press, 2012.

Gutt-Mostowy, Jan. *Podhale: A Companion Guide to the Polish Highlands*. New York: Hippocrene Books, 1998.

Lehr, Urszula. "Obrzędowość Rodzinna." [Life-Cycle Rituals]. In *Podhale: Tradycja we współczesnej kulturze wsi*, edited by Danuty Tylkowej, 305–47. Kraków: Instytut Archeologii i Etnologii Polskiej Akademii Nauk, 2000.

Paul, Linda. "A Traditional Wedding Brings the Polish Highlands to Chicago." National Public Radio. Aired October 12, 2013, 7:36 a.m. http://www.npr.org/2013/10/12 /231647523/a-traditional-wedding-brings-the-polish-highlands-to-chicago.

Schechner, Richard. "Collective Reflexivity: Restoration of Behavior." In *A Crack in the Mirror: Reflexive Perspectives in Anthropology*, edited by Barbara Myerhoff and Jay Ruby, 39–81. Philadelphia: University of Pennsylvania Press, 1982.

Szurmiak-Bogucka, Aleksandra. *Wesele góralskie*. Kraków: Polskie wydawnictwo muzyczne, 1974.

Wrazen, Louise. "Traditional Music Performance among *Górale* in Canada." *Ethnomusicology* 35, no. 2 (1991): 173–93.

INDEX

253

INNA NARODITSKAYA is Professor of Ethnomusicology at the Northwestern University Bienen School of Music. She is author of *Bewitching Russian Opera: The Tsarina from State to Stage, Song from the Land of Fire: Continuity and Change in Azerbaijani Mugham,* and coeditor of several volumes, including *Music of the Sirens.*

www.ingramcontent.com/pod-product-compliance
Lightning Source LLC
Chambersburg PA
CBHW051955270326
41929CB00015B/2668